# FEMINISM AND CONTEMPORARY ART

The impact of women artists on the contemporary art movement has resulted in a powerful and innovative feminist reworking of traditional approaches to the theory and history of art. *Feminism and Contemporary Art* discusses the work of individual women artists within the context of the wider social, physical and political world.

Jo Anna Isaak looks at the work of a diverse range of artists from the United States, the former Soviet Union, the United Kingdom and Canada. She discusses the work of such artists as Barbara Kruger, Cindy Sherman, Nancy Spero, Elaine Reichek, Jeanne Silverthorne, Mary Kelly, Lorna Simpson, Hannah Wilke, Jenny Holzer, Kiti Smith and the Guerrilla Girls. In an original case study of art production in a non-capitalist context, Isaak examines a range of work by twentieth-century Soviet women artists.

Refuting the notion that there is a specifically female way of creating art, and dubious of any generalizing notion of "feminist art practices", Isaak nevertheless argues that contemporary art under the influence of feminism is providing the momentum for a comic critique of key assumptions about art, art history, and the role of the artist.

Richly illustrated with over one hundred photographs, paintings and images by women artists, this work provides a provocative and valuable account of the diversity and revolutionary potential of women's art practice

**Jo Anna Isaak** is a writer living in New York City. She is the author of *The Ruin of Representation in Modernist Art and Texts* (1986) and the curator of the exhibition *Laughter Ten Years After*.

# RE VISIONS: CRITICAL STUDIES IN THE HISTORY AND THEORY OF ART

## Series editors: Jon Bird and Lisa Tickner, Middlesex University

Art history has been transformed as an academic discipline over the last twenty years. The 'new' art history is no longer new, and that widely used and useful label has come to seem dangerously over-tidy.

*Re Visions* responds to the arrival of new ways of thinking in art history in a series of lucid and accessible studies by authors distinguished in their fields. Each book examines the usefulness of innovative concepts and methods, not in abstract terms but through the analysis of particular art objects, ways of writing about art, and cultural institutions and practices.

Other titles in the series

Civilizing Rituals – inside public art museums
*Carol Duncan*

# FEMINISM AND CONTEMPORARY ART

## THE REVOLUTIONARY POWER OF WOMEN'S LAUGHTER

*Jo Anna Isaak*

London and New York

First published 1996
by Routledge
11 New Fetter Lane, London EC4P 4EE

Simultaneously published in the USA and Canada
by Routledge
29 West 35th Street, New York, NY 10001

*Routledge is an International Thomson Publishing company* I(T)P

© 1996 Jo Anna Isaak

Typeset in Times by
Florencetype Limited, Stoodleigh, Devon

Printed and bound in Great Britain by
Biddles Ltd, Guildford and Kings Lynn

*British Library Cataloguing in Publication Data*
A catalogue record for this book is available from the British Library

*Library of Congress Cataloguing in Publication Data*
A catalogue record for this book has been requested

ISBN 0–415–08014–2 (hbk)
ISBN 0–415–08015–0 (pbk)

# DEDICATION

My study window overlooks the St Stephen's School Playground.
The school is a private Catholic school for children from kindergarten
through grade school. It has separate entrances for girls and boys and the
children daily line up outside the doors marked "Boys" or "Girls".
One day I overheard a little boy tell a little girl she couldn't play on the
swing because it was on "the boys' side." Clearly, there was something in
the gender divide the school was underlining that the little boy
understood as privileging his sex. The little girl turned to him and said,
"This is the *playground*. There's no boys' side on the *playground*."
It is to that five-year-old future feminist, who has such an
unshakeable grasp of the fact that the playground is hers to enjoy, that I
dedicate this book.

# CONTENTS

# LIST OF ILLUSTRATIONS

# ACKNOWLEDGEMENTS

This book has been on my mind for many years. Long before I organized "The Revolutionary Power of Women's Laughter" exhibition, I had explored the connections between women and laughter in the writings of Gertrude Stein. Stein's mode of writing – transgressive, excessive, and fearlessly humorous – provided a model for looking at current developments in women's art practice. While there was never enough time to write a book during the summer, there was time to write shorter essays on individual artists. These I wrote with the theme of laughter in mind, knowing that at a later date I would integrate these essays into the book. Earlier versions or portions of individual chapters appeared in *Art Journal* (Summer 1994); *Meaning: Contemporary Art Issues* (May 1993); *Heresies* 26, 1993; *Parkett* (December 1992); *American Imago* (Fall 1991); and *Nancy Spero: Work Since 1950*, 1987. The book may have been on my mind, but it was not really conceived until the spring of 1991 when Lisa Tickner arrived at the college where I teach in upstate New York and managed to pull me out of the deep bureaucratic morass I was in as chair of my department. She looked over the proposal for the book, told me to make a few changes, mail it, and as she put it, "Bob's your uncle!" This was the first of many important contributions friends were to make to the book.

This is a book of friends. Writing is an isolated activity, but throughout the time it took me to bring this manuscript to completion, I always felt I was working as part of a collective. I am grateful to all the artists who contributed to the book. Our ongoing conversations about art and the friendships formed while working on this project have become part of the fabric of my life. I am particularly grateful to Susan Unterberg who traveled with me on my last trip to Russia to take photographs of artists' work. I would like to thank the Guerrilla Girls for the cover of the book and Kathy Grove for her work on many of the photographs in the book. Lisa Tickner, Jon Bird, and Avis Lang read the manuscript and made many helpful suggestions. Margaret McKay also read the manuscript and prepared the index, just as she did for my first book and for my PhD thesis. My niece, Joelle Sowden, helped gather together the illustrations. Finally, I would like to thank Dan O'Connell mainly because he is pretty funny, for a guy.

# INTRODUCTION

Writing in 1974, Lise Vogel posed a series of demanding questions:

> In the past decade the women's liberation movement has explored
> issues touching on virtually all areas of human experience. Why then
> do we hear so little about art? Why has art, perhaps more than any
> other field, lagged so far behind the general movement for change
> initiated by modern feminism? Specifically: Where are the books,
> articles, or collections of essays presenting a feminist critique of art?
> Why are there no monographs and virtually no articles on women
> artists written from a feminist perspective? Where are the repro-
> ductions and slides of the work of women artists? Why can't one
> find syllabi and bibliographies covering issues of women, art, and
> feminism? What is the meaning of the almost complete lack of femi-
> nist studio and art history courses in the schools? Why are there so
> few feminist art history courses in the schools? Why are there so
> few feminist art historians and critics? What are women artists today
> doing? And what are those women who consider themselves femi-
> nists doing and why? What should a feminist artist, critic, or art
> historian do? What is a feminist point of view in the visual arts?
>
> (1974: 3)

Around the same time Nicos Hadjinicolaou in *Art History and Class
Struggle* was criticizing art history for being "one of the last outposts
of reactionary thought" (1973: 4). Vogel's questions and Hadjinicolaou's
condemnation are related, but it wasn't until five years after the first publication of his book that he discovered, to his chagrin, that he was
contributing to this reactionary thinking. A reader pointed out to him that
throughout his own book art historians are assumed to be exclusively male
and that it perpetuated the customary linguistic subordination of every
grammatical person into the inclusive, but repressive person of a universal
"he." Hadjinicolaou concluded that "this proves to what extent even so-
called progressive people are victims of some very old and reactionary
attitudes" (1973; 1978 edn: 2). What was left out of Hadjinicolaou's account

1

of art history was far more systemic than what could be remedied simply by changing the personal pronoun to "she." However, the fact that his omissions were presented to him *as a problem* is a direct result of the feminist questioning of the discourse of art history, which has caused the discipline to become self-conscious. Questions asked of a subject have a way of determining the answers given. Today it is understood that any activity which addresses the logic of production (and this includes cultural production) but which neither attempts an analysis of the construction of sexual difference nor posits an alternative economy of the sexes is either naive or obtuse to the point of complicity.

Writing at the end of the 1980s, Arthur Danto surveyed the mainstream of contemporary art and acknowledged, somewhat to his surprise, that were he "to select the most innovative artists of this particular period . . . most of them would probably be women" (1989: 794). This realization caused him, in turn, to ask "whether this particular period, and hence this particular mainstream, was made to order for women, even if the work in question might not have any especially feminine – or feminist – content?" To ask if the mainstream was "made to order for women," as if this occurred by some happy accident, is to fail to realize that the very nature of contemporary art has been changed *because* of the power of the persistent critique that women have brought to bear on key assumptions about art, art history, and the role of the artist.[1] The convergence of the feminist critique, postmodernism's decentering of the subject, and theoretical reflections on gender, sexuality, politics, and representation provided the momentum for a number of feminist artists who are, indeed, the most innovative artists working today.

In 1982, more or less midway between Vogel's questions and Danto's reassessment, I organized an exhibition entitled "The Revolutionary Power of Women's Laughter." The exhibition was an early attempt to locate art within the arena of contemporary theoretical discussions. The fundamental discoveries of modern linguistics and psychoanalysis had radically affected the understanding of how all signifying systems operate. There was a growing awareness that a lot was at stake for women in these new assessments of how meaning is produced and organized in all areas of cultural practice. In 1968, when Roland Barthes pronounced the author "dead," most of the old verities associated with the confident bourgeois belief in individualism and absolute property rights died with him. For those at risk of losing their privileges, postmodernism is experienced as a crisis, but the death of the author and the consequent failure of fantasies about authoritative selfhood have wholly different implications for those who never held this privileged position. It leveled the playing field for women – and play in the new authority-free zone they did. They began by dismantling "the prison house of language" through play, or laughter, or to use the term the French have recently reintroduced to English, *jouissance*:

enjoyment, pleasure, particularly sexual pleasure or pleasure derived from the body. Included in this notion of *jouissance* is a sense of play as linguistic excess, the joy of disrupting or going beyond established, or fixed meaning into the realm of non-sense. Since, as Barthes succinctly put it, "a code cannot be destroyed, only played off," play may well be the most revolutionary strategy available.

The theme of laughter and the carnivalesque that runs throughout the present book grew out of the exhibition and is a continuation of that early project. In these chapters are references to Bakhtin's *Rabelais and His World,* in which he develops from Rabelais's writing a theory of laughter and the carnivalesque as potential revolutionary strategies; to Barthes's and Kristeva's notion of laughter as libidinal license, the *jouissance* of the polymorphic, orgasmic body; to Freud's *Jokes and Their Relation to the Unconscious*, in which an analysis of the liberating potential of laughter emerges from the workings of a witticism or a play upon language; and to Freud's essays on narcissism, which I examine in order to show why those in possession of the most radical humor may be women. I use analytic strategies developed in Althusserian Marxism, the construction of the subject formulated by Jacques Lacan, the discourses and institutions of power analyzed by Michel Foucault, and Brecht's strategies for an engaged artistic practice, and of course I draw upon the wealth of material that is currently being developed in feminist critical theory within the visual arts. To Lisa Tickner's list of the two issues central to the women's movement since the 1960s – finding a voice for women that is intelligible and separate from the patriarchal voice, and reclaiming the image of women from the representations of others – I add a third – analyzing and utilizing that particularly dense transfer point of power relations: pleasure.

To gather a group of women artists together under any rubric is to be forced into an essentialist position. Anthologies or group shows of exclusively male artists, by contrast, are allowed to address whatever organizing principle the curator or writer has in mind: a geographical location the artists may have in common, a period of time in which they worked, a particular style or medium. For example, the "New Photography 9" exhibition at the Museum of Modern Art in New York was ostensibly about new photography in general, not just from the perspective of a particular gender or race, even though every artist included was white and male. Women artists, writers, and curators have never been able to masquerade in the Emperor's clothes of universal humanity. Even if only two women artists are written about or exhibited together, the issue of gender inevitably arises. But to argue, as I intend to do in the following chapters, that women are in possession of something that men may lack is to engage in a strategic, rather than a predetermined, essentialism, to push the issue of gender past the point where it can be used to ghettoize women.

At the same time, I hope to raise doubts about any global notion of a feminist art practice. I intend to move the debate from a biological deter-minism to a consideration of gender positions occupied in the field of signs. A feminist art practice, as invoked throughout this book, is not a term designating a homogeneous group (i.e. the disenfranchised) or a fixed site (the margin) but rather an agency of intervention – an ongoing activity of pluralizing, destabilizing, baffling any centered discourse. This work, like all feminist activity, is a calculated optimistic gesture, and thus I may be accused of utopianism, or at least participation in what Steven Connor has referred to as "the romance of the margins," that is, a belief in the subversive potential of the marginal condition (1989: 228). Women are the least likely to regard their marginal condition as "romance." The romantic notion of the "outsider" artist working alone in his (*sic*) studio has continued as a convenient myth for male artists, who from time to time may affect the role, but for women artists working in isolation this myth is more likely to be a bleak reality. In the streets of New York City the Guerrilla Girls have rewritten this particular romance in a poster called "The Advantages of Being a Woman Artist." Some of these advantages include "Working without the pressure of success. Not having to be in shows with men. Having an escape from the art world in your 4 free-lance jobs. Being reassured that whatever kind of art you make it will be labeled feminine. Not having to undergo the embarrassment of being called a genius. Not being stuck in a tenured teaching position. Knowing your career might pick up after you are eighty." If women artists have been working at the margins, it is because that has been the only site available to them. But in the 1980s something quite remarkable hap-pened: using the subversive strategy of laughter, women artists began turning the culturally marginal position to which they had always been relegated into the new frontier.

I am not attempting to write an account of The Most Important con-temporary women artists. The artists discussed in the following chapters may or may not be part of what has been mythologized as the mainstream. I am not interested in valorizing a mainstream nor in exploring, validating, or reinforcing hegemony. According to Raymond Williams in *Marxism and Literature*, hegemony is a process that relies upon the mechanisms of tra-dition and the canons of Old Masters in order to waylay the utopian desires that are potentially embodied in cultural production (1977: 115–117). *The waylaid utopian desires are what I intend to explore.* What is most encour-aging about the recent influx of women into the mainstream is the changes they have made in art production itself and how successful they have been in addressing a far larger audience than that which frequents galleries and museums. At a time when the art world has generally shunned political con-tent, these artists have been producing "laboratory work" for those seek-ing to examine social realities and cultural myths. If they have established reputations in the mainstream, they have done so by undermining the very characteristics upon which it is established. They have even managed to undermine what Lucy Lippard calls "the most effective bludgeon on the side of homogeneity . . . the notion of Quality" (1990: 7). Their success is important for the way it has changed contemporary thinking about value systems that extend far beyond the art world. The constituents of "genius," "originality," "quality" are not transcendent criteria identifiable only by those in power. They are temporary, subjective, susceptible to change, and change is what this study is dedicated to.

Laughter, as it is used throughout this study, is meant to be thought of as a metaphor for transformation, for thinking about cultural change. In providing libidinal gratification, laughter can also provide an analytic for understanding the relationships between the social and the symbolic while allowing us to imagine these relationships differently. In asking for the response of laughter, the artists discussed in this book are engaging in a difficult operation. The viewer must want, at least briefly, to emancipate himself from "normal" representation; in order to laugh, he must recognize that he shares the same repressions. What is requested is not a private depoliticized *jouissance* but sensuous solidarity. Laughter is first and foremost a communal response.

While the focus is limited to women, it should be clear that the feminist "we" addressed by laughter is not gender-exclusive. It is not only women who are negatively inscribed by the symbolic function. As William Carlos Williams says of Gertrude Stein, an artist whose laughter is in many ways a precursor to the works presented in this study: "The tremendous cultural revolution implied by this interior revolution of technique tickles the very heart and liver of a man, makes him feel good. Good, that is, if he isn't too damned tied to his favorite stupidities. That's why he laughs. His laugh is the first acknowledgement of liberation" (1954: 163).

The first chapter, "The Revolutionary Power of Women's Laughter," sets out the theories of laughter that will be used throughout this book. Contrary to Dan Cameron's assertion that "post-feminism hearkens back to Lacan, who joined with Freud in proclaiming the revolutionary power of woman's laughter" (1987: 80) neither Freud nor Lacan said anything of the sort. I said it, but not in reference to something thing called "post-feminism." Nevertheless, the mistake is an interesting one. Like asking if the mainstream was made to order for women, it suggests that these philosophers paved the way for women, that the historical struggles over women's position within the institution of psychoanalysis either never took place or were inherently unnecessary. Whatever enabling theories women may be able to obtain from Freud or Lacan, they have had to wrest them from the writings themselves. Often they have done this not so much in an attempt to seize power from a phallocentric theory, but as a defence or rereading of psychoanalytic theory by those aware of its importance

5

to the understanding of women's relation to, and constitution by, any discourse. It was just such a defence that the poet H.D. tells us Freud once demanded she *not* engage in on his behalf, or on behalf of his work; he feared that it would proceed like the "inevitable course of a disease once a virus has entered the system" (1974: 86). This is exactly the kind of "defence" I plan to engage in. I intend to show that embedded in both Freud's writings and in the writings of Rabelais are the germs of a theory of laughter that will clarify why women are particularly well positioned to employ laughter as a revolutionary strategy. And since laughter, as Freud has pointed out, "is among the highly infectious expressions of psychical states" (1905b: 156), my defence of these phallocentric discourses may act as a virus once it has entered the system.

The title of the second chapter, "Art History and Its (Dis)Contents," alludes to Freud's "Civilization and Its Discontents" (1930) and to Jacqueline Rose's essay "Femininity and its Discontents" and is intended to suggest that neither femininity nor art history exists as a given; both are produced, and each may in fact be productive of the other. Lacan's famous formulation – that the woman does not exist, that femininity, psycho-analytically speaking, is constructed in relation to a series of representations – put an end to the attempts to locate an essential femininity which pre-occupied a number of feminist artists working in the 1970s. It has provided the theoretical basis for most of the feminist research on representation that has been undertaken within the last decade, informing a whole strand of artistic production. Here, in the field of representation which Mary Jacobus refers to as "the traditional arena of woman's oppression" (1986: 108), the demythologizing criticism of postmodernism has formed an oppo-sitional politic around the issues of originality, authority, production, repro-duction, meaning, mastery, the commodity, commodity fetishism, and the fetish. The feminist intervention in art history entails looking not just at the contents of that discourse, the purported premises of that history, but also at what it pretends *not* to be about, particularly the myth of its economic, political, and sexual innocence.

Chapter 3 addresses art production in what is now the former Soviet Union. This, after all, is the culture that produced Mikhail Bakhtin's *Rabelais and His World,* which argues that laughter and the carnivalesque are potent catalysts for popular revolutions. In an effort to analyze the artistic production of women working within a capitalist consumer culture, I expanded the scope of this study to include an investigation of those working outside that system. I found that in spite of the deep seriousness of the Slavic temperament and the hardships of living in a repressive regime, Russians have a highly developed *smechovja kulture* ("laugh cul-ture"). Part deconstructionists, part appropriationalists, part comedians, post-Soviet artists have become the leaders of a "ludic" postmodernism that for some time now has been mining and undermining the cultural

determinism of Soviet ideology, and will very likely enable them to nego-
tiate capitalist ideology better than we are able to. That this study was
undertaken at a historical moment when these differences are about to
disappear makes the exchange of information amongst women artists East
and West all the more urgent. We in the West need to be aware of the
work of women who are not caught in the machinations of commodity
capitalism, and they, in turn, need to know of our strategies of subversion before these differences are covered over in the seamless blanket of
homogeneity that is the hallmark of what, ironically, is known as bourgeois individualism. My analysis, both of the historic period of the avant-
garde and of contemporary Russian artists, focuses on the way these artists,
working in such different economic, political, and ideological circumstances, can illuminate contemporary art practices in the West. The issues I
address when discussing Russian women artists are not the same as those
that would be addressed by someone writing from within that culture.
Part of the great delight of researching this chapter was the opportunity
it gave me to get to know a number of Russian women, the most hospitable
and generous people I have met. Still, I will always remain outside the
culture in which they work and live, and my misperceptions will be readily
apparent to them. By the same token, they have often seemed to me to
be riddled with misperceptions about the conditions in which Western
women live and work. In the course of many long, intense conversations
that lasted well into the night, I have come to realize that our mutual
misperceptions may prove to be the most fruitful part of the interchange,
for they tell a good deal about ourselves and what we are hoping to find
in new social configurations for women.

Chapter 4, "Mothers of Invention," developed from an exhibition I
organized on the occasion of my mother's death. I found myself drawn to
those artists who, while realizing the enormous difficulty of this project,
turned to their own mothers or the figure of the mother in Western culture
in their search for ways to represent another form of love, "la mère qui
jouit." In *A Room of One's Own* Virginia Woolf said that "a woman writing
thinks back through her mothers" (1929: 96). In this sense, it may be that
this whole book was written with my mother, with our mothers, in mind.

Chapter 5, "Mapping the Imaginary," traces the way in which various
systems of representation and codification developed during the Renaissance were used by European nations in their colonizing ventures and
began influencing psychological perception. J-M. Charcot, Freud's mentor
and the discoverer of hysteria, used a number of perceptual conventions
developed in the visual arts in order to map an invisible disease onto the
bodies of the female inmates of the Salpêtrière asylum. In the process he
was able to draw upon the psychological associations surrounding these
visual codes, particularly the proprietary assumptions inherent in representation itself.

The final chapter, "Encore," exhibits an obsessional symptom: it is a repeat, a return to the origins of psychoanalysis and hysteria. Repetition may be the only way in which the history of psychoanalysis can be told – as indicated by its etymology (to analyze: to undo by going back) – as progress in regression. The question of woman addressed in Freud's early lectures and essays on hysteria is not the same as "the woman question" current at the time in which women's right *to* representation was at issue; instead the issue is the representation *of* woman. This chiasmus is more than rhetorical; the eliding of the historical and social content of this narrative is exactly what I wish to examine: just why it was that in the essays on hysteria, the canonical texts of psychoanalysis, written during a period of growing activity on the part of the women's suffrage movement, the possibility that hysteria may have social or political origins did not enter into the analytic reading. In *Studies on Hysteria* Freud does suggest that some of the symptomatic aspects of hysteria – "the pantomimic representation of phantasy" and the "clownism" documented by Charcot, for example – may be the return of repressed pleasurable features of the European carnival. The second half of this chapter looks at the work of a number of contemporary artists who in various ways enlist the hysteric's gesture of resistance and reenact ritual fragments of that festive tradition.

The end of the chapter and of the book takes us to the endgame, to dissolution, to death. If, as Hélène Cixous suggests, death and the feminine sex are for men unrepresentable, then figuring these two negatives together may be a way of asserting a positive. It may be that the most radically discursive understanding of the body, the body as site of political agency, is the body in dis-integration. This is not an apocalyptic vision; our sense of integrity is, at best, tenuous and mutable. Donna Haraway argues that "integrity" cannot reside within the "natural" body, since bodies "are not born; they are made" (1991: 208). Our understanding of ourselves as political agents should not focus on the self preserving its integrity, but should rather acknowledge the fact that integrity is a highly contingent and artificial construct – that the self is not a permanent given, but is always blurring into obscurity. In exploring the reconfigurations of their own bodies' aging, disease, or dying, these artists may be the first to understand the body's potential for embodied agency. Through this work, through the courage of their exploration, they continue to live as "activists," engaged with a society to which previously they may have been invisible.

While the diversity of artistic practices and cultural concerns addressed in these chapters makes it apparent that I am not attempting to chronicle a particular homogeneous movement in art, I am however chronicling a collective project. In June of 1994, I attended an exhibition and conference in Denmark entitled "Dialogue with the Other." In the spacious halls of the Kunsthallen Brandts Klaedefabrik, Lene Burkard brought together the work of thirty contemporary women artists and ten women writers and philosophers. The art work, made of different media and composed in various countries, and the speakers, from different countries and disciplines, addressing disparate concerns, came together in a moment of ideological self-realization to speak surprisingly clearly of our collective agenda. What projects like that exhibition or the work of the artists discussed in this book reveal is the importance of the dialogue we have been having with each other for the past two decades. Even if we have never met, we have become confident of the shared aims of our collective, and we have come to realize how one woman's work or words lead onto or enable the next woman to work or speak. The overarching intention of this book is to participate in and further this ongoing conversation so that the heteroglossae of this revolution are not just heard, but "resound."

# 1

# THE REVOLUTIONARY POWER OF WOMEN'S LAUGHTER

> In the beginning was the gest he *f* jousstly says, for the end is with woman, flesh-without-word, while the man to be is in a worse case after than before since sheon the supine satisfies the verb to him! Toughtough, Tootoological. Thou the first person shingeller. Art, an imperfect subjunctive.
>
> James Joyce, Finnegans Wake

The history of Western art begins with images of laughter – the laughter of women. In *Lives of the Artists*, the founding text for the discipline of art history, Giorgio Vasari tells us that the young Leonardo da Vinci began his artistic career by portraying laughing women. These heads of laughing women, "*teste di femmine, che ridono,*" first fashioned in clay and then cast in plaster, were "as beautiful as if they had been modelled by the hand of a master" (quoted in Freud 1910: 111). The laughing heads have been lost from the canon of Leonardo's art, but when Freud turns art historian in his analysis of the childhood of Leonardo, he returns to Vasari's account of these images of laughing women: "The passage, since it is not intended to prove anything, is quite beyond suspicion," Freud assures us, thereby arousing our suspicions (ibid.).

Something is at stake here: Freud suspects some obsessional behavior in the way Leonardo returns to images of laughing women in subsequent portraits. He examines the account of the lost fragments for a clue to the most famous enigma in the history of art – the unsolved riddle of the expression on the Mona Lisa's face. Haunted by the smile himself, Freud discovers that it has become an obsessional topic amongst art historians. He presents the early commentary on this painting as one might set out pieces of evidence in an unsolved mystery. Freud finds, as he sifts through various biographers of Leonardo, that they too have become obsessed with the enigmatic smile: "Walter Pater, who sees in the picture of Mona Lisa a 'presence ... expressive of what in the ways of a thousand years men have come to desire' ... writes very sensitively of 'the unfathomable smile, always with a touch of something sinister in it, which plays over all Leonardo's work'" (ibid.: 110). The idea that two contrary elements

11

are combined in the Mona Lisa's expression recurs in several commentaries: For Angelo Conti the smile is more than a smile; it is a laugh, and what that laugh expresses is something quintessentially female, both seductive and threatening: "The lady smiled in regal calm: her instincts of conquest, of ferocity, all the heredity of the species, the will to seduce and ensnare, the charm of deceit, the kindness that conceals a cruel purpose, – all this appeared and disappeared by turns behind the laughing veil and buried itself in the poem of her smile ... Good and wicked, cruel and compassionate, graceful and feline, she laughed" (quoted in ibid. 1910: 109).

After citing many passages of this sort, none providing a satisfactory answer to the enigma, Freud announces that he is giving up on his investigations: "Let us leave unsolved the riddle of the expression on Mona Lisa's face, and note the indisputable fact that her smile exercised no less powerful a fascination on the artist than on all who have looked at it for the last four hundred years" (ibid.: 109). But this is a ruse, for it is exactly at this moment that Freud links the smile of the Mona Lisa to the laughing terracotta juvenilia and then to Leonardo's mother: "It may very well have been that Leonardo was fascinated by Mona Lisa's smile for the reason that it awoke something in him which had for long lain dormant in his mind – probably an old memory" (ibid.: 110). Freud goes on to assert that "the smiling women are nothing other than repetitions of his mother Caterina, and we begin to suspect the possibility that it was his mother who possessed the mysterious smile – the smile that he had lost and that fascinated him so much when he found it again in the Florentine lady" (ibid.: 111).

As with the lost laughing heads, there is very little information about Caterina, whom Freud describes as "probably a peasant girl" who had her illegitimate child "torn" from her when she was very young. Her name does not appear in Leonardo's journals except in connection with a meticulous accounting of her funeral expenses. The one thing Freud feels certain he knows about her is that she is remembered by her son as laughing. "This memory was of sufficient importance for him never to get free of it when it had once been aroused; he was continually forced to give it new expression" (ibid.: 110). Freud is one of many scholars who think Leonardo strove to portray this expression in all of his works. Something about these laughing women and their enigmatic expressions has long been disquieting the discourse of art history.

Acknowledging that biographers are frequently drawn to their subjects because they feel they have characteristics in common with their "hero," Freud undertakes his own obsessional investigation of what lies behind the "laughing veil." In his essay "On Narcissism," written four years after the essay on Leonardo, Freud makes an odd series of connections. He links women and humorists in a rather bizarre sequence that includes great criminals, children, cats and large beasts of prey, as those who seem to have maintained an original, primary narcissism that the adult male has renounced. Women who love only themselves are, in Freud's account, "the type of female most frequently met with, which is the purest and truest one" (1914: 88), and he declares these characteristics in women are the greatest source of fascination for men. "It is as if we envied them for maintaining a blissful state of mind – an unassailable libidinal position which we ourselves have since abandoned" (ibid.: 89). Such women, he feels, while very charming, are the most likely to provoke complaints about their enigmatic nature. We remember that in the history of Freud's writings, the woman who provoked the most complaints of this sort was the Mona Lisa. It may be that we can read back into Freud's account of Leonardo's attachment to his mother the early outlines of the theory of primary narcissism.[1] What is important about Freud's discovery to historians of art is that it points to a breach in the assumed patriarchal contract of artistic production, which has always been a contract between father and son – the constant production of signs, by men, in furtherance of predominantly masculine perspectives, anxieties, and desires. Freud's discovery suggests that the impetus for Leonardo's artistic production derives from an attempt to recover a maternal identification, more specifically, an identification with a woman who maintained a primary narcissism.

While narcissism may seem a rather doubtful characteristic for women to claim as an asset, a number of feminist theoreticians have seen narcissism, along with hysteria, as a potential site of resistance, especially to specular appropriation. "For once," says Mary Jacobus, "Freud defines *woman* not in terms of lack but in terms of something she has; primary narcissism replaces the missing phallus" (1986: 105).[2] In his essay on narcissism Freud does not indicate what advantage women might derive from maintaining primary narcissism; in fact, he offers motherhood as a way for the narcissistic woman to overcome this condition and learn to love on the masculine model. It is not until the essay *On Humour*, written in 1927, that we begin to see the *potential* of narcissism for women. Now narcissism, rather than merely being a vehicle to elicit the admiration or envy of men, has become a laudable quality in its own right. What Freud calls the "triumph of narcissism" occurs as a result of "the grandeur" of humor. "Humour has something liberating about it; but it also has something of grandeur and elevation ... The grandeur in it clearly lies in *the triumph of narcissism,* the victorious assertion of the ego's invulnerability. The ego refuses to be distressed by the provocations of reality, to let itself be compelled to suffer. It insists that it cannot be affected by the traumas of the external world; it shows, in fact, that such traumas are no more than the occasions for it to gain pleasure" (1927b: 162).

We recall that the human beings who are able to maintain this primary narcissism into adulthood include women, criminals, and humorists. The importance of this grouping becomes clearer when, to illustrate the dynamics of the humorous gesture, Freud gives the example of a criminal, about to be hanged on a Monday, who remarks, on the way to the gallows, "Well, this week is beginning nicely." A certain rationale for narcissism now becomes apparent. The criminal, like the narcissistic woman, is outside the law; both are attempting to evade its effects, if only for a moment, by asserting pleasure. Freud assures us in the essay on narcissism that the theory was not developed out of "any tendentious desire on my part to depreciate women" (1914: 89). Freud is not, in fact, discussing biological imperatives, but rather social structures, the constraints they impose upon the individual, and the psychic mechanisms the individual develops to evade these constraints.

At the end of Marleen Gorris's film *A Question of Silence* (1983) we are given an instance of how humor may be used by women to evade the law. Three female criminals on trial for murder begin to laugh at the questions put to them by the prosecutor. This is the type of laughter Freud describes as capable of displaying a "magnificent superiority over the real situation" (1927b: 162). Their laughter "breaks up" the courtroom and, by extension, the law. It is infectious, spreading to other women in the courtroom and then out into the film audience. The women file out of the courtroom laughing and, in turn, the women in the movie theater leave laughing. This is an example of the revolutionary power of women's laughter.

In his short essay on humor Freud comes very close to delineating a political strategy for those without access to power: "*Humour is not resigned; it is rebellious*. It signifies not only the triumph of the ego but also of the pleasure principle, which is able here to assert itself against the unkindness of the real circumstance" (1927b: 163). We are reminded here of Leonardo's mother whose real circumstances were made even more unkind when her infant son was "torn" from her and given to her "better born rival." Are we then able to read in the expression portrayed in so many of Leonardo's paintings the faint outline of a case study of primary narcissism, a characteristic that enabled the young mother to refuse to suffer and transcend her real circumstance? Was Caterina possessed of this "rare and precious gift" – rebellious laughter? Was it because Leonardo was so successful in portraying the potential of this expression that later men looking upon this work have recognized in it something they both desired and experienced as a threat?

In suggesting that women have a special purchase on laughter as a strategy of liberation, Freud anticipates a number of contemporary theories linking the calculated optimism explicit in the feminist project with pleasure – particularly a sensual or erotic pleasure associated with the body. If, as Walter Benjamin suggests, "there is no better start for thinking than laughter. And, in particular, convulsion of the diaphragm usually provides better opportunities for thought than convulsion of the soul" (1978: 235), this laughter or *jouissance* may be a catalyst that could enable a break or subversion in the established representational and social structure.

A number of contemporary women artists are conducting an episte-mological investigation of the reality that, as Roland Barthes rather bluntly put it, "has already been written for us." In the only way available to them, in the guise of an amusement, they are *instancing* the continual discovery of ways to interrogate the generative nature and generative bounds of representation, making it dis-*play* through its own playful lapsus its structural elements, its inviolable conventional limits, its immanent possibilities. In this strategy the conventions and power of language are disrupted by a witticism or a pun, operating like a meta-language athwart the text – annihilating, for an instant, its domination by the challenge of non-sense.

These strategies are related to a much older and more overtly political theory of laughter: Rabelais's theory of laughter as misrule, a laughter with the potential to disrupt the authority of church and state. Such ideas may have influenced Barthes's and Julia Kristeva's notions of laughter as libid-inal license, the *jouissance* of the polymorphic, orgasmic body. While inves-tigating the revolutionary potential of the workings of the avant-garde text Barthes was pleased to discover what he called an "admirable expression" – the "body of the text." The expression stresses the corporeality of lan-guage, rather than its instrumentality or its meaning. "Does the text have a human form?" Barthes asks. "Is it a figure, an anagram of the body? Yes, but of our erotic body" (1975: 17). For Kristeva and other French feminists this erotic body is the territory of the mother, what Kristeva terms the "semiotic," verbal play, not controlled by symbolic conventions. It is the language that experimental writing liberates, absorbs, and employs, a "pre-sentence making disposition to rhythm, intonation, nonsense [that] makes nonsense abound with sense: makes one laugh" (1977: 25).

Subsequently, in *Desire in Language* Kristeva suggests it might be neces-sary to be a woman to explore the potential insurgency of this hetero-geneous body, to take up what she calls "that exorbitant wager of carrying the rational project to the outer borders of the signifying venture of men" (1980: x). Whenever an attempt is made to establish a visual practice that escapes patriarchal specularization or a specifically feminine mode of writing that is not female mimicry of male discourse, the vexed question of essentialism arises. The fear is that such theories, as Terry Eagleton puts it, "may be no more than a high-falutin version of the sexist view that women babble." Eagleton's defense of Kristeva is important to our understanding of the work of artists engaged in disruptive play: "It is important to see that the semiotic is not an alternative to the sym-bolic order, a language one could speak instead of 'normal' discourse: it is rather a process within our conventional sign-systems, which questions

15

and transgresses their limits ... On this view, *the feminine* – which is a mode of being and discourse not necessarily identical with women – *signifies a force within society that opposes it*" (1983: 190). Michèle Montrelay goes even further and suggests that it is one thing to desire, but to realize this desire, to engage in a maternal rather than a paternal identification, to enjoy Jocasta, results in the "ruin of representation." In this enjoyment "repression is no longer anything but a gigantic pantomime, powerless to assure the throwing back into play of the stake of desire. We know that, for want of a stake, representation is not worth anything" (1990: 259). Perhaps the women artists discussed in the following chapters are able to take that risk and enjoy it more readily because, as Montrelay suggests, femininity does not know repression, even though, as she reminds us, "it is femininity, not women, that can take on such a status" (ibid.: 260). Or perhaps, as women, they have nothing to lose when the "fictive" props of the social structure are removed.

## THE HERSTORY OF LAUGHTER

The first history of laughter and the carnivalesque became available to Western scholars with the translation in 1968 of Mikhail Bakhtin's monumental study *Rabelais and His World*. The study dealt with carnival not simply as a ritual feature of European culture long since past; rather, it marked out the carnivalesque as a site of special interest for the contemporary analysis of art, literature, cultural politics, and social revolt. We learn from Bakhtin that the laughter of the Middle Ages functioned as the unofficial opposition to medieval ideology – asceticism, sin, atonement, suffering, fear, religious awe, oppression and intimidation. Because it existed unofficially, outside the Church, it was marked by exceptional radicalism, freedom, and ruthlessness. "As opposed to the official feast, one might say that carnival celebrates temporary liberation from the prevailing truth of the established order; it marks the suspension of all hierarchical rank, privileges, norms, and prohibitions" (Bakhtin 1968: 10). It is ambivalent in nature, related to the underworld, to change, to revolution and renewal. During carnival, established authority and dogmas of morality or religion that pretend to be absolute become subject to mockery. People, not as individuals but in their role as vehicles of institutions, are ridiculed. Abuse is never personal, but always aimed at the higher authority. All are subject to mockery and punishment as incarnations of the dying truth and authority of prevailing thought, law and virtues. "Time has transformed old truth and authority into a Mardi Gras dummy, a comic monster that the laughing crowd rends to pieces in the marketplace" (ibid.: 213).

During the century-long development of the medieval carnival, the serious and the laughing worlds coexisted. "During carnival time [usually three months of every year] life is subject only to its laws, that is, the laws of its own freedom. It has a universal spirit; it is a special condition of the entire world, of the world's revival and renewal, in which all take part" (ibid.: 7). Throughout the Renaissance the positive, regenerative, creative aspects of laughter continued to be recognized. Laughter was understood to have a deep philosophical meaning: "Laughter purifies from dogmatism, from fanaticism and pedantry, from fear and intimidation, from didacticism, naiveté and illusion, from the single meaning, the single level, from sentimentality" (ibid.: 123).

Carnival laughter, which was not an individual reaction to some "comic" event, but the laughter of all the people, universal in scope and directed at all and everyone, was later narrowed to specific private and social vices. The Church originally adapted its calendar to the very powerful folk festivals in order to align them with "official" festivals. Beginning in the seventeenth century, state and Church encroached upon festive life, and the license formerly allowed the carnival was more and more restricted; subsequently it was banned from public life altogether. In the process, the revolutionary force of the comic was cut down and trivialized; the serious and universal could not be told in the language of laughter. Although the carnival was eventually suppressed, Bakhtin suggests that at certain historical moments, the carnivalesque as a form of social revolt would reemerge. For example, he points out that during the French Revolution, Rabelais's theories of the revolutionary power of carnivalesque laughter enjoyed a tremendous revival: "He was even made out to be a prophet of the revolution ... The men of that time well understood Rabelais's deeply revolutionary spirit" (ibid.: 119). Terry Eagleton suggests that in Bakhtin's own writing "the explosive politics of the body, the erotic, the licentious and semiotic" are pitted against that "official, formalistic and logical authoritarianism whose unspoken name is Stalinism" (1981: 144). And Peter Stallybrass and Allon White in the introduction to their book *The Politics and Poetics of Transgression* cite the women's peace encampment at Greenham Common as an instance of the contemporary carnival. In their role as "unruly women," in their independent sexual stance, in their lack of a male leader, in occupying common land in the name of the people, in being simply "matter out of place" and therefore associated with the grotesque (they were accused of such things as smelling of fish paste and bad oysters and having smeared the local town with excrement), these women are "drawing (in some cases self-consciously) upon historical and political resources of mythopoetic transgression" (1986: 24).

The example of the women of Greenham Common is an important one, for the history of laughter that Bakhtin traces is the history of the near-eradication of a potent form of social revolt, kept alive primarily by small groups of women. What remained of the ancient communal laughter after its suppression was maintained in all-women gatherings such as the celebrations at the bedsides of women recovering from childbirth. The women's conversations are recorded in what were called *caquets* or *cackles*. "The tradition of such gatherings is very old. They were marked by abundant food and frank conversation, at which social conventions were dropped. The acts of procreation and eating predetermined the role of the material bodily lower stratum and the theme of these conversations" (Bakhtin 1968: 105). Given the extreme misogyny of the ascetic tendency of medieval Christianity, it is not surprising that carnivalesque laughter, with its celebration of the body, survived the longest in communities of women.

At one point in his history Bakhtin analyzes the association of woman with the "low," or popular culture of Rabelais's day. This investigation occurs in the context of Bakhtin's attempt to defend Rabelais from accusations of misogyny. The *querelle des femmes*, the great dispute concerning women, while not a new topic, became especially controversial in France during the years 1542–50. With the new moralizing and scholastic humanistic philosophy, together with the extreme ascetic tendency of medieval Christianity, woman became more and more rigidly codified as the incarnation of sin, the temptation of the flesh. Bakhtin points out that Rabelais did not join what he calls these "enemy camps" but was instead the lone voice representing the authentic Gallic tradition – i.e. the popular and comic tradition. The gist of Bakhtin's argument is that because Rabelais was against the moralists and on the side of the popular and comic tradition, he is therefore politically on the side of women:

> The popular tradition is in no way hostile to woman and does not approach her negatively. In this tradition woman is essentially related to the material bodily lower stratum; she is the incarnation of this stratum that degrades and regenerates simultaneously. She is ambivalent. She debases, brings down to earth, lends a bodily substance to things, and destroys; but, first of all, she is the principle that gives birth. She is the womb. Such is woman's image in the popular comic tradition ... Womanhood is shown in contrast to the limitations of her partner (husband, lover, or suitor); she is a foil to his avarice, jealousy, stupidity, hypocrisy, bigotry, sterile senility, false heroism, and abstract idealism ... She represents in person the undoing of pretentiousness, of all that is finished, completed, and exhausted. She is the inexhaustible vessel of conception, which dooms all that is old and terminated.
>
> (1968: 240)

Whether or not Bakhtin is successful in acquitting Rabelais of charges of misogyny is not as important as his having realized, in the process of articulating a theory of popular culture and its connection to political engagement, that Rabelais *needed* to be on the side of women, and that to be otherwise was to be in the "enemy camp."[3] What is significant to our discussion here is that in the course of writing a history of laughter, Bakhtin reveals not just that women have historically been aligned with the popular comic tradition, but that they have a political stake in this site of insurrection.

Mary Russo, in her essay "Female Grotesques: Carnival and Theory," cites Victor Turner's and Emmanuel Le Roy's warning that the marginalized position of women and Jews placed them in danger during carnival: "Jews were stoned and there is evidence that women were raped, during carnival festivities" (1986: 217). While carnivalesque transgressions should not be idealized, they should also not be confused with attacks on women and other marginalized groups which occur when the public Law is suspended. Laughter, as Bakhtin points out, "is an idiom never used by violence and authority" (1968: 90). Acts of violence that occur when the Law that regulates a community and maintains social hierarchy is suspended need to be understood as an extension and reinstatement of that same Law. In fact, they are a more blatant statement of what is understood, but goes "unspoken" in the public Law. In Gurinder Chadha's film *Bhaji on the Beach* (1994) a group of women from the East Asian Women's Resource Centre set out to "have a female fun time" freed, as the organizer of the trip says, "from the patriarchal demands made on us in our lives ... the double yoke of racism and sexism." The first people the women meet on their quest for the carnivalesque are a group of young men traveling in a van on the same road. The men, in the spirit of charivari, pull down their pants and "moon" the women. This scene of hilarity is quickly changed when the men approach these "women on the loose" as loose women; they insult the women and spit on them. The teddyboys are revealed as just another form of the same Law the women were attempting to escape from for the day. The episode is deeply familiar to any woman who has traveled on her own, particularly in a foreign country. What is proffered as a sexual invitation is really a fascistic exertion of control over women who are perceived as having slipped outside of the control of the Law. The streets have never been available to women in the same way they have been to men. The role of the *flâneur* was open to females only as "streetwalkers," and the streets of most major cities today may be more dangerous for women than they ever have been. When women artists say they want to place their work in the streets or the marketplace, they are not naively assuming this to be some safe haven. Also, it is important to keep in mind that the artists mentioned in this book are engaged with the carnivalesque as a cultural analytic and strategy of intervention, not as an historically specific phenomenon they expect to revive.

Bakhtin's treatise on laughter and his efforts to exonerate Rabelais from the charge of antifeminism brought the *querelle des femmes*, begun in medieval times, into the contemporary discussion of feminism and postmodernism. The notion of the carnivalesque and the grotesque as elaborated by literary theorists is an instrument not only for a feminist analysis of texts, but also for feminist artistic production and cultural politics in general. The crisis of authority and value that is symptomatic of postmodernism has itself in large part been instigated by a feminist deployment of laughter.

## COMEDIAN AND CONNOISSEUR OF CHAOS

Writing in 1855 on the essence of laughter, Baudelaire described it as the collision of two contraries and linked it with the accident of the ancient Fall. Like the Original Joke, the Fall threatened the established order of things; it was a spanner, a monkey wrench in the works. Baudelaire does not mention Eve in this account, but we know the story. It seems that the mother of us all is the origin not just of chaos, but of the comic. The work of **Nancy Spero** is an extended examination of our origins, of the license and lawlessness of laughter and of women. Her entire opus writes large what Baudelaire and Rabelais only hinted at – that women have always been on the laughing side, that women have a stake in laughter's indissoluble and essential relation to freedom.

Spero's almost fifty years of work is an *œuvre* of vast energy, grotesque presences, monstrous acts, and lyric grace. It is shocking, irreverent, subversive, rowdy, unseemly, embarrassing, disturbing, but it is also reassuring and therapeutic in its profound gaiety, robust and sane in the contagion of its vitality. It is difficult: bleak, enigmatic, inconsistent, composed of hideous fantasies and, even worse, hideous facts. Spero's work is stark, perverse, obscure and capricious. Images and words are prodigally dispensed in lists and collections, piles and inundations. Hers is work of anger, knowledge, courage, and comedy.

The laughter with which Spero's work unites us is not modern in nature; it has its roots in ancient folk humor, in the carnivalesque. It is radical laughter, rooted in a much more serious and robust form of cultural politics than either contemporary parody, which is in effect a strengthening of the law, or satire, which is not laughter at all but rhetoric. When Spero speaks of her work as "carnivalesque" she is referring not only to the scrolls of lyrical dancing figures, but to all the work, from the dark chaos of the early *Black Paintings*, to the grotesque realism of the *Codex Artaud*, to the defecating figures of *Bombs and Victims*, to the printed accounts of torture in the *Torture of Women* series.

Spero speaks of the carnivalesque as the informing aesthetic principle of her work since the early 1950s, pointing out that "the figures in my carnivals are not individualized." In fact, she works entrenched within the most grotesque and fully cultural stereotypes of femininity itself. Woman is viewed as a collective subject, not a separate individual. This is true even in the *Torture of Women* series, where images of women and huge mythological creatures are juxtaposed with accounts taken from Amnesty International reports of actual women who tell of the torture they have undergone. Yet the women in Spero's work are never separate or distant "others"; they are always "us", moving in the continuous present. The stories of these women are part of the collective history of women. They take their place along with scenes of a medieval witch's hanging, a Vietnamese woman crawling with her child tied to her back, the irradiated shadow of a woman from Hiroshima, the image of a nude bound woman taken from a photograph found among the personal files of an officer of the Gestapo, the tormented imaginary daughters of Artaud. They are universal images, never individualized, private women. They are, as Spero explains, "characters in a play," part of what Bakhtin would describe as the material bodily principle, "contained not in the biological individual, not in the bourgeois ego, but in the people, a people who are continually growing and renewed. This is why all that is bodily becomes grandiose, exaggerated, immeasurable" (Bakhtin 1968: 19).[4] Spero's work is informed by an awareness of the explosive politics of the body, the way the body "speaks" social relations, the historically variable nature of the body, and the relations among body image, social context, and collective identity.

By 1974, with *Torture in Chile*, Spero began to use only images of women. She wanted to make these images function in the manner of traditional or canonical male representations of the so-called generic human – Man. "I believe I'm directly contradicting the way human beings are represented in our society. I think the universal is the male. And so in my deliberately turning this around and trying to universalize the female – the rites of passage for the woman – birth, puberty, childbirth, death would become the universal. I tried to challenge myself to look at the world as I wanted to, as a woman artist, realizing the complexities of doing so because the world isn't really that way" (Spero 1985: 51). The complexities are enormous, for everything functions as though the sign "man" had no origin and no historical, cultural, linguistic limit.

In a sense Spero had begun writing in the feminine much earlier than 1974. The black paintings of *Mother* or *Lover* or *Androgyne*, in which inchoate images of women slip back into some dark fecund embrace, or the *Codex Artaud*, in which bodies are fragmented, or possess both male and female genitalia, or have phalluses that metamorphose into tongues, were all part of earlier attempts to break up and realign a body image, to reclaim it from some predetermined representation, reproduction, and obliteration (Figure 1.1).

As Lisa Tickner points out in her catalogue essay on Nancy Spero, the major premise (and promise) of the women's movement since the 1960s has been to find a voice for woman, intelligible, yet separate from the patriarchal voice, and to reclaim the image of woman from the representations

*Figure 1.1*  Nancy Spero, *Codex Artaud XXVI* (gouache collage on paper, 109 × 42 cm) 1972.

of others (1987a: 5). Finding a language, a mode of writing – *l'écriture féminine* – has been the special problematic of the French feminists. Spero has set herself a comparable task in the field of representation, trying for what she calls *la peinture féminine*. The two projects, finding a voice and a body image, are intricately bound together. Realizing that the shattering of language is really a shattering of the body, Spero has launched a full-scale frontal attack on "things as they are," using the weapon of the fragmented female body and discovering, in the process, that laughter results from this wreckage.

When Spero did find her voice, the first words she uttered were "*Merde,*" "Fuck You," and "*Les Anes.*" These words are painted with black India ink underneath a drawing done in 1960 of the heads of women opening their mouths and sticking out their tongues. Ten years later Spero adopted Artaud's voice because, as she says, she "didn't know anything else that extreme." Artaud's abusive, vituperative language was the medium by which the poet effected his major victory: his extrication from the institutionalizing forces that sought to contain him, including language. In the special dialect of Billingsgate (foul, vulgar, abusive talk named after a fish market in London notorious for the crude and colorful language used there), Bakhtin notes that "profanities and oaths were not initially related to laughter, but they were excluded from the sphere of official speech because they broke its norms; they were therefore transferred to the familiar sphere of the market-place. Here in the carnival atmosphere they acquired the nature of laughter and became ambivalent" (1968: 17). In exploring this taboo-loaded terrain, Artaud brought language into direct contact with the body. Abuses, oaths, and curses form the basis of the grotesque concept of the body. "The importance of abusive language is essential to the understanding of the literature of the grotesque. Abuse exercises a direct influence on the language and the images of this literature and is closely related to all other forms of 'degradation' and the 'down to earth' in grotesque and Renaissance literature" (ibid.: 27). Artaud appealed to Spero because of the similarities of their pursuits: explorations of the powerful symbolic repertoires at borders, margins, and edges, rather than at the accepted centers of the social body. Artaud's writing comes the closest of all modern writing to one of the antique sources of Rabelais's philosophy of laughter – Lucian's account of Menippus laughing in the kingdom of the dead. What is stressed is "the relation of laughter to the underworld and death, to freedom of the spirit, and to freedom of speech" (ibid.: 70). Julia Kristeva describes Artaud's writing as an:

> underwater, undermaterial dive ... where the black, mortal violence of "the feminine" is simultaneously exalted and stigmatized. ... If a solution exists to what we call today the feminine problematic, in my opinion, it too passes over this ground. ... [I]t involves coming to grips with one's language and body as others, as heterogeneous elements. ... [H]aving you, *through language too*, go through an infinite, repeated, multipliable dissolution, until you recover possibilities of symbolic restoration: having a position that allows your voice to be heard in real, social matters – but a voice fragmented by increasing, infinitizing breaks. In short, a device that dissolves all of your solutions, be they scholarly, ideological, familial, or protective.
>
> (1980: 164–165)

23

Kristeva's description of a process of writing through which such risk taking could lead to the development of a voice heard in real social matters describes the trajectory of Spero's work. It is just such an underwater dive, originally an inchoate dissolution, an exploration of chaos, regression and savage violence, that gradually emerged with the discovery of a politically actualized voice. Spero speaks of her work as not being political until she began the series on the Vietnam war: "The lovers aren't political, the prostitutes and great mothers are timeless, existential figures. They're a little amorphous, going out into black space. Then I suddenly lifted them ... from the blackness and made them less and less obscure. It was clarifying, externalizing and politicizing my way of thinking, doing and acting in the world" (Spero 1985: 55).

As the work became more overtly political in its intention, it became more Rabelaisian in spirit. The *War Series* (1966–70) partakes of the ritual of charivari, a scapegoating carnivalesque ritual euphemistically described as mudslinging. In fact what was slung was offal: excrement, urine, pig's blood, etc. Angry, scratchy gouaches detailed the blatant scatological and sexual meta-discourse of war. War is rendered as a debasement of the body: bombs defecate bodies, helicopters become enormous ejaculating phalluses, women's torsos erupt into a fountain of heads and multiple breasts, bombs stick out their tongues or vomit or turn back and lick themselves in an act of self-regeneration. Spero points out that the dislocation and stylization of some of these body images have their source in medieval prototypes – the manuscript illuminations of the medieval nun Ende, who was one of the illustrators of the *Beatus Apocalypse*. Spero has carried into the modern apocalypse the ambivalent reading of the grotesque body. The lower bodily region is both the area of waste and death, and the area of genital organs, the fertilizing and generating stratum. This is the site of insurgency, of sexual energy, of regeneration and renewal.

The body that interests Spero, like the body that interests Rabelais, is "pregnant, delivers, defecates, is sick, dying and dismembered" (Bakhtin 1968: 179). Spero uses images again and again in different contexts where they play different roles and interact differently across huge extended spaces, becoming contradictory and confrontational. In each context a new historic sense penetrates these ancient, mythological or modern images and gives them new meanings, but their traditional contents are kept intact: copulation, pregnancy, birth, growth, old age, disintegration, dismemberment. Bakhtin explains that images of the material body are considered ugly precisely because they are in a constant state of change: "They are contrary to the classic images of the finished, completed man, cleansed, as it were, of all the scoriae of birth and development" (1968: 25). The examples he gives are the figurines of senile pregnant hags in the famous Kerch terracotta collection. "There is nothing completed, nothing calm and stable in the bodies of these old hags. They combine a senile, decaying

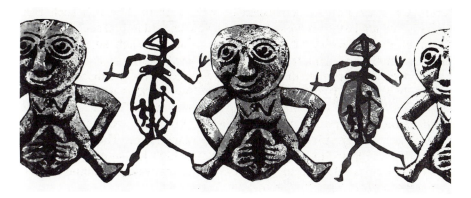

*Figure 1.2*  Nancy Spero, *Sheela and Wilma*, detail (handprinting, collage on paper) 1985 (photo: David Reynolds; Courtesy Barbara Gross Galerie).

and deformed flesh with the flesh of new life, conceived but as yet unformed" (ibid.: 26). Most important, he notes, the old hags are laughing. These are the female figures that appear in Spero's work. Sheela-na-Gig, a Celtic goddess of fertility and destruction, smiles wryly at the viewer as she reaches behind her legs to display an enormous vagina. The same obscene and humorous gesture is used by the old hag Baubo, a personification of the *cunnus*, who, when she finds Demeter in deep mourning over the death of her daughter, lifts her skirts and exposes herself, causing Demeter to laugh (Figure 1.2). "Like the Sybil of Panzoult in Rabelais's novel, she lifts her skirts and shows the parts through which everything passes (the underworld, the grave) and from which everything issues forth" (ibid.: 240). In some arrangements, Spero has Sheela link arms with a row of her identical sisters in a comic chorus line, revealing what the flounces of the tutu usually carefully conceal – the *lack* the fetishized version of female figures attempts to disavow.

Spero herself sometimes seems surprised by the peculiar capacity of these scatological images for change, renewal, and joy: "The new work has this buoyant look which worries me sometimes. Just look at the title of the new work: *Re-Birth of Venus*: That's a very positive thing" (Spero 1985: 53). In this work a very active, athletic Venus strides toward the viewer, seeming to originate from the center of the torso of another ancient fertility goddess; from one body a new body emerges. Other goddesses of death and fertility, skeletal figures from Saharan cave paintings, engage in manic dances, their tiny unborn babies curled in cavities in their bodies. In a recent exhibition Spero printed a row of "dildo dancers" directly onto the gallery wall – repeated images of an ancient Greek woman dancing with two large dildos between her legs. This figure is a more stylized version of an image that appeared earlier in *Notes in Time on Women*

*Figure 1.3* Nancy Spero, *Let the Priests Tremble*, detail (handprinting and collage on paper) 1984 (photo: David Reynolds).

(1976–79) – a woman trundling a priapus as large as herself across the scroll, as if the phallus were a piece of luggage.

These images have the opposite effect of fetishized images of women; they are not engaged in a cover-up. The laughter they provoke, like the laughter of the carnival, defeats the fears of the unknown. What was powerful or taboo or frightening in ordinary life is turned into amusing or ludicrous monstrosities. "Let the priests tremble," Spero quotes Hélène Cixous in one of her scrolls, "we're going to show them our sexts! Too bad for them if they fall apart upon discovering that women aren't men, or that the mother doesn't have one" (Figure 1.3). The fear of Medusa as the archetypal symbol of castration and the abyss is, as Cixous observes, a convenient fear. The laugh of Medusa defeats these fears; she is not hideous: "You have only to look at the Medusa straight on to see her. And she is not deadly. She is beautiful and she is laughing" (1975: 255). The dancing figures Spero weaves through Cixous's text seem to be striding forward to some future freedom, through some lighter atmosphere of liberty where the material bodily principle is revealed, where women's bodies are naked, but not fetishized.

If Spero's earlier works focused on women's pain, the later works body forth woman's pleasure and her potential. The scrolls now extend vertically as well as horizontally; the large expanses of white, the silences in the earlier scrolls, are in the later work filled with lush color, and the texts seem to have been replaced by larger, more sensual female bodies. As Lisa Tickner describes it, we enter a world where "[n]aked women are unmolested; sprinting women are never tripped; laughing women remain ungagged. The image is one of freedom from every kind of physical, mental and social constraint; a freedom we do not possess but need to nurture, as an idea or a feeling, as our talisman against the oppression of habit, the grind of everyday obligation and normality" (1987a: 16).

The disruptive, ever-renewing laughter informing Spero's work is the antithesis of the static, hierarchical conception of the world required for the maintenance of a class- and gender-based society. It travesties the established, the authorial, the didactic, the dogmatic. It is, above all, a challenge to ready-made solutions in the sphere of thought, to the accepted idea, to the established assumption and convention that construct the self-evident, what Wallace Stevens calls "the fatal, dominant X." Spero's work specifically targets what feminism has always targeted – things as they are, for things as they are are not for us.

Spero has always been out of place – ecstatic (from the Greek *ex*, "outside," and *histemi*, "place") – painting dark expressionist canvases during the minimalist years, and when expressionist painting returned, assembling fragile prints on paper, ephemeral expressions of an ephemeral freedom. "I wanted to depict women finding their voices, which partly reflected my own developing dialogue with the art world, that somehow I had a tongue and at least a part of the language of the world, there was an interchange. I'm speaking of equality, and about a certain kind of power of movement in the world, and yet I'm not offering any systematic solutions" (quoted in Bird 1987: 34). The collages, with their overprinted, fragmented, repeated polysemous images of the female body, will never resolve themselves, never offer wholeness, unity, and completion. The scrolls roll on with primordial goddesses: the great goddess of Sumer, the Egyptian goddess Nut, Artemis who "heals women's pain," Sheela-na-Gig from the façade of a ninth-century Celtic church, the great sky goddess whose skin is flayed and stretched across the sky, along with the goddesses of the silver screen all moving in the continuous present. They are repeated over and over because, as Gertrude Stein says, "It is never necessary to say anything again as remembering but it is always said again because every time it is so it is so it is so" (1935: 181). These goddesses of strength and healing, of female jouissance, these survivors, these dancers on their way to the revolution are all part of a contemporary and continuous celebration of femininity. It is utopian, it is nowhere, it is not yet, it is only the outline, the faint limning of what might be – a fiction of freedom imprinted on fragile paper (Figure 1.4).

## THE CARNIVALIZED FEMININE PRINCIPLE IN THE POSTMODERN MARKETPLACE

One afternoon, at a conference on modernism which took place over ten years ago in California, I found myself befriended by Clement Greenberg. During dinner that evening, a woman who had criticized his presentation

*Figure 1.4*   Nancy Spero, *Dancing Figure* (lithograph, 24 × 19 cm) 1984
(photo: David Reynolds).

earlier in the conference came to speak to me about my talk, but was
visibly taken aback when she saw that Greenberg was my dinner companion. Understanding her surprise, Greenberg said, "Yes, Jo Anna and
I are friends but we ceased to agree in 1939." At first I thought he meant
it was historically overdetermined, even before I was born, that I would
disagree with his version of modernism. Later I recalled that 1939 was
the year Greenberg wrote "Avant-garde and Kitsch," that last-ditch defense
of the high art of modernism against the incursions of mass culture. Unlike

many defenders of the purity and standards of high culture, Greenberg avoided ascribing a putative femininity to mass culture; he did not mention women as either consumers of culture or as cultural producers. But he was right: as a woman coming to political consciousness in the era of post-modernism, I was opposed to his notion of the great divide.

Since then, a number of critics have addressed the question of gender in the determinations of the modernism/mass culture dichotomy.[5] In "Mass Culture as Woman: Modernism's Other," Andreas Huyssen examines a notion that became commonplace during the nineteenth century – that devalued forms of popular or mass culture have historically been associated with women while real, authentic culture remains the privileged realm of male activity. In the gender inscription of the mass culture debate, women have been thought to be more susceptible to the delusions and pacifications of the institutions of mass culture. Huyssen's example of the female character caught in the lure of mass cultural *consumption* (specifically in the thrall of pulp romances) is Emma Bovary. The man of modernism is, of course, Flaubert, active *producer*, "writer of genuine, authentic literature – objective, ironic, and in control of his aesthetic means" (Huyssen 1986: 46). In spite of Flaubert's famous confession, "*Madame Bovary, c'est moi,*" Huyssen argues that Flaubert's aesthetic is based on the uncompromising repudiation of what Emma Bovary loved to read.

Huyssen sees modernism as the historical culmination of a kind of paranoid view of mass culture and the masses, both of which are associated with women:

> Thus Mallarmé's quip about "*reportage universal*" (i.e. mass culture), with its not so subtle allusion to "*suffrage universal,*" is more than just a clever pun. The problem goes far beyond questions of art and literature. In the late 19th century, a specific traditional male image of woman served as a receptacle for all kinds of projections, displaced fears, and anxieties (both personal and political), which were brought about by modernization and the new social conflicts, as well as by specific historical events such as the 1848 revolution, the 1870 Commune, and the rise of reactionary mass movements which, as in Austria, threatened the liberal order. An examination of the magazines and the newspapers of the period will show that the proletarian and petit-bourgeois masses were persistently described in terms of a feminine threat. Images of the raging mob as hysterical, of the engulfing floods of revolt and revolution, of the swamp of big city life, of the spreading ooze of massification, the figure of the red whore at the barricades – all of these pervade the writings of the mainstream media, as well as that of right-wing ideologues of the late 19th and 20th centuries. ... The fear of the masses in this age

29

of declining liberalism is always also a fear of woman, a fear of nature out of control, a fear of the unconscious, of sexuality, of the loss of identity and stable ego boundaries in the mass.

(1986: 52)

An odd recurrence of this old gender bias of modernist criticism appears in a recent essay by Rosalind Krauss on the failure of critics, more particularly feminist critics, to properly address the production processes of photographer **Cindy Sherman**. In Krauss's essay, Laura Mulvey (used as an example of feminist readers in general) is portrayed as a latter-day Emma Bovary, a victim of what Barthes calls "myth." To Krauss, Mulvey becomes one of Barthes's "petit-bourgeois *consumers* of culture" who are subject to "a naive buying-into the purported signified of a cultural phenomenon without having the distance, the skepticism, or the experience to attend to the signifiers laboring away to *produce* the mythified meaning" (Krauss 1993: 163). Instead, Krauss wants the viewer to assume Flaubert's position – objective, analytical, repudiating if not what Emma reads, then at least the gullibility with which she reads it. Wanting to focus on the mode of production is understandable, particularly when dealing with work such as Sherman's. To look anywhere else, to look *at* the photographs, to look *at* the character in the photographs is to risk absorption. To begin to construct narratives *about* the women in the photographs, as Krauss criticizes Mulvey for doing, is to position oneself precariously close to the woman *in* the photograph. The danger is especially great in Sherman's work, where from the beginning we are invited to lapse into the subjectivity of a taste like Emma's, "more sentimental than artistic . . . full of love and lovers . . . romantic intrigue, brutal crimes, vows, sobs, embraces and tears" (Flaubert 1856: 29–30). What Huyssen describes as "the loss of identity and stable ego boundaries" that results from the immersion in mass culture is only the first step; in her later work Sherman draws the viewer deep into the "spreading ooze of massification." Appropriately, the exploration is undertaken using the vehicle of her own body, which like Emma's body is capable of "disappearing in the elaboration of her attire" or materializing as the body of grotesque realism – decomposing, putrefying, emitting "a flood of black liquid . . . like vomit" (ibid.: 282). The description of Emma's body after her death would do as well for a description of a number of Sherman's self-portraits: "The corner of her mouth, which had fallen open, was like a black hole in the lower part of her face; her thumbs still dug into the palms of her hands; a sort of white dust had settled on her eyelashes, and her eyes had begun to disappear behind a pale film, a thin coating not unlike a spider web" (ibid.: 280). Sherman's body, like Emma's, seems to be capable of "gradually melting into the surrounding objects" (ibid.: 282–283). In the end it is Sherman, not Flaubert, who can say, "*Emma Bovary, c'est moi.*"

In spite of Huyssen's concluding assurances that such notions as "mass culture and the masses as feminine threat ... belong to another age" (1986: 62), the masculinist bias of Krauss's criticism repeats exactly the hidden subtext of the modernist project, both in its construction of a deluded, easily victimized, feminine (in this case feminist) reader and in its valorization of production over consumption in order to differentiate between progressive and regressive responses to cultural phenomena. While the historical specificity of Huyssen's essay is important to our understanding of modernism, I would argue that the assumptions upon which he bases his argument rest on powerful stereotypes concerning the masses, mass culture, and women: unconscious psychic associations that were in place long before the development of modernism and have not vanished with the advent of postmodernism.

Huyssen, like every critic since Adorno and Horkheimer, is careful to distinguish between modern mass culture administered and imposed from above, and working-class culture or residual forms of older popular or folk cultures. I would like to raise some doubts about these neat divisions. Although contemporary mass culture may be a long way away from the popular culture of Rabelais's day, what is apparent even in the context of Huyssen's short references to the history of the perception of mass culture as feminine is the degree to which these perceptions are a continuation of associations surrounding that older popular culture. Both mass and popular culture derive their identity in part from the pejorative characteristics attributed to them. The real or imagined threat they represent comes from the way in which those negative characteristics may be turned critically against the dominant culture. Huyssen notes that "the kitchen has been described metaphorically as the site of mass cultural production" (1986: 50), so we are not only in the domain of the feminine, we are in the realm of Rabelaisian folk traditions. "Culinary images ... were widely used in the fifteenth and sixteenth centuries; they were frequent precisely in the sphere where literature was connected with folk tradition of humor" (Bakhtin 1968: 194). Similarly, in the contemporary critical concern about rabid consumerism, we are dealing not just with consumption, but with consumption conceived as a threat, particularly the unlicensed appetites of women, for it is women who are placed in the role of preeminent consumers. This is the modern-day equivalent of the gargantuan appetites described by Rabelais – the unlicensed, potentially engulfing appetites of the material bodily principle. Baudrillard uses the term "engulfment" in describing what he sees as the radical potential of rabid consumerism. Since "a system is abolished only by pushing it into the hyperlogic. ... You want us to consume – O.K. let's consume always more, and anything whatsoever; for any useless and absurd purpose" (1983: 46).[6]

The line that divides high art and mass culture can no longer be confidently drawn, for as Huyssen puts it, "both mass culture and women's

31

(feminist) art are emphatically implicated in any attempt to map the specificity of contemporary culture and thus to gauge this culture's distance from high modernism ... where modernism's great wall once kept the barbarians out and safeguarded the culture within, there is now only slippery ground which may prove fertile for some and treacherous for others" (1986: 59). Ironically, the metaphors Huyssen chooses for his account of the demise of high culture sound like the fulfilment of warnings of the early Christian ascetics against feminine seduction and the unruliness of the masses. They were right to worry; we are now sliding about on this fertile, treacherous ground of postmodernism principally as a result of the disruptive excess of feminist interventions in the production and consumption of art. While pop art brought mass culture "up" into the realm of high art, feminist art of the 1980s trafficked in a two-way street that enabled intercourse with the politically as well as aesthetically marginalized. This has occurred as a function of what anthropologist Victor Turner rather deliciously describes as "the subversive potential of the carnivalized feminine principle," which by its very marginalized condition inevitably opens out onto the political arena:

> The danger here is not simply that of female "unruliness." This unruliness itself is the mark of the ultraliminal, of the perilous realm of possibility of "anything may go" which threatens any social order and seems the more threatening, the more that order seems rigorous and secure. ... The subversive potential of the carnivalized feminine principle becomes evident in times of social change when its manifestations move out of the liminal world of Mardi Gras into the political arena itself.
>
> (1977: 41–42)

## GRAMMATICA JOCOSA

To compound the imagination's Latin with
The lingua franca et jocundissima.

Wallace Stevens

To write a quality cliché you have to come up with something new.

Jenny Holzer

The area of common ground with postmodernism for a number of women artists is the marketplace of mass culture. While Tania Modleski cautions that women are victimized in many and complex ways by mass culture, a good number of contemporary women artists have selected this as the site of their intervention. **Jenny Holzer**, **Barbara Kruger** and **Ilona Granet** were among the first artists to occupy a terrain from which women have historically been excluded, negatively inscribed, or, if they entered, existed at "risk."

**Ilona Granet** began working, not in the studio, but in the *plein air* of the city streets. As a sign painter her work was to be found "skied" on billboards and buildings around the city of New York. She, like all sign painters, worked from a prescribed text, *The Sign Painter's Dictionary of Signs*, in which the agit-prop symbols of heroic capitalism that surround us daily are reduced and standardized by a committee of Orwellian cryptographers, expert in inducing the quick recognition and appropriate desire in the harried passersby. For "The Revolutionary Power of Women's Laughter" exhibition Granet made signs of male authority figures. *Bums/Bomb* are four monolithic figures made from a collection of codes by which male success and male power are conveyed by this culture's dictionary of signs. These superhero comix cartoons of a landowner, industrialist, media-monopolizer, and military leader are, Granet explained, "what I'm supposed to be advertising." (One of Granet's employers was the media mogul Malcolm Forbes – she painted the name on his yacht.) These corporate warriors of high capitalism were encased in four huge sarcophagus-like missiles; "stealth weapons" in the "total war" of surveillance and control. Appropriately, they were hung high over the entrance door, their long semaphoric shape, Jeanne Silverthorne suggests, recall banners in meeting halls of the Reich. But here in the site of the carnival they are uncrowned and transformed into "funny monsters" to be dunked, the melancholy clowns of pie-throwing contests.

Granet is still working in the streets, trying to make the streets a bit more tolerable for women. In 1989 she became infamous for her Emily Post Street Signs, "regulations" for etiquette in the street. The injunctions are written in English and Spanish: "No cat calls and whistling kissing sounds," or "Curb Your Animal Instinct." The image on the latter sign is of a beast straining on a leash towards a woman (Figures 1.5 and 1.6). Her work raises the obvious point: if there is a city ordinance against dog shit and horn blowing, why isn't there one against the harassment of women in the streets?

**Holzer** and **Kruger** first entered the streets surreptitiously, putting up their posters and plaques at night. The posters went up and were quickly covered over in the general pell-mell of street advertising. "I wanted my work to enter the marketplace," Kruger explained, "because I began to understand that outside the market there is nothing" (quoted in Squiers 1987: 84). Holzer speaks of the streets, particularly, as both the site of her artistic origins and as an arena she feels the need to return to – "It's necessary for me to continue to practice outside. This is where my work went originally, and where I still feel it operates best" (quoted in Ferguson 1986: 113). Over the past ten years their work has become "street clothes," appearing on building walls, billboards, movie marquees, wall plaques,

*Figure 1.5* Ilona Granet, *No Cat Calls* (enamel on metal, 61 × 61 cm) 1987 (courtesy P.P.O.W. Gallery, New York).

light-emitting diodes (LEDs), shopping bags, matchbooks, T-shirts, and baseball caps. Currently, on a dilapidated movie marquee of a now condemned building of New York's red light district on 42nd Street one of Holzer's signs asks, "What Urge Will Save You Now That Sex Won't?"

When I first wrote about Jenny Holzer's *Truisms* and *Inflammatory Essays* in 1982, I related them to the parable of the grotesque that Sherwood Anderson tells in "The Book of the Grotesque," the introduction to his 1919 novel *Winesburg, Ohio*:

> [I]n the beginning when the world was young there were a great many thoughts but no such thing as a truth. Man made the truths himself and each truth was a composite of a great many vague thoughts. ... It was the truths that made the people grotesques ... the moment one of the people took one of the truths to himself,

*Figure 1.6*   Ilona Granet, *Curb Your Animal Instinct* (enamel on metal silkscreen, 61 × 66 cm) 1986 (photo: Adam Reich; courtesy P.P.O.W. Gallery, New York).

called it his truth, and tried to live his life by it, he became a grotesque and the truth he embraced became a falsehood.

Anderson's parable of the grotesque is really just another version of the institutional alignment we all undergo in the training process of learning language and becoming socialized human beings. As Fredric Jameson points out, the symbolic order is the source of meaning and, at the same time, "the source of all cliché, the very fountainhead of all those more debased 'meaning-effects' which saturate our culture" (1972: 140). In her early work Holzer is engaged in a process of compounding cliché upon cliché, as if to beat the stultifying force of language at its own game. She plays upon the codes already in place, the reality that has already been written for us to make us aware of the ways in which those clichés have saturated us – the degree to which we are shaped by the verbal environment in which we are immersed.

35

**ABUSE OF POWER COMES AS NO SURPRISE**
**ALIENATION PRODUCES ECCENTRICS OR REVOLUTIONARIES**
**AN ELITE IS INEVITABLE**
**ANGER OR HATE CAN BE A USEFUL MOTIVATING FORCE**
**ANY SURPLUS IS IMMORAL**
**DISGUST IS THE APPROPRIATE RESPONSE TO MOST SITUATIONS**
**EVERYONE'S WORK IS EQUALLY IMPORTANT**
**EXCEPTIONAL PEOPLE DESERVE SPECIAL CONCESSIONS**
**FAITHFULNESS IS A SOCIAL NOT A BIOLOGICAL LAW**
**FREEDOM IS A LUXURY NOT A NECESSITY**
**GOVERNMENT IS A BURDEN ON THE PEOPLE**
**HUMANISM IS OBSOLETE**
**HUMOR IS A RELEASE**
**INHERITANCE MUST BE ABOLISHED**
**KILLING IS UNAVOIDABLE BUT IS NOTHING TO BE PROUD OF**
**LABOR IS A LIFE-DESTROYING ACTIVITY**
**MONEY CREATES TASTE**
**MORALS ARE FOR LITTLE PEOPLE**
**MOST PEOPLE ARE NOT FIT TO RULE THEMSELVES**
**MOSTLY YOU SHOULD MIND YOUR OWN BUSINESS**
**MUCH WAS DECIDED BEFORE YOU WERE BORN**
**MURDER HAS ITS SEXUAL SIDE**
**PAIN CAN BE A VERY POSITIVE THING**
**PEOPLE ARE NUTS IF THEY THINK THEY CONTROL THEIR LIVES**
**PEOPLE WHO DON'T WORK WITH THEIR HANDS ARE PARASITES**
**PEOPLE WON'T BEHAVE IF THEY HAVE NOTHING TO LOSE**
**PRIVATE PROPERTY CREATED CRIME**
**ROMANTIC LOVE WAS INVENTED TO MANIPULATE WOMEN**
**SELFISHNESS IS THE MOST BASIC MOTIVATION**
**SEX DIFFERENCES ARE HERE TO STAY**
**STARVATION IS NATURE'S WAY**
**STUPID PEOPLE SHOULDN'T BREED**
**TECHNOLOGY WILL MAKE OR BREAK US**
**THE FAMILY IS LIVING ON BORROWED TIME**
**THE LAND BELONGS TO NO ONE**
**TIMIDITY IS LAUGHABLE**
**TORTURE IS BARBARIC**
**YOU ARE GUILELESS IN YOUR DREAMS**
**YOU MUST REMEMBER YOU HAVE FREEDOM OF CHOICE**

*Figure 1.7*   Jenny Holzer, Selections from *Truisms* (offset ink on paper sheets, each 91 × 61 cm) 1977–82.

*Truisms* (1977–82) and *Inflammatory Essays* (1979–82) arrest the repeater of language in the act of conformity, in the conditioned acceptance of some platitude, some authoritative statement, some adage by which one habitually conducts one's life. Like Flaubert's *Dictionary of Accepted Ideas*, Holzer's *Truisms* replace thought with formulaic statements: "Don't place too much trust in experts," "Don't run people's lives for them," "Everyone's work is equally important," "You must remember you have freedom of

36

choice," "Children are the hope of the future" (Figure 1.7). It is due to the sheer multiplicity of these truths and the rapidity with which the viewer is presented with the next, equally valid but often contradictory truth ("Exceptional people deserve special concessions," "People are nuts if they think they control their lives," "Children are the cruelest of all") that the displacement occurs. The *Inflammatory Essays* have the didactic tone of the Book of Ecclesiastes, with its transcendent source of information, and they have the typeface of the *New York Times* headlines, another signifier of Truth, but the authority of the text is undermined by the sheer multiplicity of conflicting truths moving the reader in and out of the realm of the absurd.

The language and mode of presentation of Holzer's text vacillate between the look of authority (the establishment of what she calls the "upper-anonymous" voice in the commemorative bronze plaques and the large-scale electronic signs placed in such official public venues as the spectacolor boards in Piccadilly Circus, Times Square, or Caesar's Palace in Las Vegas) and the "lower-anonymous" voice of the ephemeral street posters (Figures 1.8 and 1.9). Despite the disembodied nature of the work, there is a gender specificity to these different registers of language. Holzer says she intended to make much of her work "gender neutral," but because the voice of authority and aggression in this society is associated with the male voice the work is often assumed to have been written by a male. The male voice is something Holzer admits to having "hijacked," but this verbal cross-dressing is never seamless. Signs of the feminine usually break through the normative language conventions of the public information systems she deploys. "The works had a very measured tone, a very bland, pared-down language that fits the upper-class anonymous voice" (quoted in Ferguson 1986: 113). The feminine is heard both in what is said and in where it is said. Language, when it moves away from authoritative pronouncements and into the irrational, is heard as feminine. When the voice of the marginalized or the mad predominates, when it becomes hysterical and "rants," it is heard as a woman's voice. Even when the signs are located in the gallery, language *in extremis* becomes *embodied,* and when it does, it assumes a woman's body, which speaks, as the maternal bodily principle always does, of sexuality and death. This is manifest in what has become known as the "Mother and Child" installation, first shown in "High and Low: Modern and and Popular Culture" at the Museum of Modern Art in 1990 and then at the 44th Venice Biennale. The voice never identifies itself as female, yet the words could originate only from a mother of some species. Lashing out in the darkened room they have a visceral, physical presence. Like the mother's body, it is thrown up as a protective shield between the child and the violence that threatens it. This is the word made flesh.

Holzer observes that women artists are more likely to deal with what she called "'real world subject matter" because women "do sense real danger from forces like institutions, for example. Hence we address them

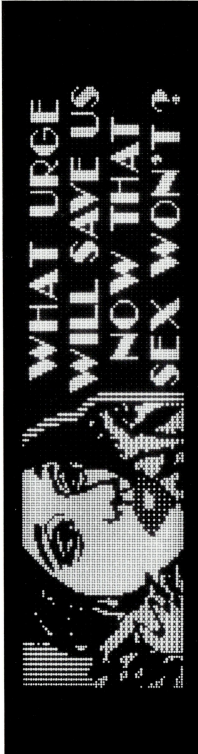

*Figure 1.8* Jenny Holzer, The *Survival Series* (Unex Signs, 77.5 × 288 × 30.5 cm) 1983 (courtesy Barbara Gladstone Gallery, New York).

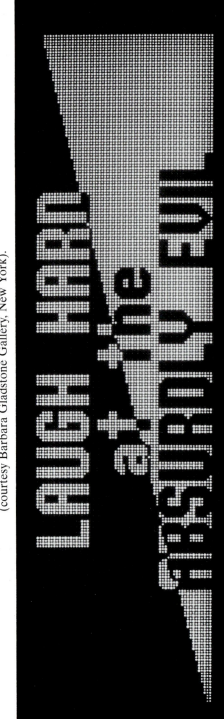

*Figure 1.9* Jenny Holzer, The *Survival Series*, 1983.

in our work" (quoted in Ferguson 1986:113). Language is clearly the institution Holzer has felt most endangered by. Her aim seems to be to push language past the point where it could exert any control over her, past sense into the realm of the sensual. In her 1989 installation at the DIA Art Foundation in New York, Holzer created a verbal sensorium. We walk *through* the language, it is printed on our bodies. We are galvanized by the electric current of letters and light, and then, like Milton's Satan, we are plunged into a "darkness visible." To enter a Holzer installation is to enter what Bakhtin calls a *grammatica jocosa*, a thoroughly material metaphysics in which the grotesque is bodied forth in the language itself. What is emitted by Holzer's light-emitting diodes is the erotic, the obscene, the materially satisfying non-sense: "I have a hot hole that was put in me. I can live with it. People made it and use it to get to me. I can hurt it too but usually I put my thinking there for excitement." The broken, repeated sentences that wash over the spectator are fragments torn from the structural dyads of carnival: high and low, birth and agony, food and excrement, curses and praises, laughter and tears.

> Carnivalesque structure is like the residue of a cosmogony that ignored substance, causality, or identity. ... It is a spectacle, but without a stage; a game, but also a daily undertaking; a signifier, but also a signified. That is, two texts meet, contradict, and relativize each other. A carnival participant is both actor and spectator; he loses his sense of individuality, passes through a zero point of carnivalesque activity and splits into a subject of the spectacle and an object of the game ...
>
> The scene of the carnival, where there is no stage, no "theater," is thus both stage and life, game and dream, discourse and spectacle. By the same token, it is proffered as the only space in which language escapes linearity (law) to live as drama in three dimensions. At a deeper level ... drama becomes located in language.
>
> (Kristeva 1980: 78–79)

Holzer has taken this metaphor of writing the body literally. Motivated by the accounts of Bosnian women being raped and brutalized she writes of the violence done to them, not in the white ink Cixous says women so often write in, but in a medium that is meant to be indelible, a mixture of India ink and blood. On the cover of the German magazine *Süddeutsche Zeitung* (19 November 1993) Holzer attached a blood-red handwritten note "DA WO FRAUEN STERBEN BIN ICH HELLWACH" (I AM AWAKE IN THE PLACE WHERE WOMEN DIE). Inside the cover are pages and pages of texts that read like violent and sexual graffiti. These words are written directly on human skin. We read of detailed accounts of violent acts perpetrated upon the bodies of women, not off the dispassionate white sheet of newspaper, but off the flesh of women.

We read through the pores, through fine hair, over moles and freckles, and experience the words as scars the bodies have endured. Articulated here is the unspeakable.

> I am interested in works that address these material conditions of our lives: that recognize the uses and abuses of power on both an intimate and global level. I want to speak, show, see, and hear outrageously astute questions and comments. I want to be on the side of pleasure and laughter and to disrupt the dour certainties of pictures, property, and power.
>
> (Barbara Kruger 1982: 221)

Like Holzer and Granet, **Barbara Kruger** puts her art out to play in the constant traffic of consumer messages – on posters, signs, matchboxes, postcards, placards, billboards, museum walls, even on the bodies of passers-by in the form of T-shirts or shopping bags. Although the early work may have been more psychoanalytically inflected, and the later work more focused on late capitalism's consumerism, it always addresses the complex interconnection of gender and the marketplace. As women, she says: "We loiter outside trade and speech and are obliged to steal language." Although she, perhaps more than most artists working today, is aware of the various and complex ways women are victimized in mass culture, she does not suffer from agoraphobia. The language she steals is the colloquialisms of the marketplace. The words printed on severely cropped commercial photographs – **Buy me I'll change your life** ... **When I hear the word culture I take out my checkbook ... Money can buy you love ... I shop therefore I am ... Put your money where your mouth is** – are commonplace speech (Figures 1.10, 1.11 and 1.12). One of the persistent criticisms of her art is that it is indistinguishable from the advertisements found in the street. This is fine with Kruger: "I don't think of art per se, I think of how words and pictures – pictures with words – function in culture. If those images on the street are seen as pictures with words on them, that is what they are. Whether they are read as art or not is really not of much meaning to me" (quoted in Nairne 1987: 157). Bakhtin makes a similar statement about the inclusion of the advertising language of Rabelais's day: "The colloquial and artistic forms are sometimes so closely interwoven that it is difficult to trace a dividing line, and no wonder, since the barkers and vendors of drugs were also actors in performances at the fair" (1968: 153). He is referring to the *cris de Paris*, the shouts of street vendors and the general verbal anarchy of the street that found its way into his novel. "The *cris de Paris* were composed in verse and were sung in a peremptory tone. The style of the barker inviting customers to his booth did not differ from that of the hawker of chapbooks, and even the long titles of these books were usually

*Figure 1.10*    Barbara Kruger, *Untitled (Buy me I'll change your life)*
(photograph, 183 × 1222 cm) 1984 (photo: Zindman/Fremont; courtesy Mary
Boone Gallery, New York).

*Figure 1.11*   Barbara Kruger, *Untitled* (**When I hear the word culture I take out my checkbook**) (photograph, 335 × 152 cm) 1985 (photo: Zindman/Fremont; courtesy Mary Boone Gallery, New York).

*Figure 1.12*　Barbara Kruger, *Untitled (**I shop therefore I am**)* (photographic silkscreen/vinyl, 282 × 287 cm) 1987 (photo: Zindman/Fremont; courtesy Mary Boone Gallery, New York).

composed in the form of popular advertisements" (ibid.: 153). The "green sauce" that Pantagruel hawks in the street offers the same promise to the consumer (restoration of youth and the cure to various illnesses, especially impotence) that is offered by Kruger's **Buy me I'll change your life**. Just like contemporary advertising, the oral advertisements of Rabelais's day played an immense role in everyday life as well as in the cultural field; elements of this familiar speech found their way into all kinds of announcements, orders, and laws and "were easily adopted by all the festive genres, even by Church drama" (ibid.: 155). High cultural forms have never been as discrete as we are sometimes led to believe. Kruger, like Rabelais, reveals their continuous and flagrant intercourse with the low cultural forms of the marketplace.

Ironically, the most vociferous complaints about Kruger's cohabitation with the marketplace came when she joined the gallery of Mary Boone. Critics who had never complained of an artist's commercial success before now became very delicate on this point. Donald Kuspit described Kruger's first Mary Boone exhibition using adjectives such as "degenerate," "degraded," and "slick" and spoke of his alarm about the possibility of a "symbolic, final 'sell out' ('sell off?')" (1987: 76). "The subtext of Kruger's big clean expensive-looking pieces now seems to be 'Buy my work . . . please,'" writes Nancy Grimes, who had, presumably, never noticed the subtext of many of the other (male) artists exhibited in this gallery (1989: 200). Both critics agree that Kruger overstepped some line; the work partakes too much of the commercial marketplace: "Now because they promise a profundity they never deliver, the works come even closer to the advertisements they mimic." And Kuspit introduces an Adornist note of condemnation when he says, "Consciousness cannot raise itself by the heels of her images because they are made of just that which degrades it" (1987: 77). When Kruger did a show that could not be sold because the words were painted directly on the walls of the gallery, critics complained that it was too loud, too authoritarian. Going directly to what had really been bothering everyone – the context – Ellen Handy claims that Kruger has "repeated herself ineffectively since she switched galleries a few years ago" (1991: 79). It was as if Kruger, who had been talking about object-lust all along, had become too explicit. It is one thing to use that old street hawker's gambit **I am not trying to sell you anything** on the Spectacolor Board in Times Square, but to write the same joke in Helvetica Bold, which, as Susan Tallman tells us, is *the* signature typeface of postindustrial capitalism (1989: 20), on the walls, ceiling, and the floor of Mary Boone's gallery seems to have offended those who did get the joke even more than those who didn't. The close-cropped photograph of the hand of God creating Adam from the Sistine chapel, accompanied by the text **You invest in the divinity of the masterpiece**; or **When I hear the word culture I take out my checkbook** printed over the face of a wooden puppet; or **You are getting what you paid for** over the image of a huge dripping baby bottle; or the image of a bratty little girl with her fingers in her ears and her tongue sticking out, accompanied by the text **Money can buy you love**, were all designed specifically with that gallery space and its audience in mind and derive a good deal of their humor from the context.

As a teller of tendentious jokes, Kruger is acutely aware of their dynamics, which brings us, as jokes so often do, to the question of gender.

> I remember watching Johnny Carson one night 15 years ago. He was telling a joke and I was laughing along with Johnny. He finishes that joke and suddenly he's telling another one – about broads. And I thought, Oh, that's me. So the jokes are never addressed *to* me, they're *about* me. I can't laugh about that. Because this is a triangulation in which we, as women, are spoken of but never addressed. We are never a subject, we are always an object.
>
> (quoted in Squiers 1987: 80)

Kruger didn't need to read Freud to understand the mechanisms of power and social motivation of the smutty joke – she just needed to be female. Freud noted that in peasant culture, the smut starts when the woman enters and that in a more highly educated and thus more repressed society, it starts when she leaves. In either case, the woman, who is taken as object of the hostile or sexual aggressiveness, is a necessary conduit for

*Figure 1.13* Barbara Kruger, *Untitled (**Your gaze hits the side of my face**)* (photograph, 140 × 104 cm) 1981 (photo: Zindman/Fremont; courtesy Mary Boone Gallery, New York).

this form of exchange between men.[7] The joke functions as a bond between teller and listener. The listener responds to the joke by laughing and is thereby won over into a pseudo-identification with the teller by "the effortless satisfaction of his own libido" (Freud 1905b: 100).

Kruger intervenes in this triangulation by telling obscene jokes of her own. By obscene I mean not just her cunt and pecker jokes, I mean overexposed, too revealing; she is "baring the device" in public. Worse, she has been doing it "in mixed company." She has been addressing an audience that included those women who were supposed to be absent. Kruger refers to her project as a "series of attempts to welcome the female spectator into the audience of men." To do this, she realized she needed first to "ruin certain representations." Freud's analysis of the mechanism of the dirty joke, which traps the listener into a pseudo-identification with the teller, is much the same as Lacan's analysis of the spectator's relation to representation: both listener and spectator are fixed in their place, "arrested" by "the dialectic of identificatory haste" (Lacan 1977: 117). Craig Owens calls this terminal moment of arrest the "'Medusa Effect': specular ruse, imaginary identification of seer and seen, immediacy, capture, *stereotype*" (1984: 104). **Your gaze hits the side of my face**, written down the side of a photograph of a stone or marble bust of a woman, illustrates the stultifying effect of the sadistic gaze (Figure 1.13). Immobility, particularly the immobility of women, is a recurrent theme in Kruger's work, as in **We have received orders not to move** printed across the image of a seated woman, hunched forward and held in place with pins, or **I am your reservoir of poses** printed below an image of a woman completely obscured by her hat. But much of Kruger's work makes it clear that, like the master/slave relationship, both positions are fixed. **You are a captive audience**, the viewer is told. Owens suggests that Kruger proposes a mobilization of the spectator. This is exactly what Kruger has been doing and she has been doing it in public. Here at last we can understand what it is that jokes achieve in the service of their purpose – "jokes produce freedom ... undoing the renunciation and retrieving what was lost. ... We can only laugh when a joke has come to our help" (Freud 1905b: 101). Although Kruger's famous accusatory "You" is specifically addressed to the male viewer, the help her jokes offer is not gender-exclusive. The "We" her work addresses is any subject seeking to shift the limits of his or her enclosure – through pleasure and laughter.

# 2

# ART HISTORY AND
# ITS (DIS)CONTENTS

Man has, as it were, become a kind of prosthetic God. When he puts
on all his auxiliary organs he is truly magnificent; but those organs
have not grown on him and they still give him much trouble at times
. . . Future ages will bring him new and probably unimaginably great
advances in this field of civilization and will increase man's likeness
to God even more. But in the interests of our investigations, we will
not forget that present-day man does not feel happy in his Godlike
character.

Freud, "Civilization and Its Discontents" (1930: 28–29)

The discipline of art history is, by slow degrees, revealing its content – its
construction of meaning, the underlying assumptions of its methodology,
the manner in which it has suppressed the evidence of its own production
– and, in the process of this self-conscious analysis, it is revealing its
(dis)contents, its *lack*. The discomposure currently afflicting scholarship in
this field occurred because the world outside this "last bastion of reactionary
thought" changed. The audience no longer shares the grand legitimizing
beliefs that, since its inception, art history has been confidently drawing
upon and reiterating. A reassessment of basic methodological assumptions
was undertaken in most other fields long ago as other voices broke through
and broke up existing conventions and established certainties. While it is
apparent that the critiques undertaken of the methodological assumptions
of other fields could be applied with similar implications to the discussion
of art history, the discipline continued to employ a methodology that reproduces the cultural hegemony of the dominant class, race, and gender. Art
history's long overdue self-analysis has been brought about, in large part,
by women artists and art historians.

Art history has masqueraded as a socially and politically *in*significant
discourse by enveloping itself in what Hadjinicolaou calls a "rhetoric of
empty eloquence." An important part of the feminist project has been to
expose that masquerade: the convenient myth that art history is an archaic,
inconsequential field of inquiry removed from the conflicts and conditions

47

of social life. As art historian Griselda Pollock announced in 1982, "We are involved in a contest for occupation of ideologically strategic terrain" (Pollock 1982: 5). Not simply the passive recording of preexisting objects, art history is the activating field for the production of art, which in turn produces a social image, which then becomes constitutive of a certain kind of knowledge and awareness – particularly with regard to women. Art history has served to rationalize the material base upon which patriarchy in capitalist societies rests: men's control over women's labor power, sexuality, and access to symbolic representation. Oil painting functioned as part of the *amour propre* of the bourgeoisie – substantiating its attitudes to property and exchange. The image of woman, particularly the nude, is the point of intersection for art, sexual discourse, and commodity exchange. As T. J. Clark notes, "The nude is the mid-term of the series which goes from *femme honnête* to *fille publique*" (1980: 24). While the nude model was replaced by the prostitute and "for sale" became the intended reading of the sign "woman," the role of male artist in this cash nexus went unremarked. When feminists began to intervene in high culture's construction of difference, which had resulted in the exclusion of women artists from art history and art exhibitions, they discovered that the dominant myth about the nature of art and artists – the celebration of creative masculine individualism found in so much art-historical discourse – was not something that could be pointed out as an example of false consciousness or as archaic and therefore susceptible to reform. Rather, it formed the heart of the discourse. Similarly, the commodity fetishism of art institutions is not an unfortunate effect of the gallery system or of some ill-conceived museum exhibition or some art magazine, but was found to be one of the major *functions* of these institutions. The following chapter is a series of unauthorized histories that explore what and whose interests have been served by art history and by art institutions as they are currently organized and attempts to locate the hidden ethico-political agenda operating this differentiation – the interest that discloses difference.

## CECI N'EST PAS UNE FEMME

> Thus, whoever would speak of woman, her ideal, her essence, her image, should simultaneously invoke the legend "This is not a woman," borrowing the strategy of Magritte's *Ceci n'est pas une pipe*.
> Mary Lydon, "Foucault and Feminism" (1988: 139)

Underneath a hyper-realistic image of a pipe, Magritte, in the precise handwriting of a grade-school teacher, writes, "This is not a pipe." The gesture is too easy – like taking candy from a baby. It simultaneously returns us to our childhood and reminds us of our earlier naive identification of words with things. Magritte's painting is redolent with nostalgia, but the old answers no longer suffice. Done in 1926, it can be read as one of modernism's declarations of independence from representational realism or, as it was painted just a few years after the publication of Saussure's *Course in General Linguistics*, it can also be read as a play upon the arbitrary nature of the sign. By now Magritte's play upon the pipe seems like a pipe-dream. We are more aware of our deep immersion in the defiles of the signifier; we know there's more at stake in representation than the presence or absence of a pipe; we know that any challenge to the image's powers of illusion and address must simultaneously engage the question of sexual difference, for "it is impossible to dissociate the questions of art, style and truth from the question of the woman" (Derrida 1979: 71).

Adapting the strategy of *Ceci n'est pas une pipe* to Lacan's famous formulation "*La femme n'est pas.*" photographer **Kathy Grove** solves the problem by removing the question: the question, that is, the woman. In her photographic sequence *The Other Series*, Grove rephotographs some of the canonical paintings in the history of Western art and airbrushes out the female figures. Masaccio's *Madonna Enthroned* and *Expulsion from Paradise*, Raphael's *Canigiani Altarpiece*, Cranach's *Judgment of Paris*, Caravaggio's *Madonna of the Serpent*, Delacroix's *Liberty Leading the People,* Ingres's *Roger Rescuing Angelica*, Velasquez's *Rokeby Venus*, Fragonard's *Lover Crowned* and *Young Girl in Bed Making Her Dog Dance*, Sargent's *Madame X*, Cézanne's *Large Bathers*, Degas's *Tub,* Bonnard's *Nude in Bathtub*, Munch's *Vampire,* Klimt's *Kiss*, Manet's *Le Déjeuner sur l'herbe*, Picasso's *Les Demoiselles d'Avignon*, etc. are all re-presented minus the bodies of the women. The effect is similar to Duchamp's gesture of painting a moustache on the Mona Lisa – the original will never be the same. Grove's gesture disconcerts by its very simplicity and its radicality. It confronts us with a very large lacuna, revealing perhaps too much about the contents of the history of Western art. Paintings of pipes, after all, are something of a rarity; their absence would not change the history of art. The image of woman, on the other hand, has become, over the past three hundred years, the obsessional subject of Western art, the shared conceptual site of Western discourse, the traditional nodal point for the conceptualization of Man, Truth, History, and Meaning. "[U]nobtrusively but crucially, a certain metaphor of woman has produced (rather than merely illustrated) a discourse that we are obliged 'historically' to call the discourse of man" (Spivak 1983: 169). Without the image of the woman, this discourse collapses.

"Unless an image displaces itself from its natural state, it acquires no significance. Displacement causes resonance" (Gokhale 1981: 11). Grove's displacement causes more than resonance; it causes a wreckage. It is too intrepid, too direct. "If you treat an indirect structure directly," Barthes observes, "it escapes, it empties out, or on the contrary, it freezes, essentializes" (1964: 156). Grove's gesture causes both to occur simultaneously.

The woman has slipped away – outwitting the unwitting. Like removing the null set in series of integers, all the other signs must shift places. They look the same but mean something else entirely. Without the imagined site of plenitude provided by the woman's body, the entire history of art changes: landscape painting reveals the pathetic fallacy we always projected onto nature; furniture awkwardly lumbers into the role of still life; sheep lose their legitimizing role as signifiers of the pastoral convention and take on the prurient interest that had once been focused upon the naked nymphs. Without some remnant of a woman, abstract expressionism occurs too early and too often, pattern painting achieves a new prominence, and mythical and biblical genres are forced to change their stories. Paris still proffers that divisive apple, but now only the horse seems interested in it; Roger and his Hippogriff seem to be gratuitously disturbing the sea rubble; family structures everywhere collapse; and so many, many beds are empty and remain unmade . . . .

Representation can't live with the woman-who-does-not-exist and it can't live without her. The image of the body of woman has served historically as the symbol of man's link with nature, his hold upon the material world, but simultaneously it has functioned as a cover-up, concealing a void, allaying his fears, his sense of lack. Woman as sign is the site of a structuring absence, designating nothing – nothing, that is, no presence.[1] But take away this irreducible alterity and the whole structure of representation collapses. With the repressed space vacated, without the play of desire that the image of woman provides, representation is no longer anything but a gigantic pantomime. Without Angelica's nude body tethered to the rocks, there is nothing at stake in Roger's battle with the Orc, or sea monster, and "we know that, for want of a stake, representation is not worth anything" (Montrelay 1990: 259).

The fact that Grove uses the medium of photography to enable the woman to make good her escape compounds the disturbance. "By nature, the Photograph has something tautological about it: a pipe, here," Barthes assures us, "is always and intractably a pipe" (1981: 5). Photography, like the woman herself, has functioned as handmaiden to the positivist vision, sustaining the referential certitude that secures our confidence in the world. By airbrushing away the image of woman, Grove destroys the documentary veracity photography has always been thought to provide – disrupting the comfortable old fallacy that the camera cannot lie.

Not only does Grove's act of tampering with the photograph call into question the credibility of photography, it may undermine the value of the painting that is reproduced. Photography has often been thought to be inimical to painting, and when it comes to photographs *of* paintings, people as diverse in their ideological outlook as Walter Benjamin and American capitalist/art collector Alfred C. Barnes agree that photographing a work of art affects the original. Benjamin maintains that when a painting or work of art is reproduced, the original loses its "authenticity," its "traditional value" within a given "cultural heritage" (1968: 222). The Barnes Foundation published a pamphlet entitled *The Lure and the Trap of Color Slides in Art Education: The Time-Released Venom of Their Make-Believe*. Written in 1986 by Violette de Mazia, the Director of Education of the Barnes Foundation, it sets out the reasons for the Foundation's refusal to allow any photographs to be taken of the art works in its collection. In extraordinarily purple prose Violette de Mazia claims that to view a colored photograph or slide of a painting is to engage in a "duplicitous collaboration" with a "defamation process." The description she gives of an art history lecture sounds more like a porn movie. The audience sits in the dark, "like a Peeping Tom" with "no fear of any recrimination or punishment to spoil that inherently enjoyable situation" (1986: 5). The photographs themselves are described in invectives usually reserved for fallen women: "brazen impostors" perpetrating "a deceptive substitute, a downright sinful dissembling, a bold-faced falsehood" (ibid.: 7).

Ironically, the technique Grove uses – that of airbrushing the photograph – is customarily used on images of women by the advertising industry to make them more seductive. In fact, this is how Grove makes her living: retouching and manipulating photographs for fashion magazines and advertising copy. The female face deemed the most beautiful is that in which the features are the most eroded, the most *in*distinguishable, the most homogeneous. Desire in this realm of representation is so inextricably linked to the effaced woman that an image of a woman that has not undergone this erosion does not signify as an object of desire. Grove takes Dorothea Lange's famous photograph *Migrant Mother, Nipomo, California*, 1936, and erases the lines and moles from Florence Thompson's face along with the holes and the dirt in her children's clothing (Figure 2.1). Two things happen simultaneously – the migrant farm worker living in a tent with her three small children disappears, as do her real-life problems. She is replaced by a fictional woman with whom we feel a greater familiarity; she has become the woman of the Calvin Klein ads, with tow-headed children in tweedy clothes. In Lange's version, Florence Thompson may have been viewed through a veil of sentimentality, but when the wrinkles, the dirt, and the worry are airbrushed away, her image is read as a-woman-to-be-looked-at. That bit of cleavage was always there, but the viewer never noticed it; not until her makeover did Florence Thompson become the object of desire. Reading bodies is a way of reading how history has been ordered; bodies record and make visible the effects of power relations. Lange's photograph is the record of a body inscribed in one system of power; Grove's erasure provides another reading, revealing the ways in which the body becomes a palimpsest of possible readings.

*Migrant Mother* was sold at Swann's auction in 1991 for a record $44,000. "I never got one red cent," Florence Thompson complained. It is not often

*Figure 2.1* Kathy Grove, *The Other Series: After Lange* (silver gelatin print, 71 × 61 cm) 1989–90.

that the woman gets to complain about her role in cultural production or her rate of remuneration as bearer of the look. Grove's alteration of Florence Thompson's class, like her removal of the woman altogether from the painting or photograph, makes woman's role in cultural production conspicuous. It causes us to think about her working conditions, the historical specificity of her job; how, for example, her absence would affect the market value of a work of art. In Grove's work the woman has gone on strike, staged a walkout from the field of representation. Like a good labor organizer, Grove is operating strategically and calculatedly at the manufacturing site of cultural production, breaking up the monopoly of Western art's production, distribution, and consumption.

## CECI N'EST PAS UN VIOLON

A joke says what it has to say, not always in few words, but in *too* few words.

(Freud 1905b: 13)

Two sound holes suspended in the air between a turban and some drapery are all that is left of *Le violon d'Ingres,* after Grove retouched a photograph taken by Man Ray in 1924 (Figure 2.2). The violin was never a violin in the first place, but the back of a model named Kiki with sound holes superimposed upon it. The legendary Kiki of Montparnasse was model to Utrillo, Soutine, Foujita and Kisling, and both model and mistress to Man Ray. She is described by Man Ray's biographer, Janus, in terms that make it very clear Kiki was exactly the kind of woman needed for the production of art: she was a "woman in love," "happy in her nudity," a "rare companion who understood the needs of an artist," "the very life of Paris between the two wars," her "intensity a distant echo of the French Revolution," "a part of France that was destined to disappear" (1980: 194). And disappear she dutifully does, from Man Ray's life at the moment most convenient for him and from the history of art. Her photograph appears again later only as part of the collection of the now obviously bourgeois and respectable Mr and Mrs Man Ray. Kiki, it seems, returned to being Alice Prin, a working-class girl from Brittany. "She died alone and poverty stricken," but, Janus continues, "always with the great honesty and dignity of a woman who was essentially innocent in every circumstance" (ibid.: 189).

The photograph, however, immediately became famous and has maintained its market value. It was an homage to Ingres, combining the back of Ingres's famous Turkish bather with a reference to his favorite hobby, violin playing, while playing itself upon the French expression for a hobby – "a violin d'Ingres" – something a man does in his leisure time. When played upon Kiki's back it resounds with the rakish old tune about playing one's mistress like a musical instrument. A back of such breadth could never be a violin – perhaps a bass viol, or a cello at best – but the quotation is what's important here, the quotation as homage: the short and sure route to becoming a classic. "Both works [Ingres's and Man Ray's] were exhibited together in 1971 in the Louvre in a show entitled '*Le bain turc d'Ingres*' ('Ingres's Turkish Bath'). Thus Man Ray's work, too, has become

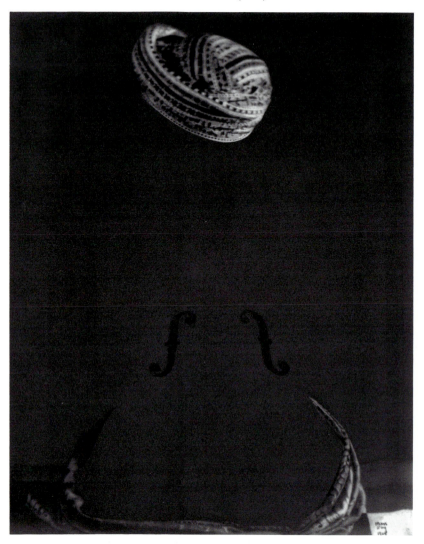

*Figure 2.2*   Kathy Grove, *The Other Series: After Man Ra*y (silver gelatin print,
46 × 41 cm) 1989.

a classic," Janus explains. How "thus"? On Kiki's back, apparently. But a
classic is not made off the back of one woman alone – to create a classic
tradition you need many, many nude women. Man Ray, in quoting Ingres,
was enlisting the service of all those broad backs of Ingres's bathers who
sit on soft cushions and gaze vacuously upon mounds of female flesh at
their toilette. Like Man Ray, Grove quotes earlier works of art, but her
photograph will not "thus" become a classic. Grove's quotation is not an

54

homage to the "original." Those two sound holes suspended in the air do not quote a classic; they place the "classic" in quotation marks.

## THE COMFY CHAIR

Art is customarily thought of as a comforting form of relaxation, a kind of reward or bonus a prosperous society is able to afford certain of its members. The enjoyment of art is a sign of affluence; it belongs to the good life; it is at once relaxing and a means of self-improvement, part of what it means to be cultivated. For Henri Matisse, the ability to provide relaxation was the very *function* of art; his most famous statement about art was that it should have the qualities of a comfortable chair: "What I dream of is an art of balance, of purity and serenity devoid of troubling or depressing subject matter, an art which could be for every mental worker, be he businessman or writer, like an appeasing influence, like a mental soother, something like a good armchair which provides relaxation from physical fatigue" (quoted in Barr 1966: 122). Matisse's concept of art reminds me of the skit by the British comedy team Monty Python in which the most dreaded sentence the Spanish Inquisition can inflict upon its victims is not the rack or the screw, but a long stretch in "the comfy chair." Recently, feminist artists have been calling into question the nature of the comfort to be had from the "comfortable chair" of culture, revealing that for some this has been the site of acute discomfort.

Matisse, as might be expected from his philosophy of art, painted many comfortable chairs. The poet Louis Aragon, a close friend of Matisse's, once wondered whether there wasn't more variety and expression in the armchairs Matisse painted than in the women. Janet Hobhouse feels that none of Matisse's figures is "half so intensely sensuous or so tenderly, passionately comprehended as certain ecstatic objects in paintings such as *The Rococo Armchair*" (1987: 65). Kathy Grove reproduces an armchair Matisse painted in 1926 (Figure 2.3). The original painting, now hanging in the Metropolitan Museum, is not called *Armchair with Green Stripe*, but *Odalisque*. In spite of the praise Matisse's armchairs have garnered all on their own merit, this armchair had an occupant. When Grove rephotographed Matisse's painting, she removed Henriette Darricarrère, whose semi-nude body with rosy nipples peeping through a transparent harem blouse frequently served as a garnish to one of Matisse's favorite armchairs. Absent, Henriette is more intriguing than when she was present. After her disappearance we wonder about her – how did she come to be in that armchair in the first place, why was she dressed as a harem girl, why this particular masquerade, why were there so many girls like her posing as odalisques at the time, where did she go when she lost her job as Matisse's model? We know that by the time this picture was painted, Henriette's time in the armchair was almost up. In 1927 the

*Figure 2.3*   Kathy Grove, *The Other Series: After Matisse*
(c-print, 61 × 53 cm) 1989.

occupant was changed to the dark-skinned, dark-haired, full-breasted Lisette, chosen, as Matisse explained, because "she brought the Orient closer to him again."

The nostalgia for a lost Orient was to become a major obsession in Matisse's life. In the winter of 1912 Matisse visited Morocco. He went for the warmth, the light, the brilliant colors, the exoticism, the sensuality, and as Delacroix had done eighty years earlier, to gather inspiration from the Orient. When Delacroix went, it was to take part in a diplomatic mission to expand French influence in North Africa. By the time Matisse went, Morocco had finally acquiesced to colonial rule. As a Frenchman and a tourist, Matisse could expect to be one of a privileged few surrounded by a large, exotic and very poor population, eager to serve wealthy visitors. However, even paradise was not perfect, or at least not easily accessible. Matisse remained for several weeks inside his hotel room. He painted the objects in his room, the goldfish in the bowl, the view from his window which overlooked not a mosque, but an English church. He painted the door to the Casbah, suggestively shaped like a large keyhole. If this journey was an attempt to encounter another culture, it was hampered by the very means of approach, for the act of figuration itself is against Islamic holy law. No Muslim would pose for him. Finally, Matisse did what Delacroix had done – he sought out prostitutes and Jews for models. His excursions through the ghettos and brothels would become romantically mis-remembered later, but at the time Matisse warned his friend Charles Camoin to keep his distance from the women: "Be careful, we have to go there like doctors making a house call" (quoted in Flam 1986: 355).

The difficulty in procuring models was only one problem. Even though France and Germany had parceled out North Africa to their mutual satisfaction, the Moroccans did not acquiesce to French rule as easily as had been expected. Matisse's reclusiveness may have been partly due to his awareness of the growing hostility towards the colonial French in Morocco. He wrote to a friend on the first of April 1912 that he had been planning a trip to Fez, but had cancelled it as the situation was growing dangerous. Matisse left Morocco just three days before the Fez massacre, during which the entire European population of Fez was murdered and their mutilated bodies hung outside the wall of the Sultan's Palace.

Matisse found that Nice on the sunny Mediterranean could provide the voluptuous sensuality he had desired from the Orient without the strain of an actual encounter with a foreign culture. In Nice he achieved a kind of touristic sublimity. With an abundance of souvenirs from Morocco – Moorish screens, rugs, textiles, turbans, hookah pipes, harem pants and, most importantly, a plentiful supply of girls – he recreated his encounter with the Orient as he wished it had been. In the comfort of a hotel room in his own country, he could play out all the psychosexual phantasms of the Western myth of the oriental pasha while he painted hundreds of odalisques. "Yes, I needed to have a respite, to let myself go and relax, to forget all the worries far from Paris. The odalisques were the abundant fruits all at once of a light hearted nostalgia, of a beautiful living dream, and of something I experienced almost ecstatically day and night, under the enchantment of that climate" (quoted in Hobhouse 1987: 61). For over twenty years Matisse painted the interior of this imaginary harem of voluptuous slave girls, nude or semi-nude, their bodies ornamented with bangles and scarves, turbans or see-through harem pants, veils or belly-dancing skirts. They pose singly or in intertwining pairs, they arch their backs, raise their arms to expose their breasts or recline passively, awaiting the whim of the owner/artist. Matisse became known as the Sultan of the Riviera. As if speaking from inside this role, Matisse comments, "I often keep these girls several years until I have exhausted their interest" (1972: 163).

While indulging in such fantasy, Matisse insisted he was working from reality: "I do odalisques in order to do nudes. But how does one do the nude without being artificial? Because I know that they exist. I was in Morocco. I have seen them" (quoted in Flam 1973: 59). "As for odalisques," he repeated later, "I had seen them in Morocco, and so was able to put them in my pictures back in France without playing make-believe" (ibid.: 135). Matisse had always claimed to be firmly committed to reality as the source of his pictorial investigations, but the claims he made for the odalisques were claims to an ethnographic authenticity, to an intimacy gained in, and over, an observed society. Matisse may have visited the ghettos of Tangier, where the wretchedly poor sold many things to Euro-pean tourists, including themselves, but he did not see a harem. Notwith-standing European fantasies about harems – fantasies of slavery, of total control without moral responsibility – harem means "the sacred." It is the most protected place in the Islamic home, the site of the feminine.[2] In wealthy Moroccan homes there is usually a large, open-air courtyard surrounded by buildings that serve as working and living areas for the members of an extended family. Men who are neither members of the family nor closely associated with it do not enter this area. If, during his brief stay in Morocco, Matisse had managed to become sufficiently well acquainted with a Moroccan to be invited to his home, he would have been entertained in the outer rooms of the compound and would not have encountered any women. Even food prepared by women would have been taken by the men of the family to the outer areas where the guests were served. However, the chances of a Moroccan wealthy enough to have a harem inviting a French tourist to his home were as slim as the chances of a French bourgeois inviting a foreigner to his Parisian home. In all like-lihood, what Matisse actually saw of a harem was what any tourist would see – the high outer walls of the compound.

Still, Matisse was correct in claiming that he had not fantasized these harem scenes, that he had seen them. But he was confusing what he had seen in paintings and photographs with what he had seen in Morocco. Far from indulging in too much fantasy, Matisse was drawing upon and dupli-cating a stereotype that by this time had deeply saturated French culture through the formulaic conventionality of harem iconography derived from Delacroix's many romantic harem scenes, Ingres's *Turkish Bath* and Renoir's *Odalisques* as well as the mass production of colonial postcards that reached their peak of popularity in 1930 with the celebration of the centennial of the French conquest of Algeria. Just like Matisse's harem scenes, the majority of these "documentary" photographs were staged in the artists' studios with models performing exotic rituals in costumes and jewelry provided by the picture-taking impresario.

## NUDES, THEY PRACTICALLY SELL THEMSELVES
### Raymond Pettibon

Most art historians mark the move to Nice in 1917 as the end of Matisse's pictorial experimentation. Having once been avant-garde, his work was now thought of as unambitious, even reactionary. Yet this period also marked a change in Matisse's relationship to the public – he became a success. Alfred Barr attributes the increase in "popularity and the commercial value" of Matisse's art of the Nice period to his "growing traditionalism and charm" (1966: 11). Though probably true, this does raise some questions about what constitutes the "charm" of this tradition. In a letter written to his son from Nice in September 1940, Matisse talks about what enabled his artistic production:

> I'm trying to stay wrapped up in my work. Before coming here I had planned on painting flowers and fruit – I even placed several arrangements of them around my studio – but this vague state of uncertainty we are still plunged into (for this country can be occupied under the slightest pretext) means that I am unable to bring myself, or perhaps am afraid, to start working *en tête à tête* with objects that I have to breathe life into and fill with my own feeling. So I've arranged with an agency for film extras to send me their prettiest girls. The ones I don't use, I pay off with 10 francs. Thanks to this system I have three or four young and pretty models. I have them pose in shifts, for sketching, three hours in the morning, three hours in the afternoon. And this keeps me in the studio.
>
> (quoted in Hobhouse 1987: 67)

What was disturbing Matisse's concentration was the German occupation of France. Matisse's wife, Amelia, who had separated from him the year before, and his daughter were now working for the Resistance. When critics claim that Matisse brought comfort and refreshment to listless and exhausted men, there was more than personal *ennui* at issue here. Matisse had begun the odalisques right after the First World War, when France began an immense compensatory undertaking for the loss of French power during the first German occupation. Matisse's harem paintings were part of a fashionable colonial discourse in which the erotic management of human subjects in cultural production thinly disguises a collective assertion of control over human subjects, territory, and property.

The odalisques, in turn, provided Matisse with an abundance of commissions, particularly from the wealthy Riviera market. An odalisque also brought Matisse his first official recognition: in 1921, when Matisse was fifty-one, the French government purchased its first painting from him. The work the government selected, *Odalisque with Red Trousers*, was remarkable because it became obvious that the political desire to assert French colonial power had extended to the acquisition policy of its museums. This painting was chosen because the subject matter was compatible with the official policy of a number of exhibitions taking place at the time, exhibitions specifically designed to give French citizens a "colonial conscience."[3] The presence of Henriette, or Laurette, or Lisette, or Antoinette, or Jeanette, or Monique, or all of their many successors promised comfort of a different nature than that which could be provided by an armchair – the reassuringly familiar connection between control of other lands and the control of female sexuality.

What happened to Henriette before Grove airbrushed away her image? She was just one of thousands of easily disposable, pretty but poor young women in France between the wars who eked out a subsistence through menial labor, modeling, or prostitution. The voluptuousness of her surroundings in Matisse's paintings tells us one story, but Matisse's housekeeper/mistress Lydia Delectorskaya tells another. By way of attesting to Matisse's generosity, she recounts how he gave extra rations of food to some of these young women because they were often poor and underfed (quoted in Wilson 1992: 19).

Grove's seemingly simple gesture prompts an inquiry into how a painting or a photograph becomes part of "that complex structure of social perception which ensures that the situation in which one social class [gender, race] has power over the others is seen by most members of the society as 'natural', *or not seen at all*" (Eagleton 1976: 5). Grove's removal of what is "not seen at all" is a play upon the discourse of art history, a pun, which reproduces *visibly* the very form of ideological imposture it catches in the act of pretending not to see.

## WHO'S AFRAID OF VISUAL PLEASURE?

"We murder to dissect" has long been the criticism leveled against the obsessional will to know. Examining something too closely, even something inanimate, may cause some damage or loss of essence to the very thing we seek to know. All looking involves risk – to the voyeur as well as the person or object of the gaze. Part of the pleasure in scopophilia is derived from the threat or guilt involved in looking at what is culturally taboo. The pleasure of watching films, particularly *film noir*, is derived from the glimpses they give of what is normally concealed, glimpses of the threatening unknown. **Dotty Attie** is an artist who isn't afraid of visual pleasure. She takes the viewer into the operating amphitheater of art history, and seduces us into watching, in sensual slow motion, the anatomy of a murder.

For over twenty years in tiny, usually no more than six-inch-square canvases, Dotty Attie has been engaging in a detailed pictorial exegesis of the meta-narratives of art history. The paintings she dissects are all well known to us; these are historic paintings, part of our visual history. We recognize that bloody hand holding the scalpel from Eakins's *Gross Clinic*, the long white prostrate boy's body from Copley's *Watson and the Shark*, the sensuous commingling of flesh and fabric from Ingres's *Turkish Bath*, those manacled limp arms from *Roger Rescuing Angelica*, the erect nipple protruding through the too adult fingers of Cupid as they clasp over Venus's breast from the great Bronzino *Allegory*. Attie, like the painters she copies, is a realist painter. To be a realist, as Barthes explains, is not to be a copier of reality, but to pastiche things already given within a culture, "to unroll the carpet of the codes" (1974: 55). Attie unrolls the codes very slowly, almost cinematically freeze-frame by freeze-frame, causing the small pieces of the painting focused upon to take on a heightened significance, making the intersection of bodies and fabric more erotically charged, making the process of viewing more sensual and making the viewer more self-conscious about the act of viewing. The realists Attie copies may have tried to be discreet about their copying, only to be outed by some art historian who recognized in Ingres the languid overripe body parts of Delacroix's harem girls, or Eakins's quotation of prostrate male bodies from Géricault's *The Raft of the Medusa*. Attie, on the other hand, is not a closet copyist. Like Bertolt Brecht, who when accused of plagiarism berated himself for being only a petty thief when what he really aspired to be was a great criminal like Shakespeare, Attie is a flagrant and promiscuous copier.

When Attie returns the stolen goods to the public domain, they seem changed. They are not quite as we remember them. Our memories are usually based upon photographic reproductions in art history textbooks, or slides, or posters – the result of the reproductive industry that has grown up around these cultural monuments. Unlike most subversive appropriationalists who rephotograph reproductions of well-known works of art, Attie repaints them, duplicating not just the image, but the act of creation itself. She reenacts all the painstaking pleasure that goes into the activity of painting: the pleasure to be had in the sensuous, viscous quality of oil paint, the rich shine of the colors, the repetitive caressing activity of the brush and the pleasure with which the images were engendered in the first place. A few painters have described this pleasure for us:

> I see my drawings as a way of caressing the woman. I use powdered pastel as a sensual lubricant for indirectly caressing unknown women. I want to stroke them via the surface of the paper. In a moment of

madness I actually dreamt up parallels between tonal drawing as a kind of foreplay and linear drawing as penetration. I once wrote about Balthus' paintings of young girls as a kind of caressing.

James Collins, 1983

Thus I learned to battle with the canvas, to come to know it as a being resisting my wish, and to bend it forcibly to this wish. At first it stands there like a pure chaste virgin . . . . And then comes the the willful brush which first here, then there, gradually conquers it with all the energy peculiar to it like a European Colonist.

Wassily Kandinsky, 1913

Paintings are made the way princes get children, with the shepherdess.

Picasso, 1923

Or, as Max Kozloff rather bluntly puts it, "the objectivity or scientific spirit of Western male artists depicting their world is underwritten by lust, a will to dominate and cruelty towards females" (1991: 105). But this story of creation most art history books discreetly try to suppress. Normally, these narratives are told subliminally, although the organization of Picasso's artistic developments according to the changes in wives and mistresses (the Dora Marr period, the Olga period, etc.) is about as obvious as you can get. In the exhibition "Picasso and Portraiture," William Rubin retells that old story of the potency of the male artist starring Picasso, the protean male genius, but Attie is not so didactic. She is not interested in writing feminist disclaimers to this myth. Her humorous interventions are made through polite and learned allusions to the history of art.

"One day I shall write a story about guilt and pleasure," promises the omniscient narrator in one of Attie's early sequences of drawings and texts. And we as readers and viewers are returned to an earlier age, that of the Victorian novel, when the realist epistemology still obtained, when narrators were all-knowing and we could relax into a good read, not obliged or expected to be resisting or critical readers. "The characters will be polite . . . unkind . . . their actions will be puzzling . . . yet understandable . . . a woman . . . a mechanical device of one kind or another." So goes the story, so goes almost any story written within the realist epistemology, which is why Gayatri Spivak has some problems with it. "The fate of Madame Bovary, the fate of Anna Karenina," she observes, "I think they are trying to tell me something about who wears the pants in the house of being." What motivates us as readers to pursue the meandering of the story is the desire to know what happens next. What motivates us to follow the unfolding of plot, based as it is on causality, is the expectation of meaning, the answer to the question that the plot posits. Ultimately, we

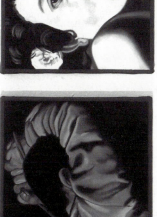

*Figure 2.4*  Dotty Attie, *A Violent Child*, detail: panels 1B and 9B (oil on canvas, 39 × 709 cm; 40 panels, 15.25 × 15.25 cm) 1988 (collection Mr and Mrs Henry Welt).

are motivated by the expectation of the end, the completion of the codes of signification. Inquiries into the function of the end, as Frank Kermode has shown in his study of formal closure, have to do with the human end, with death. Walter Benjamin claims that all narration is obituary in that life acquires definable meaning only at, and through, death:

> The nature of the character in a novel cannot be presented any better than is done in his statement, which says that the meaning of his life is revealed in his death. But the reader of a novel actually does look for human beings from whom he derives the "meaning of life." Therefore he must, no matter what, know in advance that he will share their figurative death – the end of the novel – but preferably their actual one ... *What draws the reader to the novel is the hope of warming his shivering life with a death he reads about.*
>
> (1969: 101)

Perhaps not surprisingly, a lot of realist painters Attie examines are obsessed with murder and mutilation. Caravaggio was a murderer in real life, but Attie doesn't mention this. She never points out the obvious, she only hints. She is interested in what is in plain sight but may be over-looked perhaps because it has been looked at too often. *A Violent Child* (1988) tells, in a very laconic way, of the young Caravaggio's duties as an apprentice, which involved helping his master with anatomical experiments in a secluded room (Figure 2.4). The story, which suggests an explanation for Caravaggio's otherwise inexplicable violence, is told in the context of fragments from a number of Caravaggio paintings, many of which depict bodies in pain. In this context of images even the intersection of bed-linen and blanket, or the hand holding the child, suggests violence.

*The Voyeurs* (1987) and *Masters* (1988) give us close-ups of the artists who have witnessed this horror. These are small, six-inch-square portraits of the artists, copied from their own self-portraits. They are cropped so severely that all we see is the face from the eyebrows to just below the mouth. We look at them as they have looked upon the world – as forms circumscribed by the parameters of the canvas, or as if through a small window, like the window that slides open on the door of a prisoner's cell. Stripped of their surroundings, their clothing, of all the other attributes that would suggest their character or their social status, these artists are reduced to their physiognomy. We respond like nineteenth-century phys-iognomists reading criminal tendencies in the proportions and disposition of the features.

All of Attie's paintings invite the viewer to read "into" the painting something of the character of the artist who produced it. Usually the narrative impulse of the painting is augmented by stories or brief bits of information about the artist's life. *Barred from the Studio* (1987) tells, in the context of selections from Eakins's paintings, the story of how Eakins

*Figure 2.5*  Dotty Attie, *Barred from the Studio* (oil on canvas, 28 × 86 cm) 1987, (The Brooklyn Museum, New York).

*Figure 2.6*   Dotty Attie, *Mixed Metaphors* (oil on canvas, 86.4 × 139.7 cm; 36 panels, 15.25 × 15.25 cm each) 1993 (courtesy P.P.O.W. Gallery, New York).

lost his teaching post at the Pennsylvania Academy: "Barred from the studio while male models were posing, female art students were placed in a corridor where a small window provided a distant view of the sitter's back . . . . Greatly disturbed by this, Eakins, attempting to rectify the situation, one day went too far. . . . His impulsive gesture, shocking to all, succeeded only in further sullying his reputation" (Figure 2.5). We are left to fill in the suggestive ellipse, to speculate about what Eakins revealed and his motives in doing this.

In *Mixed Metaphors* (1993) Attie looks directly at the source of the problem of representation (Figure 2.6). Using that Ur-text of representation, Courbet's *The Origin of the World*, Attie explores the latent motive behind all realist painting – the will to know, which as the title makes very clear always comes down to the desire to know our origins. (*The Origin of the World* is the title the painting acquired; Courbet had called it simply "Woman's Torso.") This painting and *The Sleepers*, in which two obviously sexually satiated nude women sleep in each other's arms, were commissioned by a Turkish diplomat: "An elegant gentleman, cultivated and artistically knowledgeable came to his studio with an unusual commission . . . his sense of delicacy made a direct explanation difficult." The paintings were intended for his private delectation: "Above the bed, hidden behind a green veil, the painting was hung." But all this discretion surrounding the paintings was violated when the diplomat went bankrupt and the paintings were exhibited for public sale. Some years later, after the defeat of the French Commune and Courbet's arrest for his part in the uprising, particularly his role in toppling the Vendôme column, the knowledge of these paintings was used by the police and the press of the newly reinstated monarchist government to discredit Courbet's character. "After Courbet's imprisonment and exile, his intense concentration, always focused so effortlessly on his work . . . faltered. . . . While assistants worked on the paintings he fitfully began, Courbet's mind darted about, finding solace in happier events of the past." Solace, Attie implies, by placing this narrative in the context of some of Courbet's most overtly salacious paintings, can be derived simply by looking at these images of women.

*The Origin of the World* went missing for many years and was found again in Jacques Lacan's country house. (Dear Reader, I sense your growing skepticism about the truth of my tale, but I hasten to assure you I am taking no liberties with the facts of this story.)[4] Like the Turkish diplomat, each owner of *The Origin of the World* was moved by a sense of decorum or *amour propre* to conceal the painting in some way. At one time it was covered by a sliding panel representing a castle in the snow and, when it was in Lacan's possession, it was concealed by an elaborate "wooden 'hiding device' constructed by the artist André Masson, representing in abstract form the elements of the first painting" (Nochlin 1988: 178). Clearly, knowledge about origins needs to be kept a secret, or revealed only to a select few. Attie, understanding the importance of the cover-up and the anxiety caused by the sight of female genitals, obscures parts of them with other images: small square paintings of the original green veil, a self-portrait of Courbet looking horrified as if he had just glimpsed the void with his own eyes.

## WHO'S "WE," WHITE MAN?

> When you name yourself, you always name another. When you name another you always name yourself.
>
> Bertolt Brecht, *Mann Ist Mann*

In a bus shelter in Vancouver I saw a poster proclaiming, "*We* are the first world, *You* are the third"— a slogan particularly pointed in the context of Canada, where native people, realizing the importance "we" place on priority, especially in relation to property, have stopped calling themselves by Columbus's misnomer and now call themselves "First Nations." (Since the name change, they have fared much better on land settlements.) The poster points with economy and humor to the power of subject positions in our speech, to how dichotomies of "we" and "they" are established, and how commonplace understandings about others form *our* identity. Women, placed in the structural role of silent Other, guarantor of the position and meaning of the Same (the Author, Man), are more likely to try to "escape" the hierarchy of speaking-subject-positions by engaging in what Bakhtin has called the "dialogical imagination" – a paratactic style of speech (and by extension mode of being) in which nothing is fixed, all relationships are contingent, subject positions are constantly changing. Like Tonto, when the frantic Lone Ranger cries, "Tonto, the Indians have us surrounded – we're done for!" They ask, "Who's *we*, white man?" Good question. What is the subject position of the second sex in the first world? Is it the same as the first sex of the third world? It's hard to compute, and *we* women are notoriously bad at math.

In "Native Intelligence," an exhibition designed to travel the US during the 500th anniversary celebrations of Columbus's arrival in America, **Elaine Reichek** manages to sidestep the dated and divisive semiotic practice which for so long now has structured Western discourse. Reichek's installations begin with information (in the sense of the Latin *informis*, without form, "un-meaning"): postcards, snapshots, magazine spreads, film stills, wallpaper, fabrics, even flour sacks, as well as various ethnographic and anthropological material culled from the Library of Congress and the Smithsonian Institution in Washington and the Museum of the American Indian, the American Museum of Natural History and the Metropolitan Museum of Art in New York. These vast storehouses of photographs, documents, and artifacts were accumulated during the encyclopedic urge

*Figure 2.7* Elaine Reichek, *Red Delicious* (oil on photograph, 122 × 150 cm) 1991 (courtesy Michael Klein Gallery, New York).

that so preoccupied the first world at the close of the last century. The burgeoning museum culture ostensibly grew out of the desire to preserve a record of peoples and customs before they vanished. But what was really at an end was the era of colonial expansionism: these are fragments we have shored against *our* ruin, not theirs.

Adopting the presentational strategy of the museum exhibition, "Native Intelligence" postulates an information-processing circuitry intended to generate intelligibility, but the vast flow of data keeps accumulating without coming to a conclusion. Metaphors compound metaphors without ever settling into the substantive. In a photocollage entitled *Red Delicious*, a reproduction of a painting by Wright of Derby from 1785 is inset with smaller, circular photographs that lead, by a process of free association, to other romantic heroines of the Wild West: Lola Albright in the Hollywood movie *Oregon Passage*, the blonde captured by Indians in *Unconquered*, the abducted brunette in *Comanche*, or that really feisty gal in *Red River*. There is a moment of Brechtian distanciation in each of Reichek's photocollages; in *Red Delicious* the "device" is "bared" in a photograph taken from behind the scenes of a movie set, revealing the cardboard canyon into which Indians chase the stagecoach (Figure 2.7).

The operations that the information undergoes, the associations that are made among disparate data, the continuities that are recognized become too profligate, suggesting a problem in the processing system. The metaphoric connections that formerly provided a reassuring sense of cosmic togetherness begin to unravel under the influence of signals from so many sources and now seem only coincidental. The activity of classification and categorization – the whole drive to stabilize, organize, and rationalize our conceptual universe – slips into irrationality, chaos, and fragmentation. We are brought too close to the margins and the marginalized, too close to what the museum has always promised to keep at bay.

"Native Intelligence" is one of a series of exhibitions in which Reichek addresses museum practices, but the project is not about the failure of the museum to produce "truth" or an objective account of other peoples. Nor is it about first-world culpability. Rather, she is accumulating texts about textuality, about fabrication and about the ways in which we are fashioned by our own fabrications. Reichek reads our documentation of other peoples for their symptomatology, for what they tell us of our needs and desires. She found two different versions of Roland Reed's 1915 photograph showing Blackfoot Indians in Glacier National Park, one in the archives of the Smithsonian, the other in the American Museum of Natural History. She also discovered that Blackfoot Indians never lived in Glacier National Park. Reed had taken a group of them there and had given them props and costumes to create scenes of the picturesque. Reichek gives us four versions of this same photo and manipulates them in various ways, inverting them, coloring them and giving them various formulaic captions such as "The Indian Suns Himself Before the Door of His Tepee," "After the Hunt," and "Shadows on the Mountain." These multiple misrepresentations are not made to expose the fraudulence of Reed's photojournalism, or the credulity of the curators of the Smithsonian and Museum of Natural History or even the pretension of the positivist vision that photography has supported for so long. If these targets are hit, they are only collateral damage in a search-and-destroy mission against anything that is already culturally determined. Reichek is not the Ralph Nader of a museum culture, demanding correct consumer information.[5] She is an eccentric and generous reader who finds herself constitutionally alienated from divisions like "fact" and "fiction" and doesn't hold the text or the teller accountable for the misinformation they generate. Instead, "errors" become cracks that provide an opportunity to look behind seemingly transparent texts to the culture that requires them. Read through Reichek's methodology, Margaret Mead's *Sex and Temperament in Three Primitive Societies* would be the story of a young American girl who writes an enormously popular book in 1935 about her desire for a more sexually liberated culture, one in which women are not linked to property exchange.

There is a flagrant and funny feminism weaving in and around Reichek's reworking of ethnographic, anthropological, and museum exhibition practices. It is most overtly manifested in her choice of the medium of knitting, which she uses to reproduce documentary photographs of native peoples and their dwellings (Figures 2.8 and 2.9). Knitting is an "inappropriate" tool for this purpose – so unscientific, one of those typical feminine misunderstandings, as if some dotty old woman had gone on an anthropological expedition equipped with wool and knitting needles instead of a camera and notebook; or one of those comic cross-cultural misperceptions, like the moment in the 1930 documentary film *First Contact* when a New Guinea Aboriginal puts on a Kellogg's Corn Flakes box as a headdress. The culture that Reichek is misreading is her own, but her misrecognitions mark her distance from it and, at the same time, her deep familiarity with the machinations of its codes. It is as if she had taken literally Barthes's metaphor of the textuality of the text: "*Text* means *tissue*, but whereas hitherto we have always taken this tissue as a product, a ready-made veil, behind which lies, more or less hidden, meaning (truth), we are now emphasizing, in the tissue, the generative idea that the text is made, is worked out in a perpetual interweaving; lost in this tissue – this texture – the subject unmakes himself, like a spider dissolving in the constructive secretions of its web" (1975: 64). Barthes's metaphor almost seems to be a reworking of a story told by Jimmie Durham in his catalogue essay for Reichek's exhibition – the Cherokee fable of Grandmother Spider, who sits unnoticed in the corner weaving, yet in the tale she is the most important character, for it is her activity that makes the yarn.

*Figure 2.8* Elaine Reichek, *Polkadot Blackfoot with Children* (wool, oil on photograph, 2 parts, 172.8 × 198.25 cm) 1990 (private collection, New York).

The knitted men in "Native Intelligence" are derived from Edward Curtis's turn-of-the-century photographs of Apache Gaun, or "devil", Dancers and a Mandan dancer. The three-dimensional knitted versions hang beside large-scale prints of the original photographs. The knitting reproduces the information in the photograph in a way that is at once precise and quite *un*signifying. It is not just that knitting, being "women's work," is out of place in this context; it is that as a discourse knitting is not, as Foucault would put it, "*endowed* with the author function" (1984: 107). By miming and thereby undermining those more well-endowed discourses that claim to provide significance and a purchase on property, these knitted versions reveal the tenuousness of the web of lexical or indexical certitude that secures our confidence in the world.

The process of transcoding or reweaving of texts reveals the bias of the original fabrication, what the anthropological and ethnographic accounts have tried to cover up: the body of the text, or rather, the bodies

*Figure 2.9* Elaine Reichek, *Mandan* (wool, oil on photograph, 3 parts, 162.2 × 264.3 cm) 1991 (courtesy Michael Klein Gallery, New York).

of the natives in the texts. Narratives of exploration and discovery are about nothing if not the human body. They habitually describe natives' bodies as monstrous, riddled with all manner of libidinal excess – naked, sexually licentious, and commonly engaged in every form of Western taboo from incest to cannibalism, a people *sans roi, sans loi, sans foi*, in short, just what the Europeans unconsciously wanted to be.[6] The agenda of the narratives of discovery was to inscribe these people in Western systems of representation, a project that had something of a missionary aspect to it, as if the very act of encoding them would bring them into the realm of "normality."

A significant side-effect of this inscription was that native peoples could then be made to disappear at the will of the author. Early explorers of the Americas invariably described the land as "wilderness," unoccupied empty space to be claimed for some European monarchy, yet the central enigma of the wilderness was always the body of the wild man. We still have trouble seeing these "others." A photograph in the *New York Times* of 18 September 1990 shows in the foreground a row of three men. The identifying caption reads, "Napoleon A. Chagnon, left, American anthropologist, and Charles Brewer-Carías, Venezuelan naturalist at Konabuma-teri." But the man at the left wears a loincloth and feathers; the two white scientists stand center and right. To the *Times* editors the native is not there, even though *his* is the body we are really interested in; his body is the reason for the scientific study and the newspaper's story.

The bodies in "Native Intelligence" take on a presence, stand three-dimensionally, cast a shadow, have human stature. It is *our* erotic body that "Native Intelligence" invites us to explore. Instead of the detached, fetishistic pleasure to be had from viewing a photograph, the knitted bodies offer the pleasures of texture and proximity. They have a plenitude, a warmth, a sensuality. Their tactility implicitly invites us to touch or rub these nude or semi-nude fuzzy bodies, compelling ambiguities of cuddly life-size dolls and dark, enigmatic, even slightly threatening Others. There is a *frisson* to the encounter, and those who accept the invitation to transgress or regress will be provoked to laugh.

Everything presented in Reichek's work is familiar to us; in fact, we are awash in the comfort of the familiar. The final installation in "Native Intelligence" is redolent with nostalgia. We are returned to our childhood, and to the childhood of our grandparents, when little girls labored over embroidery samplers and, in the process of learning their ABCs, learned homilies of constraint, a constraint perhaps more anxiously imposed on women during pioneer times because of the proximity of "savages" on the frontier. Here, however, instead of those stultifying adages by which we were taught to pattern our lives, other voices speak through. Whereas the original samplers contained maxims such as "She walked with God and He was her support" or "Religion should our thoughts engage," now

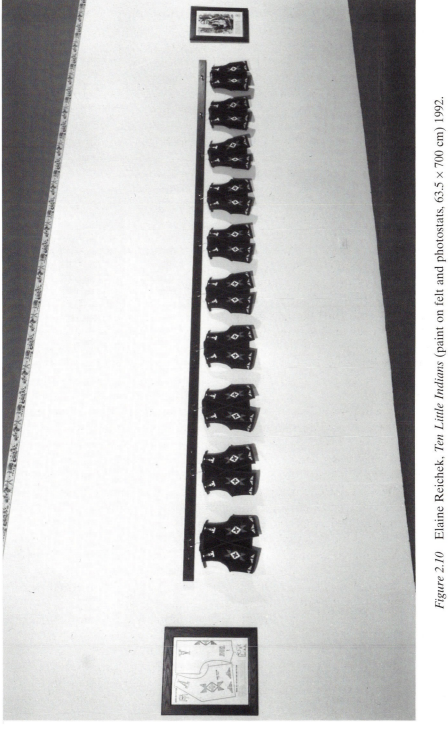

*Figure 2.10* Elaine Reichek, *Ten Little Indians* (paint on felt and photostats, 63.5 × 700 cm) 1992.

Mahpwa Luta (Red Cloud) says, "When the white man comes to my country he leaves a trail of blood behind him," or Yellow Wolf says, "Only his own best deeds, only the worst deeds of the Indians, has the white man told." That these voices have infiltrated embroidery samplers suggests a deep defection. If women, occupying a marginal position within the symbolic order, have come to represent the necessary frontier between man and the supposed chaos of the outside, there is always the disconcerting possibility that they will identify with the marginalized. It looks now as though the patriarchy's worst suspicions are confirmed – Big Eagle, Yellow Wolf, and Red Cloud came to tea and chatted!

While little girls embroidered their ABCs and learned their position in the symbolic order, little boys learned the same lessons playing cowboys and Indians. Childhood is the time we learn about the great divides – between *he* and *she*, between *us* and *them*. A remark by General Norman Schwarzkopf embroidered on cowboy-pattern curtain material shows just how formative those years were for him: of the Gulf War, he says, "It was like going into Indian country!" An old poster reproduced in another work depicts one little boy's quest to find out "Why Don't We Live Like Indians?" The poster is in French, attesting to the internationality of this fascination with Native Americans.

Ironically, even Indian kids play cowboys and Indians. My childhood playmates were Kwakiutl and Comox Indians, though I didn't know them by those names then, and I doubt that they thought of me as Caucasian. One Hallowe'en we all dressed up as Indians, making fringed buckskin jackets and skirts out of burlap potato sacks. I remember this not because any adult pointed out the absurdity of our choice of costumes, but because a firecracker landed in my skirt and the whole burlap outfit instantly caught fire. Our childhoods divided when they were sent to the Indian school in Alert Bay and I had to stay home and take correspondence courses. Years later, when I was a student at the University of British Columbia, Claude Lévi-Strauss gave a series of lectures on the kinship relations of the Kwakiutl. As he spoke, at times in rapid French and at times in an almost impenetrable English, of "native conceptions" that were clearly to be understood as something other than his and the audience's own, the divide between "us" and "them" seemed to grow into an abyss.

Reichek's work offers a sense of reparation, of some amends made, like the knitting up of rent fabric. Perhaps it's the care with which ten-little-Indian vests hanging on the wall have been stitched together from the patterns in an Indian craft catalogue (Figure 2.10). They seem to offer another chance at childhood, a chance to do it over again and get it right.

# 3

# REFLECTIONS OF RESISTANCE: WOMEN ARTISTS ON THE OTHER SIDE OF THE *MIR*

Reading how woman is constructed as sign in what was, until recently, Soviet society is like entering the Russian futurist play *The World-backwards*. Like many letters of the Russian alphabet that seem reversed to us, the ways in which "woman" is represented are frequently the mirror inversion of the representation of woman in the West. In looking at the image of women on the other side of this mirror, we have an opportunity (almost as we could with computer image programming) to see how our lot would differ if our image was different.

The project of feminists in Russia today is to initiate an exploration of contemporary representational systems that have determined the social production of sexual difference and gender hierarchy and to raise questions about how women speak and are represented within these systems. To undertake this task of writing and "righting" in the context of the powerful patriarchal syntax of Soviet culture is to initiate a more difficult project than that undertaken in 1968 by the French feminists or by Western feminists in general. Psychoanalytic theory, so instrumental in the development of the theoretical formulations of the women's movement in the West, has, until recently, been unavailable to Soviet feminist theoreticians. As a result of its suppression, they have been working without an account of the cultural construction of gender. Russian women do not share the forty years of feminist intellectual work that followed upon Simone de Beauvoir's 1949 statement, "One is not born, but rather becomes, a woman." Without this intellectual history and without a theory of the construction of subjectivity, discussions of gender take place within the circularity of essentialist, biological paradigms, or collapse into the sexual "in-difference" of totalitarian androgyny.

Even among the intelligentsia and artistic groups in Russia, there is still a strong resistance to shifting the intellectual debate about gender equality away from its deadlock within binary oppositions (men vs. women) and facile formulations. In a recent interview the prominent Russian writer Tatyana Tolstaya claimed that feminism was really a consequence of the commonplace habit in the West of thinking in terms of stereotypes: "You know what feminists invented: they invented the idea of phallocracy – that the world is bad because it is ruled by men. That is completely ridiculous because, for example, England is ruled by a woman" (1991: 26). Tolstaya speaks from within the limitations of essentialist thought, and her statements reveal both the limitations and the sexisms inherent in construing femininity in these terms. The fact that her opinions are similar to those that would be expressed by the least informed and most unsympathetic members of our society gives us some indication of how widespread are the misgivings and misunderstandings about feminism.

The artist **Natalya Nesterova** (b.1944) was reluctant to be included in an all-women's art exhibition. She clearly felt the need to distance herself from the category "woman artist": "I haven't got a high esteem for female artists, apart from a few exceptions. Men happen to be more intelligent. Professions that require a lot of wit and intelligence should be done by men, and art is as much a matter of the mind as it is of the heart." When asked about herself, she said, "Me, I am an exception" (quoted in Michgelsen 1991: 26). In spite of such statements, Nesterova is not at all an unsympathetic woman. She wants only the right to live forgetfully, to forget herself as woman, but her own comments reveal that to do so she must participate in the exclusion or negation of other women. Nesterova is an official artist, highly favored by the now defunct Soviet Artists' Union, to which she was admitted in 1969. Her views are commonplace among the few women who have achieved prominence within male-dominated institutions; the cost of their success can be read in such denigrations of their own sex.

Soviet women can be the strongest proponents of male chauvinism. Galina Starovoytova is the only woman in Boris Yeltsin's administration. Rather than see herself as a forerunner of the equitable participation of women in political life, she repeatedly refers to herself as if she were an aberration, saying that women have no place in political life, thereby making her presence as unthreatening to her male colleagues as possible and deterring other women from entering the political arena. At the same time, there are many highly politicized Soviet women who, while being very supportive of their female colleagues, would resist being categorized as "women artists" or "women writers" and would not accept the terms of Western feminist debates. Their resistance is grounded in a complex postrevolutionary and postwar intellectual history.

Feminism stands in a particularly vexed position *vis-à-vis* a number of conflicting currents within both official and unofficial Soviet ideology. With the 1917 revolution came the most extensive social restructuring in modern history, one that arguably, even to this day, articulates the most progressive programs of emancipation for women.[1] The women and men engaged in working out these reforms were not involved in feminist activism in the usual sense; they were not a disenfranchised group with little power, working to improve the condition of women in general. The women's section of the Bolshevik party, or Zhenotdel, was not an oppositional group, but rather an integral part of the government. A separate feminist movement outside the party was discouraged on the grounds that it could lead to a contingent of labor breaking away from the common class struggle. It was under charges of bourgeois individualism that the Zhenotdel was dismantled in 1930, and these charges resonate in the lives of women today who are sensitive to the notion that feminism (which they associate much more with current Western feminism than with their own historical women's movement) is somehow "selfish." While they may be acutely aware of women's daily hardships, they are less likely to rectify those wrongs through collective action with other women than to work on behalf of their family or immediate community. Women are quick to point out that conditions are not good for men either. Also, many Soviet women would avoid participating in a feminist movement because they have developed a deep distrust of all political movements and collective identities, seeing them as infringements on the autonomy of the individual rather than as vehicles of group empowerment. This may be particularly true for women artists and writers who have found in the activity of art-making a venue for personal, subjective expression – something denied them in most other areas of their lives. The idea of organizing to secure for themselves and for other women a different kind of treatment or visibility is often seen by them as inimical to what is most important to them in their activity as artists – the exploration of their own subjectivity. I have visited the Soviet Union five times since 1981 and once after it became a Commonwealth. During scores of studio visits I came to understand that a good deal of the art I was seeing was political, if only in its assertion of the validity of the personal.

As we become more knowledgeable about the history of the women's movement in the Soviet Union and more conscious of the obstacles faced by contemporary feminists in these chaotic times as the Commonwealth of Independent States takes shape, our admiration for this fledgling feminist movement will increase. It may need to recapitulate some developments of Western feminism, including some of our mistakes; it is also possible that the dialogue begun with Western feminists may speed them past pitfalls in which we have floundered. On the other hand, these women may help us out of some of our own ruts. There is much to be gained from looking beyond our American or Eurocentric points of reference, to look, not for more problems, but rather for alternatives to our own practices. We know very little about cultural production in countries that are not capitalist or not, at least not yet, completely caught up in the machinations of commodity fetishism. It is only within the past ten years that the discipline of art history in the West has begun to expand its analytical perspective to include non-Western versions of modernism, such as the Russian avant-garde. Western feminist artists and art historians have not yet begun to fathom the importance of the role played by women artists in the development of that practice, nor why the roles for Western women artists were so much more circumscribed during the same period. Our concerns have been conditioned by the conversation of our own feminist community, which at times contributes to our confinement; inevitably we have worked from within a given set of intellectual, political, and artistic paradigms. We now have the opportunity both to access that important period in the history of women artists and to engage in a dialogue with a rapidly developing contemporary feminist cultural practice. This is an invitation to expand our conversational community, widen our frame of reference, and look forward beyond the present impasse known to us variously as late capitalism, postmodernism, or postfeminism.

## WOMEN ARTISTS OF THE AVANT-GARDE

What amazes Western viewers when first introduced to the art of the Russian avant-garde is the women – the prodigious amount of work produced by the many, many women artists who belonged to this revolutionary art movement of, loosely, 1910 to 1930. *It is the first historical epoch in which women were able to freely contribute as cultural workers, theoreticians, and art educators, and they did so in large numbers, producing works of exceptional merit.* The reviews of the Costakis collection shown at the Guggenheim in 1981 focused on what for Western critics was a novel phenomenon: the achievements of women artists. Hilton Kramer wrote, "The Russian avant-garde was the only movement of its kind in which the achievements of women were unquestionably equal to their male colleagues" (1981: 54). The question that presents itself is why, at this particular historical moment, women came to the forefront of the avant-garde in large numbers and why this did not occur in the West.

Even their contemporary critics were awed by these women. Writing about the women artists of his generation, Benedikt Livshits said, "These were the real Amazons, these Scythian riders" (1933: 143). He is referring to the earliest historical accounts of women in Russia, invoking a legendary society of women who dominated the south of ancient Rus. Information about them comes from early Greek texts, which describe them as skilled riders and warriors as well as astute linguists. It is interesting that Livshits, who himself worked with the women artists of Russia's avant-garde, collaborating on what was to be one of the most fascinating chapters in the history of art, describes them in these mythic terms, as if they were legends in their own time.

The myth of the strong Russian woman, like all myths pertaining to women, is something to be wary of; nevertheless, it may have functioned as an enabling myth compared to the debilitating constructions of woman as the "weaker sex," "the angel in the house," or the *"femme fatale."* In the case of women artists, these alternative constructions become particularly significant. Rozsika Parker and Griselda Pollock have persuasively argued that in England and Europe by the nineteenth century, with the consolidation of a patriarchal bourgeoisie as the dominant class, femininity was constructed as exclusively domestic and maternal, despite the fact that more and more women were of necessity entering the labor force. At the same time, evolving bourgeois notions of the artist associated creativity with everything that was antidomestic, and the Bohemian model of the free-living, sexually energetic, socially alienated "genius" became the stereotype of the artist who was, by this definition, male (1981: 99). Art was represented as the ideal of self-fulfilling, creative activity, and its antithesis was proletarian alienated labor, but its full opposite, suggests Pollock, "is the repetitive and self-effacing drudgery of what is called 'woman's work'" (1982: 4). Through such constructs, artists and women were allotted almost antithetical, yet equally marginalized, roles within Western bourgeois culture.

This historical bifurcation, between woman and artist on the one hand, and artist and participatory member of society on the other, did not take place in Russia because Russia lacked a bourgeoisie of the sort that provided the impetus for developing a comparable ideology of domesticity. In contrast with the middle class in industrializing Europe and America, which had begun to idealize family life, most progressive Russians found such an ideal self-centered. The novelist Nadezhda Khvoshchinskaia spoke for many of them when she wrote that family happiness is the "vulgar happiness of locked-up houses, tidy and orderly; they seem to smile a welcome at the outsider, but they give him nothing but that smug and stupid smile. These oases are simply individual egotism united into family egotism. They are orderly, temperate, and self-satisfied – and totally self-involved" (quoted in Engel 1987: 54). This antifamily sentiment was widespread, and many Russian women began to seek out ways of participating in public life. During the late nineteenth century, numbers of doctors, teachers, artists, and other members of the intelligentsia – hundreds of them women – travelled to the countryside to work toward ameliorating poor living conditions in peasant communities. The women in particular took on this work with the altruism of a religious campaign. Utterly dedicated, living in wretched material conditions, often without the comfort of family or personal relationships, they devoted their lives to improving the lot of the Russian peasants. While these were not feminist movements (these women were more interested in improving the conditions of the peasants than in improving their own circumstances), the women's movement emerged from their activities and resulted in advances for women in higher education, particularly medicine, and in the high visibility of women in leadership positions within later revolutionary groups.

Several artists' colonies and art schools, some established by women, were based upon a similar hybrid of philanthropic and democratic strivings. Long before the revolution, there was a well-developed tradition of social commitment on the part of both women and artists. A good deal of the work made by the artists in these colonies was based upon folk art and crafts and was intended to be of use to the local population. One of the most prominent members of the early avant-garde was **Natalya Goncharova** (1881–1962), whose paintings of 1909–12 depicted the cyclical life and labor of the Russian peasantry (Figure 3.1). Goncharova's work was deeply influenced by Russian folk traditions, such as the popular woodblock print (*lubok*), semi-abstract embroidery patterns, ancient Scythian sculpture, wood carvings, and icon paintings. Unlike the cultural appropriations of French artists, who were at this time exploring primitive art imported from France's colonies, the interest in primitive art in Russia was based upon indigenous art forms and fueled by nationalist sentiment. Such attitudes had considerable influence on the inception of abstract art, which in Russia was to follow a vastly different trajectory from that of abstractionism in the West.

*Figure 3.1*  Natalya Goncharova, *Planting Potatoes* (oil on canvas, 11 × 132 cm) 1908–09.

In 1913 Goncharova wrote a remarkable manifesto in which she distinguished Russian art from Western art expressly because of the West's adherence to archaic notions of individuality and genius: "I shake off the dust of the West and I consider all those people ridiculous and backward who still imitate Western models in the hope of becoming pure painters . . . Similarly, I find those people ridiculous who advocate individuality and who assume there is some value in their 'I' even when it is extremely limited." One of her objectives was to "fight against the debased and decomposing doctrine of individualism, which is now in a period of agony. . . . In the age of the flowering of individualism, I destroy this holy of holies and refuge of the hidebound as being inappropriate to our contemporary and future way of life" (quoted in Bowlt 1976: 57–58).

Goncharova's critique of modernism as it was emerging in the West is remarkably similar to that undertaken in the past ten years by many Western feminists, who have worked to dismantle bourgeois notions of individuality. This work is central to the feminist project because, as Pollock has pointed out, "it is only feminists who have nothing to lose with the desecration of Genius. The individualism of which the artist is a prime symbol is gender exclusive" (1988: 11). In its radical reassessment of the *function* of the artist, the Russian avant-garde is arguably one of the most significant manifestations in the history of art for both women and women artists.

Following the Russian revolution, no radical shift in roles was necessary for artists, influenced by utilitarian craft traditions, to turn their energies to such things as housing, clothing, daycare, and training in hygiene and basic literacy. They addressed themselves to mundane material domestic needs, to the petty yet pressing problems of daily life that in Russian are called *byt* and affect women most directly. For this reason it can be argued that a utilitarian or materialistic art practice is inherently a feminist art practice. A good number of women artists took part in this broad-based feminist activity, and it may be precisely because of their participation that the Russian avant-garde was able to move so quickly from a high art practice to the utilitarian modes of Productivism and Constructivism. Many Constructivist designs for housing, furniture, transport, etc. were never built due to lack of resources and materials, and Soviet industry did not welcome Constructivist artist-engineers. Nevertheless, those artists who addressed themselves to resolving the mundane problems of the home and workplace were the most likely to see their designs realized. Soviet art historian Ludmilla Vachtova argues that women artists were much more successful in implementing their aesthetic principles than were their less practical male colleagues: "Logically, since a book, dress, or cup obviously appealed more directly to the next door comrade than a painting, almost all women artists in Russia ventured into the field of the 'applied arts' and industrial design. . . . [They] never considered themselves to be heroines or the victims of a cruel fate, but were happy to assert with an unshakable grasp of the facts that they were only 'in the lines of the workers at the art front'" (1979: 43–44). **Liubov Popova** (1889–1924) and **Varvara Stepanova** (1894–1958) were instrumental in opening the First State Textile Print Factory in Moscow, where they then designed clothing according to Constructivist principles – made from simple components, functional, versatile, practical to wear, easy to mass-produce, hygienic, and undecorated except for essentials like pockets, seams, buttons, etc. (Figures 3.2 and 3.3). The actual test of Constructivist principles was in whether or not they appealed to the consumer. In a memoir Popova recounts one of the happiest days of her short life, the day women workers at a factory outlet store selected her clothing over more traditional designs. Rather than the usual trivialization of women's "handwork," this meant success in Constructivist terms, and it marks the distance from the individualism at the heart of the Western avant-garde.

Another difference between Russian and Western art is apparent in the most casual walk through the Russian Museum in St Petersburg – they do not share the same tradition of the nude. The trajectory that went from the Italian Renaissance's glorification of the male body as closest replica of its divine maker, to the predominant use of the female nude in the eighteenth-century Academy paintings, to the nineteenth-century equation of the female nude with the sexual availability of the artist's model/prostitute, to the frequent use of the fragmented or dismembered nude female form in the canonical works of modernism – this is not repeated in the history of Russian art. Even during the eighteenth and nineteenth centuries, when Russian art was most influenced by the French Academy, there was great reservation when it came to depicting the nude body in general and the female body in particular. One notable exception to this general tendency was the proliferation of neoclassical nudes during the period of Social-ist Realism. It is interesting to note that aside from the sculptors **Sarra Lebedeva** (1892–1967), who produced a bust of the now infamous founder of the KGB, Felix Dzerzhinsky, and **Vera Mukhina** (1889–1963), most well known for her gigantic sculpture the *Laborer and Collective Farmer* (1937), Socialist Realism is remarkable in the history of modern Russian art for the *lack* of women artists. It may be that its very representation of woman precluded their participation. Recently feminist art historians have specu-lated that Western women artists may have been deterred from participat-ing in the Western avant-garde specifically because so much of the work is modeled upon the distorted, debased, or otherwise fetishized bodies of women.

The European Academy's obsession with the nude functioned to deter Western women artists in another way. The ability to paint the human figure in historical, mythological, or religious subjects gradually became institutionalized as the fundamental criterion of artistic greatness, and the academies exercised control over this criterion of success as well as

*Figure 3.2*  Liubov Popova, Work uniform designs for actors at the Free Studio of Vsevolod Meyerhold, State Higher Theater Workshop (GVYTM) 1921.

*Figure 3.3*  Varvara Stepanova. Costume designs for *The Death of Tarelkin*, 1922 (photo: Jo Anna Isaak).

the means of achieving it. Young ladies were excluded from the life study classes out of a consideration for decorum. In Russia, on the other hand, the nude was not the *sine qua non* of artistic training; other genres, particularly landscape painting, were highly esteemed, as were the applied arts.

Many artists were strong supporters of the Slavophile movement, which stressed Russian themes, particularly landscapes and genre scenes, and asserted their independence from the Academy, which had always been identified with Western art, which at that time meant a stultifying neoclassicism. As early as 1840 a series of administrative reforms gradually gave Russian women direct access to art education. In 1842 the first art school for women opened – the Women's Section of the St Petersburg Drawing School (Figure 3.4). This was quickly followed by the Stieglitz School and the Stroganov School in Moscow (Hilton 1980: 142). By 1870, women were admitted to the Academy of Arts. A collective painting by the students of Ilya Repin (1844–1930), depicting his life study classes, which he held from the late 1880s until he retired in 1907, shows male and female art students working together in the presence of a live nude model (Figure 3.5). By this time there was a growing population of women doctors, and the idea of women in anatomy classes was not so unusual. (In 1886 at the Pennsylvania Academy of Fine Arts, where women had customarily been given cows as models, Thomas Eakins was dismissed for bringing a nude male model into a female life drawing class.) The hegemony of the St Petersburg Academy had been undermined long before Repin began to reform it. Numerous other organizations provided artistic training and exhibition possibilities. In 1882 seventy-three women painters in St Petersburg formed their own association to support women artists (Sobko 1886).

The relative ease with which women gained access to art education in Russia meant that the women who participated in the avant-garde were the second or third generation of professionally trained artists. This becomes particularly important when we realize that artistic training in the Soviet Union was frequently passed on from one generation to another like a craft or a trade. **Vera Miturich-Khlebnikova** (b. 1954) speaks of her earliest artistic training as part of a family tradition: "At a huge desk of my father's, artist Mai Miturich, there was a special place for me. That's how I began to paint thirty years ago. That is also how my father himself began, when the table belonged to his father, Petr Miturich, an artist and inventor" (letter to the author, April 1989). Vera is the granddaughter of Petr Miturich and **Vera Khlebnikova** (sister of Victor Khlebnikov) – all were artists of the avant-garde. **Irina Starzenyetskaya** (b. 1943) is the daughter of the well-known stage designer **Tamara Starzenyetskaya** (b. 1912). For many years mother and daughter have been involved in theatrical collaborations. The costumes and curtains Irina designed for her mother's sets have influenced her own landscape paintings, particularly in their capacity to convey deep recessional spaces. For several decades now

*Figure 3.4* Ekaterina Khikova, *Women's Classes at the St Petersburg Drawing School for Auditors*, 1855 (Russian Museum, St Petersburg).

*Figure 3.5* Collective Painting, *Model Study in the Studio of Ilya Repin at the Academy of Arts*, 1899–1900 (Research Museum of the Academy of Arts, St Petersburg).

*Figure 3.6* Irina Starzenyetskaya, *Entrance to Jerusalem* (egg tempera on wood, 50 × 40 cm) *in situ* in church in Tarusa.

*Figure 3.7*   Dzemma Skulme, *The Near and the Far*, 1979 (courtesy International Images Sewickley, Penn).

Irina has been working both as a painter in a contemporary mode and as an icon painter with the icon painters' cooperative in the ancient church of the Resurrection of Christ in the village of Tarusa, where she lives most of the year (Figure 3.6). In a conversation with the artist **Dzemma Skulme** (b. 1925), head of the Artists' Union in Latvia (Figure 3.7), I learned that not only had her father and mother both been well-known artists but that her son and daughter were artists as well. When I remarked on how infrequently this occurs in the West and how common it is in the Soviet Union, she responded, with a matter-of-factness that reveals a world of difference, "On our passports we are called workers, not geniuses." Clearly the cult of genius was undermined long ago.

I have taken this quick run through the history of Russian art to examine the ways in which alternative somatic and social texts affect the ways in which women assume the roles of woman and of artist. Although conditions have changed a great deal since the period of the avant-garde, some of these historical developments still exert considerable influence upon contemporary conditions for both women artists and Russian women in general.

*Figure 3.8* David Attie, from the series *Russian Self-Portraits*
(black-and-white photo, 51 × 61 cm) 1977.

# WOMAN AS SIGN IN *THE WORLD BACKWAЯDS*

As part of an American–Soviet cultural exchange that took place in Kiev in 1976, David Attie installed a large Polaroid camera where visitors to the exhibition could take their own portraits (Figure 3.8). The studio was equipped with a full-length mirror so participants could arrange their appearance as they wished and assume whatever expression they considered most suitable. They were given the cable-release bulb and they decided when to take the shot. What is fascinating about these photographs is what they reveal about the way in which the image of the self is constructed by images in the environment. The participant seems uninformed about the whole system of representation into which she has unwittingly entered. It is as if she had not thought of herself as an object to be looked at before. She doesn't adopt any of the stereotypical poses we would arrange ourselves into; she doesn't even think to smile. When transported to the West, images such as these become rich fodder for the comic. A TV commercial for Wendy's hamburger chain used a woman who looked a lot like one from Attie's collection as its model. The woman lumbers down a designer runway modeling fashions for the season, but each season she wears the same unhappy dress – with only the addition of a beach ball for summer. How does this sell hamburgers? The pitch – at Wendy's you get to choose what toppings you want on your hamburger. The ad is perfect of its kind. In it, the freedom to choose lettuce, onions, or tomatoes is equated with freedom itself, and we are invited to congratulate ourselves on the limitlessness of our freedom compared to that of those poor hapless Soviets. Ostensibly the issue is mustard versus relish, with a meta-textual reading of capitalism versus communism, but the contested *site* of this ideological warfare is the body of a woman – a body, perhaps not incidentally, that won't "make it" in today's market economy.

When I first went to the Soviet Union in 1981, I was struck by the fact that women are not "hailed," to use Althusser's term, by ubiquitous images of women on billboards, posters, cinema marquees, shop windows, and magazines. Images of women were not used as part of the continuous barrage of exhortation and entrapment that, as Susan Sontag puts it in *On Photography*, a capitalist society needs "to stimulate buying and anesthetize the injuries of class, race and sex" (1973: 178). But now, as they move toward a market economy, a proliferation of images is preceding and directing actual social change. As advertising images fill the streets, the bodies of Russian women are undergoing enormous rewriting. In the winter of 1991 I came upon a billboard in St Petersburg in which a bikini-clad woman in a pin-up pose was juxtaposed with an image of a computer (Figure 3.9). The caption read, "Shaping – It's the Style of Life for the Contemporary Woman." In this self-improvement poster addressed to women the role of the computer was unclear; it could simply have been

*Figure 3.9* "Shaping – it's the style for the contemporary women," billboard in St Petersburg, 1991 (photo: Susan Unterberg).

the signifier of all that was progressive, like the tractor in Soviet posters of the 1930s. Now the emphasis was on the appearance of the woman, not on her work. In real terms, however, this image is no less about women and work than Socialist Realist posters. As job opportunities arise in the emerging entrepreneurial sector and in Western businesses, the call is for young, attractive women to occupy predominantly low-paying, decorative jobs in the service "industry." As the free market brings unemployment in its wake, the education, training, and professional skills of women are being sacrificed first – at the moment it is estimated that between 75 and 80 percent of the newly unemployed are women.[2] The subliminal message of this ad aimed at women is, "Either make yourself look like this, or you'll be out of a job."

Formerly, women in the Soviet Union were depicted as heroic workers – tractor driver, construction worker, road worker, engineer, vegetable farmer. Coming from a culture in which images of women signify sale and sexual titillation, I found these pictures of active, strong women at work refreshing. But Soviet women, conscious of the violation inherent in so overdetermined an iconographic program, do not. They recognize in this stereotype of the all-capable and resilient woman a strategy to colonize a workforce. Here the Equal Rights Amendment has been in effect since 1917. Women do not have to go to court to assert their right to jobs such as fire fighter or garbage collector, as they have done in the US, and women are well represented in such professions as medicine and engineering. All of this seems progressive to us, but what we want the right *to do*, they want the right *not to do*. "Emancipation is dreadful," says **Ira Zatulovskaya** (b. 1954). "I am a victim of emancipation. So are all women here. I've tried my heart out to understand you Western women, but obviously I just can't. In the Soviet Union it is us women who are obliged to do everything."

The word that comes up most frequently in conversations with women is *peregruzhennost*, "overburdening." The myth of the strong woman, the amazon, is a myth that has recurred in different forms throughout Russian history when agrarian, economic, or military considerations have made excessive demands on the contributions of women. As one woman wrote in *Moscow News*, "Yes, a woman can do everything, but she just doesn't want to anymore," and proceeds to compare Soviet women's emancipation within the labor force to "Atlases putting all their load on the shoulders of caryatids" (quoted in Gray 1990: 37–38). Although it is demonstrable that Soviet women assume more than their share of the burden of labor, the actual power exercised by most Soviet women is severely constrained to a certain familial and ideological zone.

Artist/critic **Anna Alchuk** has pointed out some of the images of heroic womanhood found in the Moscow metro. For example, in Baumanskaya station there is a female figure on a pedestal stepping out of a bay of red

*Figure 3.10*   Anna Alchuk, *Untitled* (black-and-white photos) 1990.

marble, wearing a wind-blown, quilted worker's jacket and girded with a holster and revolver. In one hand she holds a grenade, in the other a machine gun. All eight figures on this station, which was built during the Second World War, have the same aggressive stride, the same menacing look, and all of them are armed (even the "intellectual" brandishes sheets of paper). But none of them looks so fanatical, none is armed so thoroughly (a grenade, a machine gun, *and* a revolver) as the woman. In Avtozavodskaya station there is a fresco in which amidst several gray male figures a female silhouette stands out. Wearing a scarlet dress, this woman proudly pushes a huge handcart of coal (Alchuk 1991: 49). In a manner somewhat like Louise Lawler's investigation of the ways in which a work of art is altered by its context, Alchuk critiques these monuments to heroic Soviet womanhood by photographing them and putting them on display in a gallery. As reliefs and even as large-scale statuary placed in busy public thoroughfares, these images are almost unnoticed by the masses who flow past them. "Their function is not to be read," Mikhail Ryklin points out, "but to exert an influence" (1993: 57). When converted to photographs their original didactic function is undermined. Reduced in scale, framed, and hung on the gallery wall, they are transformed into objects of contemplation for private viewing, and other embedded readings emerge. What is most striking is the sense of human redundancy. Whatever the activity, whether it be the harvest, or industry, or the war, vast numbers of people are depicted taking part. The individual is subsumed into the undifferentiated body of the masses; even the distinction between male and female is obfuscated. Female bodies with hypertrophied shinbones and muscular arms become metaphors of an ideal collective body merging into the sexual "indifference" of totalitarian androgyny. In the molded panels at the Electrozavodskaya metro station which depict the various phases of labor there is a triad of female figures, the three graces of labor (Figure 3.10). The women are holding, almost caressing, propellers or cannons. The phallic and fecund symbolism of this trinity is repeated in a relief showing three fists holding a hammer – the apotheosis of the labor process. What Alchuk's work points out is that throughout the period of Socialist Realism, labor was increasingly depicted as if it were experienced ecstatically, as if erotically charged. The eroticism was generated and then harnessed, as if it were a natural resource to be expended in "exultant" labor.

Ironically, the period of Socialist Realism, as we have seen, was the historical period in which Russian art drew most heavily upon the Western tradition of the nude. A 1991 exhibition of Socialist Realist art at the New Tretyakov Gallery in Moscow displayed more nudity in one room than can be found throughout the entire collection of Russian art in the Russian Museum, St Petersburg. Although Andrei Zhdanov, as Minister of Culture under Stalin, led campaigns against the representation of sexuality, images

*Figure 3.11* Aleksandr Samokhvalov, *After Running*, 1934, Russian Museum, St Petersburg (photo: Susan Unterberg).

of nude women were nonetheless officially encouraged. As in Germany under National Socialism, there were many images of female fecundity; bare-breasted harvesters or nursing mothers were very popular, as were nude female athletes or bathing scenes that allowed the artist to depict the nude in numerous postures. Alexsandr Deineka's *Football* (1932), for example, depicts three nude women chasing a ball. The title provides the same pseudo-rationale for viewing these women from various vantage points as the theme of the judgement of Paris did for the painters of the French Academy. Alexsandr Samokhvalov's *After Running* (1934) is a classic of this genre (Figure 3.11). It depicts a female athlete drying her moist, semi-nude body; her panties are pulled down to reveal a little of her pubic hair. The obsession with the healthy athletic body as a form of sexual sublimation during the Stalinist period is remarkably similar to the mechanisms of libidinal alignment used on us today – twenty pounds lighter, and this girl could be in an ad for Evian water. In Western culture the iconographic appropriation of the female body facilitates the construction of difference, whereas in Soviet culture it contributes to the notion of the undifferentiated collective body. Yet both representational systems serve to control women's sexuality and to guarantee manageability in the workplace.

## THE PERSONAL AS THE POLITICAL

For the most part, the Soviet art I saw in the 1980s was made for private reasons and was seen only by a small group of friends. Exhibition space was difficult to come by and had to be arranged through the Artists' Union, an organization that didn't seem to bestir itself too often even on behalf of artists who were members, and most of the artists I met were not members. When I first started visiting artists' studios in the early 1980s I found a small and very generous artists' community, one that was tightly knit and highly supportive. One artist would invariably take me to see the work of another. While the work suffered from lack of materials and lack of critical attention, the fact that these women were working in relative obscurity had its advantages. As one artist put it, "No one sees this work, so it can be totally free." On the other hand, the constraints placed upon official artists manifested themselves in various ways. During the 1970s, a period of relative liberalization, a number of women artists were admitted to the Artists' Union; Nazarenko, Nesterova, Nasipova, Bulgakova, Tabaka, and Vint are among the most well known. No one declined an offer to join the Artists' Union; the benefits (salary, studio, and art supplies) were too great. The price paid for this acceptance was that the artist was to some degree expected to work in the service of the state. Responses to this obligation ranged from identification with the institution, to small, sanity-preserving subversions.

99

**Tatyana Nazarenko** (b. 1944) is a figurative painter who was admitted into the Artists' Union in 1969 and was awarded the Komsomol prize in 1972. Like other members of the Artists' Union, she was sent on field trips to study the life of Soviet people. Her painting of the women construction workers of the Moldavin Hydro Power Station (Figure 3.12) was a typical assignment, yet it shows that interesting work can be produced within the confines of the requirements of Socialist Realism. Like Léger's merging of men and machines, the tubular structure of the huge pipes is echoed in the dwarfed bodies of the women who climb amongst them, patting on insulation by hand. Many of Nazarenko's works, particularly the large-scale historical paintings, can be found in the Tretyakov. In her studio, however, one can find traces of Nazarenko's resistance to her "success." *Circus Girl* (1984) (Figure 3.13) is a portrait of herself dressed in a bikini doing a precarious high-wire act. Below her the officials of the Artists' Union politely applaud her act, which is all the more remarkable because she is working without even a wire. On her return from a recent trip to the United States, she painted a record of her experiences. Her body is served up in a large chafing-dish while a strange assortment of exotic creatures, part animal, part bird, part man, stare down upon her. A man with the head of a pig and predominant teeth leers at her while another man, metamorphosing into an as yet indeterminate animal, starts to carve the dish with his fork. Nazarenko's private and comic resistance to the various molds she was being fitted into is typical of the responses of the women artists who were accepted into the Artists' Union during the 1970s.

Some of the more recent work, particularly that done by the younger women artists, is overtly political, critical, and controversial. **Natalya Turnova** (b. 1957) painted large-scale, brightly colored cartoon caricatures of the icons of the Afghanistan war – the soldiers and sailors and the legitimizing slogans and banners under which they marched. Seen together, everything seems to partake of the innocence and gaiety of a game for small boys. The slogans are fragmented and abstracted almost to the point of unintelligibility, yet enough remains of questions such as "Who Sold Us to Afghanistan?" or the familiar Stalinist slogans "Who is with me?" and "The party decides everything" to cause them to be censored from a group exhibition at the Palace of Youth in 1988. In 1989 Turnova began a series of rather irreverent portraits of then famous, now infamous, public figures. This work takes on a prophetic dimension in the context of the statue smashing and the proliferation of posters and cartoons attacking public figures that took place after the failed coup of August 1991. In another work large-scale portraits are cut out and installed as free-standing sculptures throughout the gallery so that viewers can walk around them, get a sense of their flatness, even have their own photos taken alongside them (Figure 3.14). These are portraits of powerful men – Ryazhsky,

*Figure 3.12* Tatyana Nazarenko, *Women Construction Workers at the Moldavin Hydro Power Station* (oil on canvas, 100 × 80 cm) 1974 (courtesy Norton Dodge).

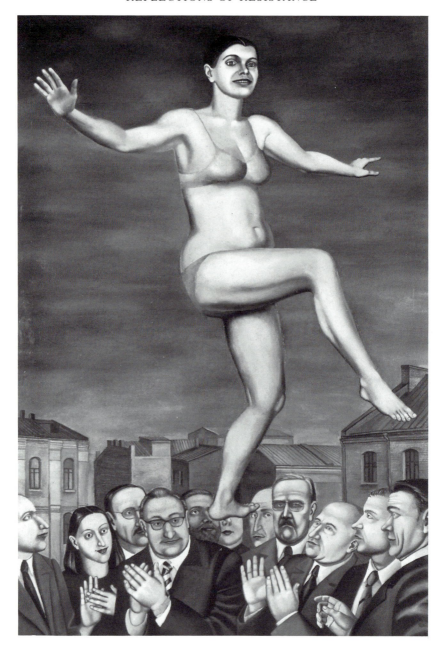

*Figure 3.13*   Tatyana Nazarenko, *Circus Girl* (oil on canvas) 1984.

*Figure 3.14* Natalya Turnova, *Portraits of Civil War Heroes and Contemporary Leaders* (oil on cardboard) 1990, installation, Minsk.

Voroshilov, Ordzjonikize, Lenin, and Gorbachev – but the homogeneity of treatment causes the men to become almost anonymous, almost interchangeable. Masculinity is explored as masquerade, and power itself is revealed as a put-on. Turnova's portraits are provocative and confrontational; in part this is a result of reducing these public icons to comic caricatures and in part a result of the context – Soviet citizens, at least until 1991, were not used to seeing their public figures "sent up" in this way. What is most disturbing about Turnova's portraits is that they are given smiles and made to look a little jaunty, almost what in America would be called "fun loving." The effect is truly sinister.

While the political content of Turnova's work is banner bold, the messages in the paintings of **Elena Keller** (b. 1951) are coded and arcane, more like the half-intelligible traces of a prisoner furtively trying to communicate with the outside world. Seemingly abstract paintings reveal themselves to be political allegories. A random splattering of red against a yellow background becomes, on closer examination, a map of the Soviet Union; in the center a stick figure lies in a grid, or is it caught in a trap? Is this a reference to the internment camps located throughout the Soviet Union, or is the Soviet Union understood to be one large prison? Both map and trapped human figure are repeated in another painting called *Great Expectations* (1988); this time golden bars rain down upon the figure – a reference to Danae and the shower of gold, or a hope for some spiritual infusion from above, or are these golden bars hard currency coming in from the West? Readings are multiple and ambiguous. Often words or letters interconnect with iconic signs. *To the Decembrists, Your Affectionate Brother* is a series of red and blue markings that can eventually be read as AKATUI, the initials of the Decembrists.[3] *A Letter* (1987) is a pictograph, the addressee and message unclear. At times the iconography is so personal, so solipsistic, it precludes any conversation with the outside world. What is clear is an almost primitive desire to make a mark, to leave a trace, to let someone, anyone, know you exist. Keller is writing in the universal morphology of the human condition; the text is subject to repeated misreadings. In *Runes* (1987) (Figure 3.15) the hieroglyphic markings on one side of the canvas are as unintelligible as the markings on the other side, which may or may not be human figures; what we see may be only our desire to see something formed in our image, or our desire to decipher, to find or impose meaning. In *Constellations* (1987) an intertwined couple may be locked either in an embrace or in combat. Like the game of cat's cradle, the viewer can see either a cat or a cradle as the hands manipulate the strings. In a painting done in 1988 one can discern the epigraph to Kurt Vonnegut's book *Cat's Cradle* – "Give me the strength to change what I can, the grace to leave alone what I can't, and the sense to know the difference" – which would serve well as the epigraph for Keller's own work.

*Figure 3.15*   Elena Keller, *Runes* (oil on canvas, 200 × 150 cm) 1987.

Much of the work I saw during my first visits in the early 1980s was heavily embedded in a conversation that Soviet people were just beginning to have with foreigners. This is a country in which many people are absent: they died in the war, they died in the purges, they died during the collectivization, they were sent to prison camps, they emigrated. **Svetlana Bogatir** (b. 1945) creates a translucent surrealist world of outlines emptied of content; a volumeless world whose objects and figures float somnambulantly through space, receding into the vanishing point (Figure 3.16). These are mute tracings of those who have disappeared yet seem to have a presence, not just in people's memories but in the streets, the buildings, and interior objects where something of their physical aura seems to linger. They are made of light; luminous contours of the place they hold in space now, in the past, or in the future. "I feel that in this room there have been many people here before me and after I am gone there will be others. We meet now by chance. We live in the space of people with whom we have associated. You know and I know that it was not possible to speak about these things. Each of us is just minutes in transit, only moments in light. Everything is fragile and transparent – so now I don't paint people, only places for people in light" (conversation with the author, Moscow, July 1988).

A good deal of the work, especially that done by women artists, seems to be engaged in an investigation of the representation of the self. Unlike many Western women artists, they are not seeking to deconstruct the images of woman that have been mass-produced by advertising. Instead, many Soviet women artists seem to be engaged in a private, almost obsessive recording of the self. For example, **Clara Golitsina** (b. 1925) painted seventeen self-portraits over a period of forty years. When seen together these self-portraits, tracing the narrative of a life in almost novelistic terms, provide a record rarely available to us in paint. They begin with the self-portraits of the artist in young womanhood, in which she seems to be trying to see herself as others see her. If it were not for the steadfast stare of the young woman, these works could be Impressionist paintings of a pretty young woman in a sun hat. The gaze, directed at the viewer, will be a constant throughout the years. In later paintings she becomes more purposeful, more direct, the woman now addresses the viewer more confidently. Her hair is cut short, the clothes are simpler, the hat more functional than stylish. Later, the viewer is not provided with distractions; the face fills the picture frame. There is no longer any question; these are self-portraits (Figures 3.17 and 3.18). Although the recording of time upon the face progresses with unflattering objectivity, these are portraits of someone obsessed not with aging, but with the process of painting. As viewers of Golitsina's portraits, we are caught up in this obsession. Like readers of a narrative, we feel obliged to try to read "off" the repeated physiognomy some meaning, to seek the meaning of another's life, to come to some closure. The portraits do not suggest varying emotions, with one exception – a series of expressionistic, haunting works done in the 1980s after the death of her husband. Afterward there is a hiatus. The last self-portrait I saw was done in 1988; the gaze is now directed towards a book in the artist's hand, the hat has a colorful bow, a bird sits on her shoulder. The face is of indeterminate age; were it not for the date on the back, this self-portrait could easily be confused with those of earlier days.

*Figure 3.16* Svetlana Bogatir, *Walking People* (oil on canvas, 97 × 116 cm) 1987.

**Elena Figurina** (b. 1955) also seems to be engaged in an extended self-analysis. Figurina received no formal artistic training; until recently she worked as an aircraft engineer. Figurina began painting in 1980 with a series of portraits, some of friends, one of Van Gogh, and several self-portraits. These early self-portraits were crude expressionist works, the features highly stylized and distorted, executed with broad simple strokes; the colors, reduced to a primary palette with red and yellow predominating, are used arbitrarily, and green blotches, reminiscent of Matisse's Fauve period, appear on the face. Figurina's explorations of the self expand to

*Figure 3.17*   Clara Golitsina, *Self Portrait* (oil on canvas) 1965.

include family groupings of the artist with her mother, father, and sister. All distinguishing features are minimized and all members of the family come to look alike. In later works this family resemblance is extended. Groups of people all resembling one another, yet all resembling the artist, are engaged in activities such as walking, picking apples, standing in fields with cows, catching birds, cleaning fish, dancing, playing in the sand, or just standing, either engrossed in quiet contemplation or looking out at us (Figure 3.19). In a painting called *Masks* (1989) four figures, carrying bright yellow masks, are as devoid of distinguishing features as the masks. Like

*Figure 3.18*   Clara Golitsina, *Self Portrait* (oil on canvas) 1982.

characters in folk tales, they interact with animals, who in turn take on human characteristics, looking inquisitively or balefully at the humans painted in the same primary colors. People and animals carry out their activities in the bright, indefinite, and timeless background of Matisse's dancers, and like Matisse's figures, their physical bodies are extended or distorted in such a way as to harmonize with their activity or to convey emotion. Stylistically, Figurina's work is closely associated with Russian primitivism and the folk art revived by artists such as Goncharova, Larionov, and Malevich at the turn of the century. Her figures are engaged in the same

*Figure 3.19*   Elena Figurina, *The Red Fish* (oil on canvas, 122 × 97 cm) 1987.

tasks and are as simplified and generic as Goncharova's peasants. Figurina's paintings, however, are not a celebration of peasant life; the characters are engaged in the exploration of subjectivity or the contemplation of something external to the scene in which they find themselves, and they do this with the indefinite determination of characters in a Beckett play.

**Vera Miturich-Khlebnikova** has also been exploring her own family in her recent work. She has been recycling all the memorabilia, the quotidian accumulations of their lives – papers, bills, documents, newspaper clippings, old photographs, etc. As many members of her family belonged to the group of Russian Futurists, their personal papers and documents provide a

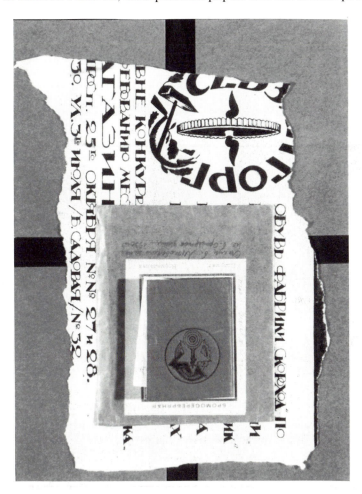

*Figure 3.20*   Vera Miturich-Khlebnikova, Vera Khlebnikova's rifle-shooting test scores (collage contaning silkcreen) 1991 (photo: Susan Unterberg).

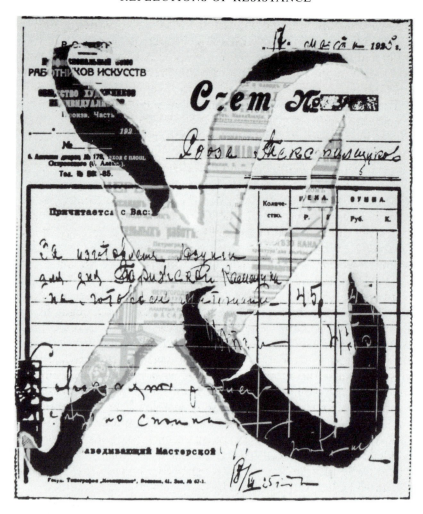

*Figure 3.21*   Vera Miturich-Khlebnikova, Alexander Miturich's receipt for art
supplies (silkscreen) 1991 (photo: Susan Unterberg).

fascinating record of the impact of political changes upon the daily life of an
artist. One collage contains her grandmother's (Vera Khlebnikova's) record
book with the test results of her rifle shooting, an activity in which every
good Soviet citizen (male or female) was expected to excel (Figure 3.20). In
a series of silk-screen prints and collages made of her relatives' papers and
correspondence with the Artists' Union, one can discern the fate of the
avant-garde: receipts for art supplies, invoices for commissions, and finally
the unemployment card issued by the Artists' Union in 1927, the official way
of informing artists their services were no longer required (Figure 3.21).

The work of husband and wife team **Ludmila Skripkina** (b. 1965) and **Oleg Petrenko** (b. 1964), known as **The Peppers**, is so deeply immersed in the banality of *byt* that the mounds of potatoes, pots of peas, and jars of pork seem about to overwhelm the life they are intended to sustain. In a 1991 installation of their work at the Ronald Feldman Gallery in New York, 800 pounds of potatoes filled one small room. The walls were covered with a series of paintings devoted entirely to potatoes; potatoes, like faces in a crowd, recede into the horizon, crowding out everything else. Eruptions of peas flow out of canvases, pots, aprons, even bones and breasts (Figure 3.22). But the abundance suggests only boredom and repetition, not plenty. The obsessional nature of the activity of gathering and preserving the food destroys the idea of enjoyment in eating, just as all sense of pleasure is absent from the charts and graphs documenting such things as the number of hours people spend engaged in what would be considered pleasurable activity: reading, listening to music, going to a museum or the circus or a movie or a concert. As Skripkina explains, "They were studies made of workers in the Severski Factory in Sverdlovsky, a town I grew up in. It is an industrial town that is located at the midpoint in the Soviet Union between Asia and Europe. It is thought of as an average or medium point. They were studies done to increase productivity. If a worker went to a concert, did it increase his productivity? If music was played in the workplace, did that increase productivity? Reason controls pleasure. This is not science, but pseudo-scientific communism" (all quotations are from conversations with the author, September 1991). The charts are comic in their ludicrous ineffectuality and depressing if one thinks of the amount of time wasted in compiling them. Another piece involves a book about the production and distribution of electricity, embedded in an accordion. "The accordion is a comic folk instrument," Petrenko explains. "Playing it causes the book to wheeze *er-er-er-er* back and forth with the old saw of productivity under socialism."

Every so often in the midst of these compilations and charts written in various registers of language, one encounters a sinister note. Diagrams documenting the breakdown of movement coordination, olfactory, and other essential faculties in a dog, caused by the removal of various parts of his cerebellum, suggest the enormous amount of damage done in the name of science. By far the most sinister are those studies done on the reproductive function of women. Petrenko discounts any feminist agenda to their work. "Many Western critics make the mistake of thinking that we are addressing women's problems when we deal with abortion procedures and use these charts of women's gynecological diseases, such as in our *Types of Leukorrhea according to Mandelshtam*, but we are not really concerned about women's problems. We are interested in the language of science, the context in which this language is produced, and the way this language constructs an ideology." There is a certain irony in

*Figure 3.22* Ludmila Skripkina and Oleg Petrenko (The Peppers) *Bone Marrow* (6 pea-filled porcelain pipes, cloth apron, 109 × 38 cm) 1989 (photo: Dennis Cowley; courtesy Ronald Feldman Fine Arts Inc.).

this disclaimer, for while it may be true that the Peppers' expressed intentions were "to explore the metaphorical workings of the language of science [and] the way ideology works deep inside language," the fact remains that the most powerful examples of these interconnections come from the pseudo-scientific material they have collected on the medicalization of women's bodies. The *Chart of Relia*, "Data Concerning Discharge

114

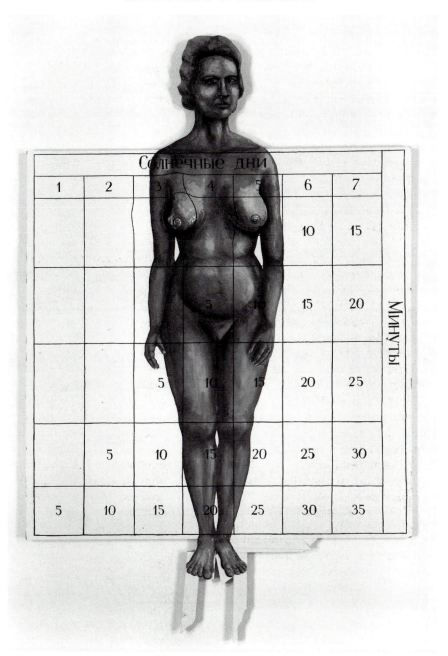

*Figure 3.23* Ludmila Skripkina and Oleg Petrenko (The Peppers) *Chart of Relia*
(enamel paint and mixed media on masonite, 164 × 122 cm) 1989
(photo: Dennis Cowley; courtesy Ronald Feldman Fine Arts Inc.).

115

as Related to the Degree of Vaginal Cleanliness According to Hermin" (Figure 3.23); "Classification of Retrodeviation of the Uterus according to Elkin"; the "Diagram of Fallopian Tube Permeability with the Aid of Chemograms Obtained through Insufflation with the 'Red Guard' Device" (the Red Guard being an actual gynecological device for examining women); "Methods of Provocation," which seem to be ways thought to expand the cervix, including "Gegor's Widening Device," "Placement of Kafka's Cover on the Cervix of the Uterus," or "To Drink Some Beer," are too hilarious and too cruel to be made up. They reveal what feminists in various fields have been exploring for some time: the fantasy link between femininity and the pathological, an important component of the political unconscious as it developed within patriarchal configurations. Categorizing femininity as diseased, a source of contamination, or simply enigmatic, serves to regulate sexual mores and to establish state policy on public hygiene and state control over women's labor and reproductive activity. While the Peppers may not categorize their activity as feminist, their exhibition reveals that any charting of the complex nexus of language, science, and ideology has historically been mapped on the terrain of the female body.

In her recent work **Irina Nakhova** (b. 1955) has been exploring the construction of gender as a by-product of all cultural production. For several years Nakhova has been examining the interstices between process and completion, between fragmentation and wholeness, between the extant and the ruined, between renewal and decay. This began with a series of paintings called *Scaffoldings*, in which the image was of the scaffolding itself, the structures of restoration, not on what was being restored – a natural response to a culture caught up in *perestroika*. After her visit to Italy she began another series exploring the ruins and remnants of classical antiquity. The perfect beauty of classical art with all its images of the finished, completed man, outwardly monolithic, is re-presented by Nakhova as inwardly riven. In her work the classical body is subject to aging and decay just like the material body. In this re-presentation of classical art Nakhova seems to have discovered, almost as if by accident, the gender assumptions upon which it is based. In 1991 she painted a series of pairs of male and female faces or torsos from antiquity (Figure 3.24 ). As classical statuary they show the effects of time upon them in chips and broken limbs, and as material beings they show them as sags and wrinkles. All the pairs are cracked; in one set the cracks appear in a random pattern suggesting age or accident, in another the cracks appear along the lines of a perfectly symmetrical grid. The cracks are identical so that the viewer can exchange the pieces like a jigsaw puzzle, and in doing so, the dichotomies between the material body, with its close association to the maternal body, and the classical body, with its claims to completion and perfection, become as apparent as the

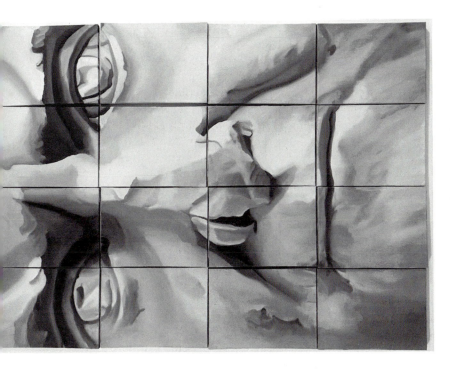

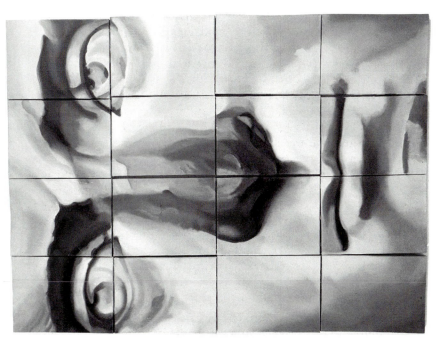

*Figure 3.24* Irina Nakhova, *Untitled* (diptych, oil on canvas, 102 × 76 cm) 1991 (courtesy Phyllis Kind Gallery, New York and Chicago).

*Figure 3.25*  Irina Nakhova, *Aphrodite* (oil on cloth) 1994.

differences between the male and female bodies to which these dichotomies are inextricably associated. In her recent work Nakhova paints the torsos of ancient Greek statuary on old overcoats (Figure 3.25). The viewer is again invited to interact with the work. This is readywear art, the viewer can try it on for size like coats in a second-hand shop. In other cases, when the coats are on display on dressmakers' dummies, simply

*Figure 3.26* Maria Konstantinova, *M.K.K.M. (Maria Konstantinova/Kasimir Malevich)* (mixed media, 101 × 40 × 17 cm) 1990 (courtesy Phyllis Kind Gallery, New York and Chicago).

touching them causes them to talk back to the viewer – vituperative, seductive, nonsensical or foreign language emanate from these coolly classical body-coats.

**Maria Konstantinova** (b. 1955) also reveals some of the gender assumptions of high art by turning painting into women's work – making a pillow of Malevich's Suprematist *Black Square* (Figure 3.26). To underscore the

119

inversions of identities she signed this piece with both her own and Kasimir Malevich's initials: *M.K.K.M.* In a prophetic work of 1989 Konstantinova made a large cushion of a red star, propped it against the wall in such a way that it assumed humanoid features (somewhat like a drunk sprawled against a wall), and draped across it a funereal banner reading "Rest in Peace" (Figure 3.27).

*Figure 3.27*   Maria Konstantinova, *Rest in Peace* (mixed media installation, 152 × 152 × 102 cm) 1989
(courtesy Phyllis Kind Gallery, New York and Chicago).

Nearly the entire history of writing is confounded with the history of reason, of which it is at once the effect, the support, and one of the privileged alibis.

(Cixous 1975; 1981 edn: 249)

The work of **Svetlana Kopystianskaya** (b. 1950) is in a very literal sense the ongoing act of finding a language. The subject matter of her paintings is texts – readymades of a reality already written for her, the barrage of bureaucratic language she found herself daily overwhelmed by. "I don't go in for political activity," she says. "I'm very far from politics, but you see, all our newspapers and magazines of the so-called period of stagnation were absolute nonsense. It was absurd. The information they contained had nothing to do with reality, with real life. Several years ago I just copied out from a newspaper a most banal text about a communist *subbotnik* [someone who is a hard worker for the revolution – working on Saturdays, for example]" (interview with the author, December 1989). One version she called a text with meaning, the other she called a text with no meaning. The lyrical flow of Kopystianskaya's hand-painting of the letters is the only difference. This act was not as apolitical as she thought, for as her husband, Igor, points out, when Svetlana began selling her works abroad, officials were very suspicious: "All the other paintings passed with no problems, but at the Sotheby's auction a very high-ranking official from the Central Committee of the Communist Party came, he looked at the works with texts, and he got very nervous wanting to know what was said in the texts. Someone made a joke that the texts were significant state secrets. This just illustrates the fact that all texts are treated from the political point of view. For example, it's forbidden to take xerox machines into the USSR, but you can bring cameras and video-cameras."

It was in the midst of this textual overproduction and censorship that Kopystianskaya began her subversion of language. In her landscape paintings (Figure 3.28), composed of handwritten texts, she reverses the viewer's habitual relation to language – rather than looking *through* the printed word to the meaning it is intended to convey, the viewer is invited to look *at* it. The language in Kopystianskaya's paintings is not the self-effacing medium that permits the reader's gaze to pass straight through it to rest on the background of illusionistic literary conventions. In this manipulation of attention, the materiality of language is foregrounded. Her intention, however, is not just to reduce language to its surfaces, but rather to investigate the condition of any sign's visibility. To see the landscape and to read the text are two incompatible operations that exclude one another because they require different adjustments. The texts are passages from famous Russian novels that have so described the Russian landscape that it is impossible to perceive it except through this screen of language which turns all into a *paysage moralisé* – a landscape onto which one

*Figure 3.28* Svetlana Kopystiankaya, *Landscape* (oil and acrylic on canvas, 79 × 158 cm) 1985 (courtesy Phyllis Kind Gallery, New York and Chicago).

Svetlana Kopystiankaya, *Landscape* (detail).

projects and from which one extracts meaning. It is not the "real" that Kopystianskaya intended to reclaim; she was motivated by the sense that her voice, her vision, had been silenced by what she describes as "the oppressive role of literature in the Russian visual arts; literature drives the visual properties of an artwork into the background." In Kopystianskaya's landscapes the viewer is asked to let go of the imposed significance and focus instead upon something far more elusive.

## THE ICON OF OUR TIMES

As the old order of art production, distribution, exhibition, and critical reception collapses, those with the requisite energy, commitment, and enthusiasm are finding that for the first time their projects can be realized. Ironically, the closest historical comparison is to the activities of the avant-garde just after the revolution. When Lunacharsky, the commissar of culture, came to Lenin for funds to support the avant-garde, Lenin replied that in such difficult times, artists would have to live on the energy produced by their own enthusiasm. Today, as in 1918, enthusiasm seems to be very rich fare. Currently there are almost no government funds to support artistic activity, yet paints, paper, and building materials are gathered, exhibition sites are rehabilitated, and volunteer labor is in abundance. As a result, this is a time rich in creative exhibitions and publications.

Making a joke of their straitened circumstances and of the anxiety over food shortages, two artists put on an exhibition at the Marat Guelman Gallery that included a huge table loaded with fruit, bread, and sausages they had transported from Odessa; at the opening the audience was invited to feast at the groaning board. As official art institutions flounder, independent curators and critics have been quick to take advantage of the opportunities chaos has created. At the Dom Khudozhnika, or Artists' House, in the New Tretyakov, Yelena Selina and Yelena Romanova were able to organize an exhibition of contemporary art unlike most previous exhibitions sponsored by that institution in that it was political, provocative, and at times very witty.

Many of these artists find humor in the empty excesses of totalitarian ideology, the emptiness of the official ritual. **Anna Alchuk** rephotographs and enlarges sections of a poster advertising the VDNkh, the Exhibition Palace of Agricultural and Economic Achievements of the USSR. The photograph Alchuk appropriates was taken during Stalin's day: a crowd of rejoicing figures circle around his statue (Figure 3.29). What strikes us about this image is its excess, the hypervitality of the crowd, the exaggeration of their enthusiasm. All the images in the photo reinforce and reiterate one another, and each person seems to be a replica of the next. Alchuk selects two faces from the crowd and enlarges them; each wears the same ecstatic expression – the "bliss of conformity" so

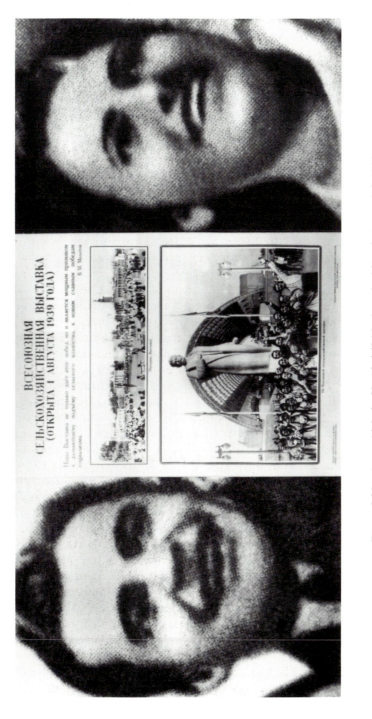

*Figure 3.29* Anna Alchuk, *Untitled* (3 black and white photographs) 1990.

common in group scenes of that time. What is revealed by Alchuk's gesture of individuation is how *de*personalized these people are. This kind of "absolute depersonalization lures the 'spectators' into the maelstrom of their own nonexistence . . . the ontological profundity of the elimination of loneliness" (Ryklin 1993: 58). What is also revealed is the unreality of the photograph. Obviously, such scenes could never have been "documented" by a camera.

This brings us to a key distinction between our own use and expectations of photography and the use and expectations of photography in the Soviet Union. Although we are continuously brought up against the error of our assumptions, we still think of photography, at least documentary photography, as maintaining a link with its referent. In the Soviet Union, documentary photography was quite candidly given the task of shaping society and the photographer granted the mandate to *create* a potential reality. Anatoly Lunacharsky described the function of photography as "not merely a chemically treated plate – but a profound act of social and psychological *creation*." The "validity" of staged documentary photography is a vexed issue in Soviet photographic history, one that usually gets stuck in the quagmire of creativity, credulity, conformity, and complicity. Alexander Rodchenko's 1930s series of photographs documenting the construction of the White Sea–Baltic Canal has recently come under criticism. These dramatic, formally dynamic photographs were intended to convey pride in Soviet technology. The workers were prisoners who were to be rehabilitated by performing socially useful labor. Rodchenko's photographs included scenes of an outdoor orchestra entertaining the workers while they worked. Later, it was revealed that this was a forced-labor camp with poor living conditions and a very high mortality rate. "What did Rodchenko see? What could he have done about it anyway?" Paul Wood asks in "The Politics of the Avant-Garde" (1992: 21). Moscow photographer Alexander Lapin has also begun to question Rodchenko: "What he was doing in the thirties, as it turned out – not only I but others noticed this too – was using his form for Stalin's content. Maybe Rodchenko was earnest about his belief in the party line. But it's nevertheless disconcerting that he so totally embraced and followed Stalinism" (quoted in Bendavid-Val 1991: 13). The complaints of both Wood and Lapin stem from the continuing belief in the aesthetic of objectivity that has been constructed around documentary photography. If documentary photography were not caught up in this pseudo-bind with "reality," they would not think to complain about Rodchenko's photographs on these grounds any more than it would occur to someone to complain that Hollywood westerns, for example, did not accurately portray the genocide of the indigenous populations.

Russian photographers are still shaking our confidence in the candid camera. A *Time* (21 June 1993) special report on childhood prostitution was accompanied by a series of photographs taken by Alexei Ostrovsky. The photo essay shows various scenes of an older man with two pubescent Russian boys made up to look like girls. In one scene the older man is feeding the boys dinner in his apartment, in another he is putting make-up on one of them, in another he is displaying them openly, like market goods, in Red Square. These scenes of the new Russian decadence were, it turns out, staged by the photographer. The hoax was exposed by Jeannette Walls in *New York*'s "Intelligencer" (19 July 1993: 7). Ostrovsky, like his Soviet counterparts before him, was dutifully producing the kinds of images that were called for – *Time* wanted images of the new Russian decadence. What Ostrovsky didn't understand was that magazines like *Time* still want to represent photographs as fact. Ironically, the exposure of Ostrovsky's staged photographs will probably only serve to support the notion that all the other photographs that appear in *Time* are factual and that deceptive photographs will be caught out.

Almost the entire photographic heritage of the Soviet Union consists of manipulated or constructed social and documentary photography. Today, a number of contemporary Russian artists are looking back upon the artistic tradition in which they grew up and incorporating it in their work. Leah Bendavid-Val in her book on recent Soviet photography claims that the intention of these artists is "to expose the hollowness and cruelty of past illusions" (1991: 29). If exposing past illusions is the intention of these artists, they are in for a lot of work and a large dose of future disillusionment as they enter the vortex of the ideological apparatus of Western capitalism's cultural industry. However, the work of contemporary artists suggests that Soviet artists were never so credulous.

*At the Source of Life*, an installation done in 1990 by **Elena Elagina** (b. 1949), addresses the utopian desire of heroic communism (Figure 3.30). The title is taken from the autobiography of Olga Lepeshinskaya, a famous Soviet scientist. The autobiography is illustrated by numerous photo-ops, or rather photo-props, of Lepeshinskaya working with schoolchildren, overseeing research in some laboratory, and so on – scenes that were either staged or constructed through photomontage. Lepeshinskaya, one of the early feminists, rejected the wealth of her mine-owning family and dreamed of becoming a doctor who would improve the lives of poor miners. She began her medical training in St Petersburg, where she met and married Lepeshinsky, a friend of Lenin's. In 1921 the Communist Party established her in a scientific laboratory. In her fifties she began to make a series of highly publicized experiments for which Stalin awarded her various prizes and the title "Academician of Medicine." We now know that Lepeshinskaya's amazing experiments could never be scientifically repeated and that she was instrumental in bringing about the demise of a very important school of genetic research. In Elagina's installation three photographs of Lepeshinskaya are presented as they might have been

*Figure 3.30* Elena Elagina, *At the Source of Life* (installation), 1990.

*Figure 3.31* Elena Elagina, *Iksisos* (wood, glass, electric light, 225 × 125 × 12 cm) 1991.

exhibited in biology classrooms, where dreary, pedantic photographs such as these "decorate" the walls. The large portrait of Lepeshinskaya in the center is given a little lipstick, and a thin tube connects her mouth to an aquarium filled with turbulent water and an empty egg. The installation is a parody of her most famous experiment, the "synthesizing" of albumen. The trajectory of Lepeshinskaya's career – the early revolutionary impulse converted into bogus heroic deeds which hinder progress – is marked by the deep pathos of utopian desire.

In *Iksisos* ("sausage" spelt backward), done in 1991, Elagina raises the sausage to its appropriate place in the Russian collective consciousness – as "the icon of our times" (Figure 3.31). The price and availability of this item are daily topics of conversation, discussed regularly on radio and television as if they were one of the leading economic indicators. Elagina takes a string of sausages made of wood and draps them like rosary beads over a wooden cross. Where traditionally scenes from the stations of the cross would be located, there are instead back-lit photographic transparencies

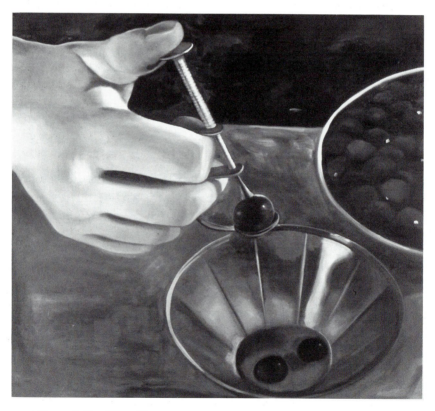

*Figure 3.32*  Olga Chernysheva, from *The Book of Wholesome Food*
(oil on canvas) 1991 (photo: Susan Unterberg).

130

of illustrations taken from a book distributed to food-service employees during the 1950s. The book is a safety manual instructing people on proper procedures for the handling and cleaning of huge food-processing equipment. There is an implied threat to the humans working with this equipment and consequently something suspect about the content of the sausages. The icon itself is an ironic comment on all the devotional knick-knacks and souvenirs that are appearing everywhere in the wake of religious "freedom" and the rise of interest in the occult.

**Olga Chernysheva**'s (b. 1962) work also focuses on culinary cultural conditioning. Using the recipes from *The Book of Wholesome Food,* a cookbook found in every household during the Stalin era, she creates sculptural versions of the complex confections every good communist woman was expected to be able to bake. Gessoed canvases coated with what look like layers of cream become sculptural realizations of such Old Masters as *Cake Napoleon* or *Baiser Rodin.* Using a star-shaped pastry cutter (a favorite motif in this cookbook) she makes Soviet pot pies. Along with these sculptural realizations of what was always a utopian art form because the ingredients for these elaborate dishes were never available, Chernysheva repaints illustrations from the cookbook – oddly reified and cropped photos of women's hands and midriffs. These fragmented body parts shift in connotation from the clinical, as the hands work with strangely complex equipment (Figure 3.32), to the erotic, as they knead and shape bread dough into breast and vulva formations (Figure 3.33).

## THERE ARE NO NYMPHETS IN POLAR REGIONS
### Nabokov, *Lolita*

Historically, Soviet artists have been very reticent in the exploration of erotica or sexually explicit imagery. Not only nudity but also even sexually suggestive material were forbidden to artists in several directives issued by the Ministry of Culture during the Stalinist era. Obviously the ban acted as a deterrent, although as early as 1968 **Nonna Gronova** (b. 1935) and her husband Francisco Infante staged an outdoor performance in the snow called *Forest Ritual* in which Nonna posed in the nude while candles melted the snow castle built around her (Figure 3.34). This early performance, documented in a series of photographs, was important as a transgressive public gesture involving the nude body, but it was not intended to be an exploration of sexuality. While it is impossible to generalize about an entire country, it is fair to say that Soviet culture has not regarded sexuality as the locus of subjectivity. It is not that the majority of the population embraced Clara Zetkin's "glass of water" theory of the naturalness and relative insignificance of sexual desire, but rather they were not conditioned by advertising's eroticization of everyday objects to conceptualize their subject relations primarily in terms of the sexual.

131

*Figure 3.33* Olga Chernysheva, detail from *The Book of Wholesome Food* (oil on canvas) 1991 (photo: Susan Unterberg).

Sex is not constructed as the key to their individuality, the sole means of expressing their most intimate selves or understanding the subjectivity of another. Today, however, in the logic of de-repression, which always considers the most censored to be the most significant, many artists are exploring sexuality and sexual taboos. Not accidentally, the exploration of sexuality is most commonly conducted with a camera.

For so many photographers the stranglehold of Soviet officialdom on creative life meant that they were prevented from using their medium in the manner it seemed intended for – the exploration of the "truth" of the visual. Skepticism about the truth of Soviet documentary photography did not extend to the medium of photography itself. "Present-day Soviet photographers have a score to settle with the past," argues Bendavid-Val:

> In making the link between photographs and reality a basic question, they are challenging past representations. By examining the relationship between picture and truth, photographers are forced to think of their own role differently. The photographer of the past was a craftsperson hired to deliver a specific product. The new photographer is an artist with unique vision, and that vision must be acknowledged in the search for truth.
>
> (1991: 29)

*Figure 3.34*   Nonna Gronova, *Forest Ritual* (performance) 1968
(courtesy International Images, Sewickley, Penn.).

Bendavid-Val writes as if photography's claim to function in certain contexts as recorder and source of "truth" and in other contexts to assume the artistic privilege of "unique vision" had never been questioned. Nevertheless, she is describing the intention, however nostalgic, of many photographers in the former Soviet Union. Cut off from recent discussions of sexuality, surveillance, and the deployment of what Foucault calls "the technologies of power" that bear directly and physically upon the body – like the camera's gaze – a number of contemporary Russian photographers repeat unselfconsciously, perhaps unwittingly, the acts that have historically made photography a tool for control and repression.

Relating Foucault's conceptualization of the science of sexuality to the early history of photography, Linda Williams in her study of pornography argues that the role of photography in the drive for knowledge is always pornographic in nature. The exploration of the ever more visually available female body was one of the unexpected pleasures of the medium of photography. Using Muybridge's photographs of naked and nearly naked male and female bodies to illustrate Foucault's point that the power exerted over bodies *in* technology is rendered pleasurable *through* technology, she argues that power and pleasure are exerted differently upon female bodies, even when the male and female bodies perform many of the same tasks. "If Muybridge's prototypical cinema became rather quickly, for the female bodies represented in it, a kind of pornographic girlie show

*Figure 3.35*    Bella Matveeva, diptych (oil on canvas) 1991.

that belied its more serious scientific pretensions, it is not because men
are naturally voyeurs and fetishists and that these perverse pleasures overwhelmed science" (Williams 1989: 45). Rather, she stresses the importance
of the social apparatus, "which is ultimately what constructs women as
the objects rather than the subjects of vision, for it is what places women
in front of the camera and what determines the repertoire of activities in
which they will engage." While the males in Muybridge's studies, like the
animals, simply go about their business performing tasks or engaging in
sports, the women become self-consciously visible in the camera's address.
Williams also notes that among the early audience of sportsmen-scientists
there were no women in a position to speak critically about the "truth"
of the fetishistic visions that were being constructed about them. "There
is nothing very startling in this observation, since women's bodies are
fetishized in social existence as well. . . . The transparent draperies, flirting
fans, superfluous props, and narcissistic gestures of Muybridge's women
could simply be viewed as part of Western art's long tradition of representing the nude woman" (ibid.: 40). In reminding us that photography
and psychoanalysis are both historically determined – and determining –

mechanisms of power and pleasure, Williams is speaking rather pointedly to contemporary conditions in the former Soviet Union, where a radical change is taking place in the social apparatus.

The quest for the "truth" of the visual undertaken by many photographers in the former Soviet Union today frequently degenerates into something close to Muybridge's pornographic girlie show. In many cases, as with the series done by Georgii Kizevalter in 1984, the artist's newfound freedom to explore his "unique vision" quickly rigidifies into cliché. Kizevalter poses a nude young woman in a series of incipiently ingratiating pin-up postures. The model arches her back, throws back her head, and opens her mouth seductively in studied imitation of "Western art's long tradition of representing the nude woman." Anna Alchuk explains that this work was favorably received by Russian artists, both male and female, when it was first exhibited: "It was a time when there was an interdiction on representations of the body. [The] Soviet person existed as abstract productive force without sex" (letter to the author, 8 June 1993). It is true that the woman in Kizevalter's photographs is represented as a sexual being, but as Foucault points out, images of bodies produced by machines effected a diminution of sexual plurality, and "scattered sexualities rigidified, became stuck to an age, a place, a type of practice" (1978: 12). Instead of a gesture of liberation, in this work the cultural determinacy of one ideology is replaced by that of another. I would also argue that the moment women cease to be represented as part of the labor force is the moment that they should start to worry about job security. Kizevalter's photographs may be the avant-garde of the social apparatus that will naturalize the gender inequality attendant upon commodity capitalism.

Not all Russian artists are miming the representational "traditions" of the West. In some cases, representation of the nude body and shifting sexual norms is part of a process of emergence. Members of the gay and lesbian community in St Petersburg have effectively used erotically charged material in art exhibitions and performances to announce their existence, to counter stultifying assumptions of normality, to celebrate the body, and to liberate it from its previous incarceration in the de-eroticized Soviet communal body. A number of artists in St Petersburg have adopted a gay public identity both as a gesture of solidarity with this small and, until recently, very beleaguered community, and because this is the most transgressive gesture available to them. Putting their bodies into the arena of identity politics, they carefully maneuver the rhetoric of their art toward ambiguities of desire and display. The collaborations of painter/film-maker **Bella Matveeva** (b. 1961) and photographer **Vita Buivid** (b. 1962) explore androgyny and homoerotica. Matveeva paints highly stylized androgynous nudes and semi-nudes (Figure 3.35). Buivid photographs the installation of these paintings accompanied by the models who posed for them, so that the photographs then become documentations of a performance (Figure 3.36). By themselves the paintings seem to be uncomplicated offerings of visual pleasure in which threatening knowledge is allayed by the beauty of the images; but the presence of the actual people used in creating them interferes with the illusion of art, revealing how these fixed positions of separation–representation–speculation are classically fetishistic, and this disturbs what Stephen Heath has called the "safety of disavowal" that photography usually provides for the viewer: "The photograph places the subject in a relation of specularity – the glance, holding him pleasurably in the safety of disavowal; at once knowledge – this exists – and a perspective of reassurance – but I am outside this existence ... the duality rising to the fetishistic category *par excellence*, that of the beautiful." (Heath 1974: 107). The high degree of self-conscious reflexivity of this work (by which I mean all its parts: paintings, photographs, installation, and performance) locates it in the context of Western feminist discussions of representation and the construction of gender, while at the same time its extreme artificiality is oddly – and significantly – reminiscent of staged Soviet documentary photography.

It may be that some artists will be able to draw upon the historical legacy of Soviet photography to utilize the techniques now most derided, the potential of utopian display to envision, if not, as Foucault would have wished, "new relationships, new forms of love," then at least to create an excess of ambiguity, what in electronic warfare would be called "jamming" – the overproduction of meanings so that no one meaning can be fixed and no truth congealed. In the process they may disabuse us of some of our own favorite illusions whereby so often "representations are taken as perception" (Baudry 1986: 314).

# 4

# MOTHERS OF INVENTION

The mother is the faceless, unfigurable figure of a *figurante*. She creates a place for all the figures by losing herself in the background.
                    Jacques Derrida, "All Ears: Nietzsche's Otobiography"

"Paternity may be a legal fiction," Joyce speculates in the episode of *Ulysses* in which the proprietorial assumptions of man, both in the act of begetting and in the act of authorship, are brought into question. "Fatherhood, in the sense of conscious begetting is unknown to man. It is founded upon the void, upon incertitude, upon unlikelihood. *Amor Matris*, subjective and objective genitive, may be the only true thing in life" (1922: 205). Motherhood may be the only fact of life about which we can be confident. A mother's love, the dyadic relationship in which the mother and child are undifferentiated beings, oblivious to the outside world, complete unto themselves can, however, only be experienced nostalgically. We can only know it, attempt to articulate it, when it is over. Thus the adult fantasy of a self-less love is always marked by a sense of loss. For all the biological certainty of birth what mother, desiring briefly something beyond the child, has not wondered if this were really her child, and what child, unsatisfied with this site of origin, has not thought that her real mother must be someone/somewhere else? "Whatever the individual mother's love and strength," Adrienne Rich writes in *Of Woman Born*, "the child in us, the small female who grew up in a male-controlled world, still feels, at moments, *wildly unmothered*" (1976: 225). Motherhood may also be an invention – an invention born of necessity whose role it is to save us from the void, the incertitude that patriarchy is based upon.

The following artists, all in different ways, are engaged in the process of reinventing motherhood. It is not that they seek to replace this idealized misapprehension with representations of the truth about maternity and originality. For even if a truth were to be found, it would not satisfy. Freud tells us how his own mother attempted to provide him with, if not the truth, then at least as good a fiction as any other:

139

When I was six years old and was given my first lessons by my mother, I was expected to believe that we were all made of earth and must therefore return to the earth. This did not suit me and I expressed my doubts of the doctrine. My mother thereupon rubbed the palms of her hands together – just as she did in making dumplings, except that there was no dough between them – and showed me the blackish scales of the epidermis produced by the friction as proof that we were made of earth. My astonishment at this ocular demonstration knew no bounds and I acquiesced in the belief.

(1900: 205)

Like young Sigmund, man has tended to resist such mundane accounts of his origin, preferring something spiritual, something with a little transcendence to it. In Christian cultures this desire was fulfilled by the relationship between the Madonna and Child which became the model for all maternal relationships in Western society. As the cult of the Virgin became intertwined with courtly love a whole range of other sexually overdetermined relationships developed out of the maternal, from sublimation to asceticism and abnegation. Julia Kristeva argues that "Christianity is no doubt the most sophisticated symbolic construct in which femininity, to the extent that it figures therein – and it does so constantly – is confined within the limits of the *Maternal*" (1986: 99). In addressing the construction of motherhood we are not dealing with a biological given, still less with an essence, but with a complex set of representations which imposes itself as reality – a set of representations suited to the needs of a particular social order which circumscribe women's lives.

As mothers, as daughters, as artists, but most of all as women we all have a stake in displacing the bio-maternal determinism that lies hidden in the seemingly benign representations of motherhood. Women artists have always worked in a Catch-22 situation and the catch is motherhood – an "original" division of labor: women have babies; men create art. Sublimating the maternal, or primary narcissism, has always been the necessary precondition for artistic achievement. Historically, the representation of motherhood has been in the hands of male artists or authors. What men have created is an image of woman so mired in the nature side of the culture versus nature dichotomy that a woman who attempted to be a cultural producer was perceived as a category error. This may also account for why in the two main stories of the family (in which we in Western culture find ourselves inscribed, no matter what our personal beliefs may be), Christianity and Freudian theory, the function of the mother is represented as the "conduit" from the father to the son. In Christian iconography, the Virgin Mary is represented as the unwitting "interval" from the Name of the Father to the Son, with any traces of matrilinearity expressly disavowed. Motherhood, according to Freud, is premised on the woman's desire for the phallus, a compensation for her perceived deficiency as a woman: "Her happiness is great if later on this wish for a baby finds fulfilment in reality, and quite especially so if the baby is a little boy who brings the longed for penis with him" (1933: 128).

What does it mean to be a mother, Mary Jacobus asks, "when mothers are the waste product of a sexual system based on the exchange of women among men?" (1986: 142). A great deal has happened in the postmodern period to disrupt the set of assumptions upon which such an exchange system is based. The question asked by the artists discussed here is what motherhood would look like when women have a hand in shaping its representation. Even to pose this question is to effect a figure–ground reversal, to suggest that in the economy of representation the mother's part in the system could be more than "the faceless, unfigurable figure of a *figurante*."

The most problematic issue for feminist artists has been the attempt to gain some control over the way women are represented in this culture. The first and most obvious "front" to attack has been pornography, for it represents the most visible arena in which women are shaped into commodities of commercial exchange, but for various reasons women artists, searching for ways to represent women, or looking for evidence of themselves, have been slow to turn to what would seem to be an obvious source of reference – the image of their own mothers. Perhaps because it was not an image they want for themselves, or perhaps it was an image of woman that simply was not presented in art or anywhere else. As May Stevens acknowledges about the images of her working-class mother: "I think there are some people who don't want to look at this woman. They don't think she should be in art; in fact, they don't think she should be anywhere." Just to present these images of their mothers – ordinary women who are neither particularly young nor beautiful – is to disturb.

In so far as motherhood has been represented in art, it has been mainly represented as a relationship between mother and son. The second reversal effected by the artists in this chapter is to install the mother–daughter relationship in place of the mother–son relationship, to start to explore what has gone largely unrepresented and undiscussed: the relationship of the woman to the mother and from there to the relation of women amongst themselves. Freud deals with female sexuality only very late in his writings, having assumed until then that the sexual development of the little girl followed somewhat the same development as the boy. When he does turn to the little girl, he is surprised at the importance and intensity of the original attachment of the girl to her mother: "Our insight into this early, pre-Oedipus, phase in girls comes to us as a surprise, like the discovery in another field of the Minoan-Mycenean civilization behind the civilization of Greece" (1931: 226). Freud acknowledges that the phase of exclusive attachment to the mother possesses a far greater importance in women than it does in men. In his too brief exploration of this earlier lost matriarchal civilization he finds not only the repressed relation between mother and daughter, but also clues to what was not understood of women's sexual life.

This brings us to perhaps the most disquieting issue raised by this work: the representation of what Kristeva calls the most severely repressed "feminine" figure in Western culture – the mother who knows sexual pleasure. Although the Virgin Mary is said to be "alone of all her sex," unique in her ability to be both virgin and mother, Western Christendom has projected this fantasy onto all women. Rather than a fecund and sensual goddess reveling in her own sexuality and the pleasures of procreation, our culture may be unique in constructing an asexual model of motherhood. In opposition to this impossible ideal **Niki Berg** presents images of her own and her mother's nude body: the bodies are voluptuous and sensual, an expanse of pink flesh like that which became the hallmark of Renoir's sensuality, but these bodies are so alien from the standard images of the fetishized female body it is doubtful that the sensuality of the bodies will be seen as such; instead they will be read as transgression, a breach of decorum, even more so because these are the bodies of a middle-aged woman and her mother (Figure 4.1). Femininity, as it is constructed in this culture, is only a brief moment in a woman's life. Middle age marks the loss of the only version of femininity this culture offers women. Berg's photographs call into question the whole relationship between femininity and its limited and limiting representations. The disturbance is caused simply by representing the repressed – the middle-aged woman and the mother who knows sexual pleasure. For a middle-aged woman to present both herself and her mother as sexual beings, to want to be able to represent themselves as women's bodies that are both desired and desiring would require the displacement of the maternal function as it has been constructed/constrained by this culture.

**Mary Scott**'s *Imago* series repeats fragments of two found images (Figure 4.2). One, the head of a woman, is taken from a full-length semi-nude photograph in *Penthouse*. The head is tipped back, mouth open, eyes closed – the stereotypical pose thought to represent female sexual ecstasy constantly portrayed in magazines, films, advertisements, and so forth. The other image is taken from a drawing by Leonardo da Vinci, "Studies of a Virgin adoring the Infant Christ" (*c.* 1486). In Leonardo's drawing the Madonna is kneeling before the Infant Christ, but in Scott's reworking of the image the mother is absent; only the baby boy remains. The images presented at either end of a long torn fabric represent the two poles of woman's alienation and are subtitled "Who Isn't There," making it clear that this is the site of woman's absence, where woman exists only as the possibility of mediation, transaction, transition between men. In placing

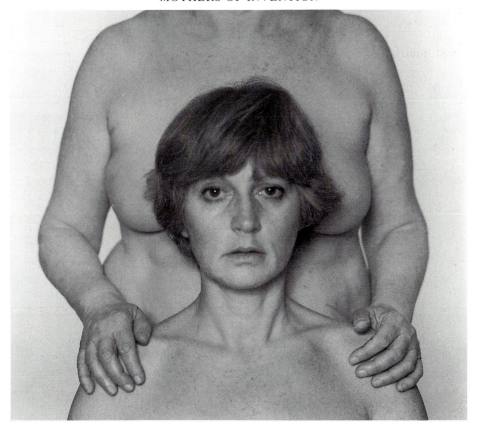

*Figure 4.1*   Niki Berg, *Self Portrait with Mother, III* (C print 39.5 × 39.5 cm) 1982.

these images on woven fabric Scott may be alluding to Freud's remark that "women have made few contributions to the discoveries and inventions in the history of civilization; there is, however, one technique which they may have invented – that of plaiting and weaving" (1933: 132). This preoccupation with clothing and veiling is a natural preoccupation for women, Freud concludes, because they must cover their shame, conceal their genital deficiency. In *Studies on Hysteria* he had said that "the disposition to day-dreams to which needle work and similar occupations render women especially prone . . . [are introduced] into waking life in the form of hysterical symptoms" (1895: 12–13). Evidently, concealing a "genital deficiency" is linked to the hysterical symptom. In Scott's work the fabric is shredded, as if to tear apart this whole fabrication.

**Janice Gurney**'s work also is an unraveling of the texts and the veils of various systems of representation which create for women a self and subjecthood – the manipulation of photographs, the coercive effect of the

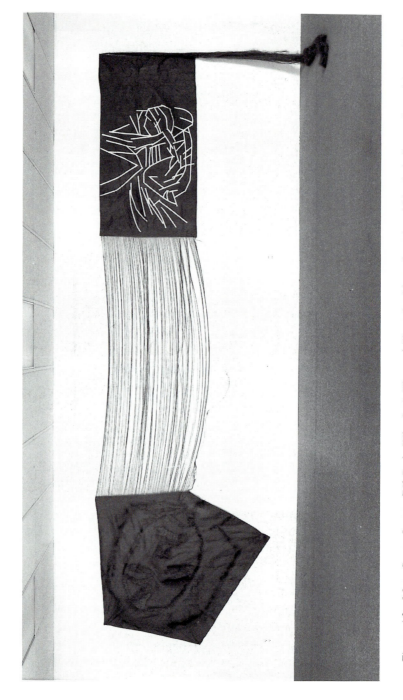

*Figure 4.2* Mary Scott, *Imago [V] Red «Who Isn't There»* (silk embroidery thread, gold leaf, shellac and varnish on silk, 165 × 1065 cm) 1987 (photo: John Dean).

*Figure 4.3* Janice Gurney, *For the Audience* (found painting, photostats and plexiglass, 112 × 194 cm) 1986 (photo: Cheryl O'Brien; collection Winnipeg Art Gallery).

cinematic gaze, the fatality of narrative. Her work is a record and a revelation of an ongoing activity of extrication. *Screen* (1986) is a six-part work which combines images from film, found photographic studies, found text and mechanically reproduced textures of fabric. The film still is of a child or woman of ambiguous age, taken from the film *Foolish Wives* (1921) by Erich von Stroheim. She is seen through a scrim filter which distances her image and begins to break it up. On either side are partially repeated passages from Marguerite Duras's novel *The Lover*; the doubling calls into question the identity of the woman in the text, or in the image. *For the Audience*, from 1986, consists of a framed watercolor of the artist's grandmother as a young girl, a photograph of the artist, a still from a 1917 Abel Gance film of a woman standing in front of a framed painting of another woman, and a still from a 1944 Fritz Lang *film noir* of the reflected image of a woman looking at a framed painting of herself (Figure 4.3). "The original contexts of the different images are blurred together as they construct a new range of reading – film stills, time periods, familial descent, looking out, being looked at, and private and public documents interact within the confined space of the work," Gurney explains. "I have included an image of myself produced by someone other than myself, so that in using it in the work, I too become subject to this process of representation."

**Elizabeth Mackenzie** sketches large-scale drawings of herself and her own daughter directly on the walls of the exhibition space. She too becomes subject to the process of representation and, as the work will eventually be painted over, she will be erased. Her work deals with everything from issues of gender formulation to sexual stereotyping, and desire, self-identity, camouflage, masquerade, voyeurism, and narcissistic exhibitionism. All the figures, whether mother or daughter, male or female, fat or thin, nude or clothed, watching or posing, are self-portraits. It also deals with women's problematic relationship to food, entangled as it is with sexuality, an unattainable body-image, desire, self-denial, and virtue. In *Identification of a Woman* (1986) Mackenzie masqueraded as her own mother; but because this is what the woman becomes when she herself becomes a mother, it is not really a masquerade (Figure 4.4). This may just be preparation for the next installation in which she is the mother – the not-good-enough mother, not sufficiently nurturing, perhaps because she is an artist: "I've been working on a series of projects about food and eating for the last two years. Three months ago I gave birth to a daughter. I was convinced that I would breastfeed this child, but had extreme difficulty in having her accept the breast for feeding. I struggled with her for weeks before we finally got our problems sorted out. Even so, we still have minor skirmishes from time to time, and I don't always feel confident that she is getting enough to eat. I worry that my own ambivalence about food and eating has passed itself onto her."

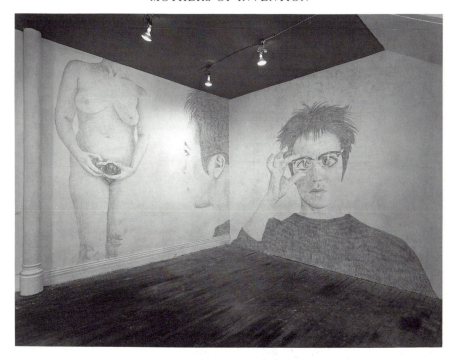

*Figure 4.4*   Elizabeth MacKenzie, *Identification of a Woman*, detail of left corner,
installation view, 1087 Queen Street West Toronto (graphite on existing walls;
ceiling height 12ft) 1986 (photo: Peter MacCallum).

What strikes us first about **Susan Unterberg**'s photographs of mothers
and daughters is their extraordinary honesty, an honesty that could only
come with age, with difficulty, with a willingness to relinquish the advantages and security that an idealized version of motherhood provides, an
honesty that perhaps could come only from a middle-aged woman. The
images are straightforward, unaltered, unposed close-ups; the subjects look
directly at the viewer and do not smile. A series of seven photographs of
each daughter is juxtaposed with seven images of her mother. They are
not constructed as narratives, yet they tell stories of pain, frustration,
anger, ambivalence, even loneliness. In looking back and forth from mother
to daughter we see the physical resemblances, the effects of aging, the
similarities in gestures and expressions, stories of what was and what will
be, but also signs of resistance and acceptance – the degree to which the
daughters resist or accept their mothers' fate, the mothers' own rage or
acquiescence. All the photographs are of white, upper middle-class women.
The signs of the class background can be seen in the clothing, cosmetics,
and hair styles, in the masks of respectability which in some cases seem
to be slipping. While the photographs are revealing, Unterberg explains

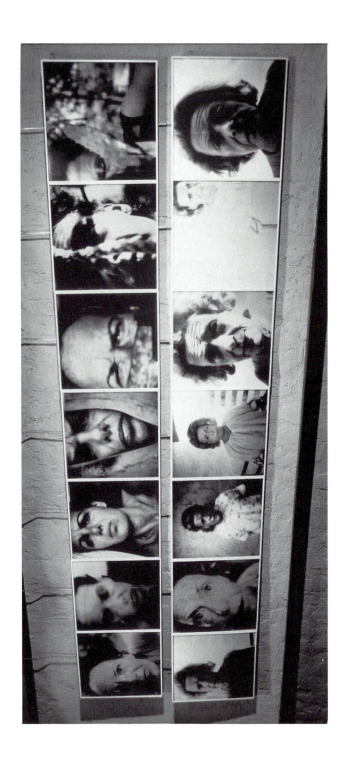

*Figure 4.5* Susan Unterberg, *Self Portrait/Mother Series* (color C prints) 1985.

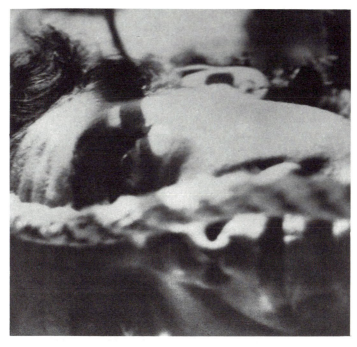

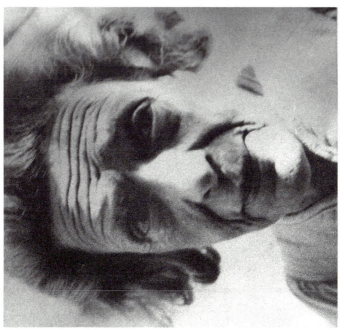

Susan Unterberg, *Self Portrait/Mother Series*, two details.

they are "total manipulations," just like all photographs. "The process of image making is preeminently an art of decision making so I spend a lot of time sequencing and editing. Clearly the work speaks about me." An earlier series of photographs of dogs was also an exploration of the constraints an upper middle-class life imposes upon women: "Quite unconsciously, I had picked only pedigreed specimens and photographed them in a way to reveal their vulnerability, pain, and constraints. This was not unlike the way I had experienced my own upper middle-class life of enforced conformity." The first portraits of the mother/daughter series are of herself and her own mother (Figure 4.5). Her statements about the photographs speak of her identification with her mother, with her mother's pain, the pain of her mother's illness and her unarticulated anger. At the same time she says, "I am trying hard not to become my mother," not to accept the rules which governed the mother's life, rules which demand that the daughter be "pretty, pleasing, placating, find a husband and have children." The aim of this installation is to reveal the real cruelty such a trivialization masks. There is a kind of exhilaration in this unflattering presentation of self ("unlovable, an old woman and bummed out") and worse yet, the presentation of all that we resist in our mothers, the self we will become in old age. Contrary to Sartre's claim that after forty we get the face we deserve, women after forty get the face they have the courage to present.

**May Stevens**'s work has long been important to a broad range of feminist-socialist practices because she deals directly and incisively with class. For over ten years Stevens has been formulating a disjunctive, disrupted dialogue between her own working-class mother Alice (housewife, mother, washer and ironer, inmate of hospitals and nursing homes) and Rosa Luxemburg (Polish/German revolutionary leader and theoretician, murder victim) – *Ordinary/Extraordinary* (1977–86). In "Two Women" (1976) images of Alice and Rosa are juxtaposed – from their childhood when they look very similar, full of some great expectation, to early womanhood (Alice awkwardly holding her first child, May; Rosa, at about the same age, at the height of her influence in the German Social Democratic Party, wearing a stylish hat, yet for all that strangely vulnerable), to the two women at the end of their lives: Alice old, overweight, legs swollen from years of hard work, sits silently in her room in a mental hospital; the last image of Rosa is a photograph taken after her bludgeoned body had been retrieved from the Landwehr Canal, her open eyes staring directly at us (Figure 4.6). These are the bare bones of the two stories which Stevens tells over and over again in images and texts, the activity of telling and retelling undertaken as if the ritual would incrementally restore a subjectivity to these women. The texts include Rosa's writings on social inequality and injustice, her letters to her lover, her desires for an ordinary life of intimacy, family, friends, "and perhaps even

Rosa Luxemburg, zwölfjährig

Rosa Luxemburg, about 1907

Rosa Luxemburg's corpse, March 1919. Probably an official photograph

*Figure 4.6*  May Stevens, *Two Women* (collage) 1976 (courtesy the artist).

a little, a very little baby? ... Despite everything you've told me ... I keep harping on the worn-out tune, making claims on personal happiness. Yes, I do have an accursed longing for happiness and am ready to haggle for my daily portion with the stubbornness of a mule" (letter to Leo Jogiches, 1899). Alice was not a writer or public speaker. Over the years she spoke less and less, and for many of the last years of her life she was silent. Her story is told as remembered conversations, disjointed comments, letters, and her daughter's account of her life:

> Sexism and classism, male authority and poverty-and-ignorance were the forces that crippled my mother; the agent in most direct contact with her was, of course, my father. But the equation cannot be written as two equal forces of sex and class focusing their oppressive powers through one man onto my mother. Poverty (class) ground her down from the beginning (when it took a bright child out of school to make her a mother's helper to the rich folks on the hill) and used male dominance to do it (her brother was kept in school) and religion to sanctify the arrangement and squelch her own desire. She was taught to be good. ... She was always good – until she painted the kitchen red in the middle of the night and screamed at passing cars.

*Figure 4.7* May Stevens, *Forming the Fifth International* (acrylic on canvas, 198.2 × 292.3 cm) 1985 (courtesy the artist).

A more recent work, a painting entitled *Forming the Fifth International*, done in 1985, is oddly gentle, restorative almost (Figure 4.7). Alice and Rosa sit together in a lush green landscape; the title implies that their conversation is political, important, but the disparity in the images suggests that perhaps no dialogue is possible, or else is not to be so easily achieved, not even, as Stevens notes, in the fictional and easily manipulated realm of representation: "The still-great distance (in color, in time) between them admits no easy solution but holds out, tenuously, promise, and necessity. A sad humor, illogical and vague hope play here with utopian intensity."

**Lorraine O'Grady**'s work is an ongoing act of reclamation – the reclamation of the black female body which as she herself describes it is a body "outside what can be conceived of as woman" (1992: 15). O'Grady's performances are an exploration of her position as an eccentric, inconceivable subject, doubly displaced. Looking for her likeness O'Grady found it reflected back to her in Egypt's contemporary heterogeneous cultural and racial amalgam as well as in its ancient monuments. On a visit to Cairo, she was constantly mistaken for an Egyptian, but since all identity is based upon a misrecognition, O'Grady turned this mistake into the basis of an ongoing meta-narrative on racial/cultural encounter, dispersion, and hybridization. Egypt, particularly because of what it represents to African-Americans, provided a fertile terrain for O'Grady's project of reclamation. Egypt's relationship to Black Africa – as a Black mulatto cultural antecedent to sub-Saharan, Greek and European cultural development – has long been a feature of black nationalist thought. In an ongoing series involving both photography and performance, O'Grady creates correspondences between the women of her own family and the women in Egyptian Queen Nefertiti's dynastic line. *Nerfertiti/Devonia Evangeline*, first performed in 1980, uses her own family to trace the African-American diaspora through both contemporary American culture and ancient Egyptian art and mythology. From this performance evolved the *Miscegenated Family Album* series of 1980/1988. In this work mother and daughter relationships are formed which link, not just generations, but centuries of mixed-race women (Figure 4.8). O'Grady juxtaposes images of her sister, Devonia Evangeline, with the Queen Nerfertiti; images of herself with Nefertiti's younger sister, Mutnedjmet; and images of Devonia Evangeline's two daughters with images of Nefertiti's two daughters, creating a sense of an ancient and ongoing matriarchal descent based upon uncanny physical resemblance as well as similarities in family history. O'Grady is fully aware that the quest for "origin" and "identity" is problematic from a poststructuralist point of view; nevertheless, for displaced persons the development of an effective relationship to place or to a lost ancestry becomes a means of recuperating a personal and cultural identity. "Genealogy, as an analysis of descent, is thus situated within the articulation of the body and history. Its

*Figure 4.8* Lorraine O'Grady, "Sisters IV", from *Miscegenated Family Album*, (cibachrome diptych, 71 × 99 cm) 1980–88 (courtesy Davis Museum, Wellesley College).

task is to expose a body totally imprinted by history and the processes of history's destruction of the body" (Foucault 1977: 148). O'Grady is not so much concerned with writing a story of origin, or finding a lost matriarchy, as with writing over the narratives and images of a colonial culture that obliterated a previously extant culture and that wrote her, as a black woman, off. Her own idiosyncratic quest for subjectivity is used to politicize an aesthetics of identity.

What the work of these artists reveals is that the mother, precisely because of her materiality, her body, whether that body is too old, or too fat, or too worn down by poverty, or too riddled with the incest taboo, or simply the wrong color, is a body that has gone missing, is not represented, has slid off the social map. What they also intimate is that the selflessness of the mother's role – creating "a place for all the figures by losing herself in the background" – may be both a way out and the only place from which to conceive new life. It is the mother's marginal position – the ulterior, the secondary, the unstressed, and the repressed – that may transform the perspective from which the center is seen. The mother's body, the body that expands, splits open, oozes fluids, gives birth, the body that is in flux, aging and dying, in fact female reproductive power itself, as Susan Bowers points out, "is a natural preoccupation of an art form that loves to transgress boundaries, and pregnancy is an ideal metaphor for feminist grotesque art" (1993: 27).

In spite of the unsentimental, even at times brutal, image of motherhood presented in these works, the artists engaged in this project in their mothers' names, to honor them. It is an act of reparation, an attempt to restore to the mothers' lives something they never had, and like all reparations, it comes after the fact, too late. It may, however, come just in time for some daughters. For they are engaged in tracing an alternative genealogy, and necessity after all is the mother of invention. "And so is born imagination, the ability to see to the edge of self and beyond." Motherhood, as Bowers puts it, may be the ongoing act of giving birth to what we want to become – "a miraculous grotesque erasing of boundaries, the metamorphosis of lack into possibility and then into actuality" (1993: 26).

# 5

# MAPPING THE IMAGINARY

As a woman, I have no country.

Virginia Woolf

While the psychoanalytic study of art is as old as or older than psycho-analysis itself – even before Charcot's essays on art there were interpreta-tions of art that could be considered psychoanalytic in approach – it is only in recent years, principally through the application of the theories of Lacan, that the psychoanalytic concept of the subject has become part of the study of representation. The Cartesian *cogito*, in which the subject, presumed to exist outside the systems of signification, apprehends himself as thought, has been afflicted by a sort of methodological doubt by the implication of representation in thought. "I think, therefore I am" becomes "I see myself seeing myself." As Lacan warns, "In this matter of the visible everything is a trap" – interlacing, intertwining, labyrinthine; the world becomes suspect of yielding the subject only his own repre-sentations, his own misrecognitions (1977: 93). "We are beings who are looked at in the spectacle of the world. That which makes us conscious-ness institutes us by the same token as *speculum mundi*" (ibid.: 75). It is in the context of reflexivity that I wish to explore the relationship between the invention/discovery of the unconscious and the invention/discovery of various modes of representation in art, particularly perceptual codes used to map unexplored terrain and representational systems used to codify the female body.

## FEMININE HYSTERIA / TERRA INCOGNITA

What is man that the itinerary of his desire creates such a text? Why has it been necessary to plot out the entire geography of female sexuality in terms of the imagined possibility of the dismemberment of the phallus?

(Gayatri Spivak 1983: 190)

156

Psychoanalysis began with hysteria, a disease occasioned by a problem of representation. The two early explorers of this unmapped terrain saw the reflecting relation differently. Pierre Janet believed that paralysis occurred in the hysteric because she was unable to form the image of her limbs and thus was unable to move them, whereas Charcot believed the hysteric was unable to obliterate a preexisting image of paralysis. For both, hysteria was a problem of representation – the incongruence of image and thought. Charcot's photographs of the hysterics of Salpêtrière are the record of an attempt to make visible a disease that cannot be known except through representation. Because the underlying pathology is invisible, Charcot was concerned that hysteria might not be classifiable as a disease at all. It was in order to *anchor* this invisible, mobile disease that Charcot enlisted the aid of photography. Photography, then being theorized as both the product and handmaiden of positivism – objective, unmediated, actually imprinted by light rays from an original – was the ideal representational mode to bring the disease into a discursive framework.

Although the *photo-graph* (as Lacan fragments the word) became the major mode of documentation at Salpêtrière, Charcot, himself an artist, began by making many sketches and paintings. Freud described Charcot as "not a reflective man, not a thinker – he had the nature of an artist – he was, as he himself said, a 'visuel', a man who sees" (1893: 12). This image of Charcot, as a man distinct from his fellow beings by virtue of his keener insights into the visual, links him with the Romantic notion of the artist.

The Romantic artist that Charcot is most indebted to is Théodore Géricault, who explored the influence of mental states on the human face and believed that the face accurately revealed the inner character, especially in madness and at the instant of death. He did studies of inmates in hospitals and institutions for the criminally insane, where he himself spent time as a patient. His work, like Charcot's, instituted the subject into the visible. As Norman Bryson points out,

> The Géricault portraits of the mad: from the first a contradiction, if the historic purpose of the portrait genre is to record the precise social position, a particular instance of rank in the hierarchy of power; the portrait of the insane is, therefore, an impossible object, a categorical scandal since the mad are exactly those who have been displaced from every level of the hierarchy, *who cannot be located on the social map*, whose portraits cannot be painted; Géricault fuses the categories together, of privilege and placelessness, society and asylum, physical presence and juridical absence.
>
> (1983: 143)

What Charcot learned from works such as Géricault's *Insane Woman* (*Malicious Mischief*) or *Insane Woman* (*Envy*) (Figure 5.1) was not how malicious mischief or envy would manifest itself on the human face, but

*Figure 5.1*   Théodore Géricault, *Insane Woman (Envy)*, 1822–23
(Musée des Beaux-Arts, Lyons).

what the photographs at Salpêtrière should look like (Figure 5.2). The
indefinite backgrounds, the luminosity of the lighting, the lack of distinguishing clothing all draw attention to the facial expression. Each picture
is captioned as though the physiognomic determined the reading rather
than the other way around. Thus, when looking at Géricault's *Envy* the
art historian Louise Gardner sees it as follows:

158

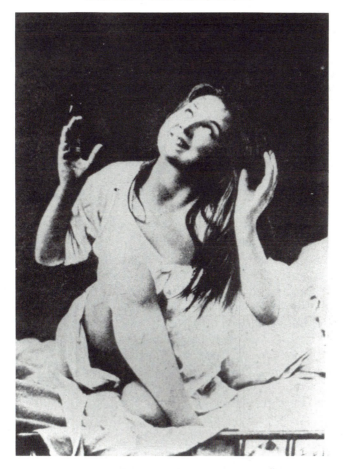

*Figure 5.2* Jean Martin Charcot, "Attitudes Passionnelles: Menacé,"
photograph from *Iconographie photographique de la Salpêtrière*, 1877–80.

Géricault's *Insane Woman* (*Envy*) her face twisted, her eyes red-
rimmed, leers with paranoid hatred in one of several "portraits" of
the insane subjects that have a peculiar hypnotic power as well as
astonishing authenticity in presentation of the psychic facts. The
*Insane Woman* is only another example of the increasingly realistic
core of Romantic painting. The closer the Romantic involved himself
with nature, sane or mad, the more he hoped to get at the truth.
Increasingly, this will mean for painting, the *optical* truth, as well as
truth to "the way things are."

(1980: 737)

But if this painting were called *Portrait of the Artist's Mother*, the "optical
truth" would be altered. What Charcot, an art historian in his own right,

159

learned from Géricault was not authenticity in presentation of psychic fact; what he learned was *how to make images produce already established readings*, how to institute a system of perceptual codes.

With Paul Richer, Charcot published two books on art: *Les Démoniaques dans l'art* in 1887 and *Les Difformes et les malades dans l'art* in 1889. The illustrations in the latter book are organized into categories, such as dwarfs and pygmies, cripples, epileptics, syphilitics, and the possessed. For the most part, the selections were made from Renaissance paintings or from paintings that utilized Renaissance perceptual codes: chiaroscuro, the exploded view, the cutaway, linear perspective, and the grid. Linear perspective achieved what Panofsky called a decompartmentalization of the old medieval categories and a recompartmentalization of the natural and physical world into forms adaptable to scientific study. The grid was thought to facilitate "mathematical, exact, impersonal, objective statements ... producing identical meanings in all [viewers], referring to accumulative and repeatable effects" (Edgerton 1980: 182).

Renaissance perspective, based on projecting a grid plane to a single vanishing point, has always been credited with enabling a new *realism* in picture-making, but it is more important for influencing psychological perception and for the way it began to structure the physical world. The cartography of Ptolemy and Toscanelli demonstrated that "once the surface of the earth was conceptually organized into a rectilinear grid, it took on a new sense of conformity. It was no longer to be thought of as a heterogeneous assemblage of frightening unknowns" (Edgerton 1974: 225). Although the actual geography of Ptolemy's maps was extremely erroneous, this device by which the world could be schematically represented was extremely useful to Europeans, who needed to develop a visual language of property or territory in order to inventory their "discoveries," both actual and potential. This representational system was understood as the paradigm of divine order, as a device for the conquest of the physical world, and as a practical tool for an imperialist venture. "It may seem bold to link the introduction of perspective to the discovery and conquest of America," writes Tzvetan Todorov in his book *The Conquest of America*," yet the relation is there, not because Toscanelli, inspirer of Columbus, was the friend of Brunelleschi and Alberti, pioneers of perspective ... but by reason of the transformation that both facts simultaneously reveal and produce in human consciousness" (1984:121–123). (Todorov goes on to discuss Cortes's semiotic strategies and he notes that perhaps it was not coincidental that the first grammar of a modern European language was published in 1492; its frontispiece reads: "Language has always been the companion of Empire.") The ascendance of scientific cartography became possible only when the language of property became so taken for granted that it lost visibility; that is, it came to seem natural to divide and lay claim to portions of the world once the world

*Figure 5.3* Albrecht Dürer, "Draughtsman Drawing a Nude," from *Underweysung der Messung*, 1538 (Lessing J. Rosenwald Collection, Rare Book and Special Collections Division, Library of Congress.)

*Figure 5.4*   Nicole Jolicoeur, *La femme en hystérie (d'après Charcot)*, 1980
(photo: Louise Bilodeau).

could be divided by longitudinal and latitudinal lines. This is what Lacan
calls that

> *belong to me* aspect of representations, so reminiscent of property
> ... that bipolar reflexive relation by which, as soon as I perceive,
> my representations belong to me ...
>
> It was Dürer himself who invented the apparatus to establish per-
> spective. Dürer's 'lucinda' is ... a trellis that will be traversed by
> straight lines – which are not necessarily rays, but also threads –
> which will link each point that I have to see in the world to a point
> at which the canvas will, by this line, be traversed. It was to estab-
> lish a correct perspective image, therefore, that the *lucinda* was
> introduced. If I reverse its use, I will have the pleasure of obtaining
> not the restoration of the world that lies at the end, but the distor-
> tion, on another surface, of the image that I would have obtained
> on the first, and I will dwell, as on some delicious game, on this
> method that makes anything appear at will in a particular stretching.
>
> (1977: 81, 87)

## THE OCCUPATION OF AN IDEOLOGICALLY
## STRATEGIC TERRAIN

On the maps drawn by men there is an immense white area, terra
incognita, where most women live. That country is all yours to
explore, to inhabit, to describe.

Ursula K. Le Guin (1989: 158)

**Nicole Jolicoeur** examines Charcot's discovery/invention of hysteria as
well as his son's explorations and mapping of Antarctica in terms of the

162

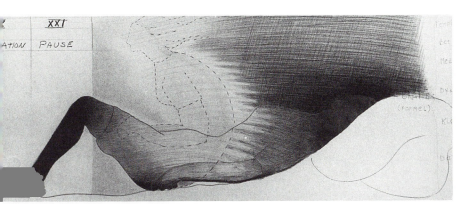

imposition of representational determinism that both projects imply. Her first work in the series, large-scale vividly colored gouaches entitled *La Femme en hystérie (d'après J-M. Charcot)* (1980) rework Charcot's sketches of the stages of an hysterical fit – what he calls the *grande attaque hystérique complète et régulière* – with typical positions and variations (Figure 5.4). These sketches of women in various contorted positions were arranged and codified by Charcot into twelve columns labeled alphabetically and then numerically subdivided into four phases: *période epileptoïde, période de clownisme, période des attitudes passionelles, péroide de délire*. Jolicoeur replaces Charcot's systems of classification with musical notations by Stockhausen. The horizontal axis reads: Evolution, Spiral, Adoration, Pause; the vertical axis reads: Tempi, Bet-gesten, Melodie, Dynamik, Klangfarben, Davern. This abstract and arbitrary meaning system imposed upon the images discloses the way in which the choreographed bodies of women were made to function at Salpêtrière as part of the performance of a mimetic theater. As the scroll progresses, the images of the women's bodies become increasingly more colorful, chaotic, and indeterminate as if the subjects were seeking to elude Charcot's inscription. In *La Vérité folle* (1989) Jolicoeur continues to explore the alignment that bodies undergo when confronted with the codification of images. In this installation the religious lithographs from Charcot's *Les Démoniaques dans l'art* (1887) are reworked in juxtaposition with the photographs of the hysterics at Salpêtrière. What Charcot learned from the religious iconography is what gestures the women at Salpêtrière should adopt and, concomitantly, what gesture *he* should adopt. For example, Jolicoeur superimposes a lithograph from *Les Démoniaques dans l'art* of Saint Philippe de Néri delivering a possessed woman onto André Brouillet's painting of Charcot lecturing with his patient Blanche draped over his arm as pedagogic prop.

*Figure 5.5*  Nicole Jolicoeur, "Polaire, BITCH," from *Charcot: Deux concepts de la nature*, 1985.

Charcot here has assumed the same position as the saint, and both saint and doctor coalesce in the same image of master and saviour (see Figure 6.4). An earlier work done by Jolicoeur in 1985, entitled *Charcot: deux concepts de nature*, is based on a series of seemingly accidental associations between photographs, sketches, charts, and diagrams made by Charcot at Salpêtrière and those made by his son Jean-Baptiste Charcot documenting his experience as an Antarctic explorer (Figure 5.5). Jolicoeur appropriates the explorer's charts of "natural resources" (the winds, the sea currents, the stars, etc.) as well as various cartographies of the Antarctic. In some cases, Jean-Baptiste has named undiscovered and unexplored terrain after himself, his father, or his ship, the *Pourquoi Pas*. These are drawn together in such a way as to suggest their similarity to J-M. Charcot's eroticization of the hysteric's body – hysterogenic zones, passionate attitudes, arcs of circles; in short, the whole hystericization of the woman's body. Photographs of icebergs, ships, explorers, and dog teams are photocopied, extended by color and drawing, and aligned according to their horizon lines. They are then linked with a unified vanishing point to provide a complete picture of the terrain in much the same way that J-M. Charcot put together several images of different women with "incomplete" hysterical attacks in order to complete the desired cycle, fill in the "clinical picture," and provide an image of wholeness. The maps made by the son are understood as a continuation of the exploration of the father, revealing the connections between the mapping of "feminine hysteria" and "terra incognita" and the assumption of mastery that mapping brings with it.

The phallogocentric impetus of map-making is addressed by **Dorothy Cross**, one of a number of Irish women artists who have adopted a humorous approach to the cult of nationalism and the sometimes stultifying tradition of Irish landscape poetry and painting. Cross sculpted two bronze maps (one of Ireland and one of England) into latrines, installed them in a derelict underground toilet in the East End of London and invited locals to use the facilities (Figure 5.6). The reopening of this public convenience which had long stood idle was Cross's contribution to *Edge 92*, an international biennale of innovative visual art which took place in the economically and racially mixed neighborhood of Spitalfields. Cross's site-specific installation is an interactive art work; as with all public toilets, choices must be made before you enter, but on this occasion the signs over the doorway do not discriminate along the usual gender lines, instead they read "IRISH" and "ENGLISH." The signs recall the "Colored" signs on public conveniences in America or "help wanted" advertisements with caveats such as "no Irish, Jews, or Italians need apply." Ironically, or perhaps inevitably, like all signs suggestive of such neat divides, these signs lead you astray, as both entrances lead to the main toilet area. On the wall where the Victorian loos have been removed hang the two bronze urinal/maps. The participant/patron can both assert a national identity and lay claim to another country in the simple and satisfying manner of a dog staking out his territory. Once again, however, the choice offered is illusory, for whether one chooses to relieve oneself in the basin shaped like Ireland or the one shaped like England, the drain pipes protruding from the bottom of the bowls, which are cast in the shape of penises, point towards each other in such a way as to pun, in good Joycean fashion, upon the meaning of "the meeting of the waters."

Like Dorothy Cross, **Kathy Prendergast** has been schooled in the traditions of Irish landscape painting and poetry in which for decades connections have been woven between gender and geography. Within this tradition Ireland has always been thought of as female, more specifically a colonized female subject: Mother Ireland mourning the loss of her land/children. This metaphorical family drama played out between Ireland and England subtly exerts control over the bodies of Irish women today. Cultural preservation, land and language reclamation, the Gaelic revival, Irish nationalism in general cannot be thought of separately from the

*Figure 5.6*  Dorothy Cross, *Attendant* (cast bronze and hand-painted signs) 1992.

notion of Irish womanhood. All manner of anxieties about geopolitical instability coalesce in the Church and the state's attempts to maintain strict control over female sexuality. Prendergast's rationalist mapping and renaming of the female body is a reminder of the nineteenth-century British mapping and Anglicization of place names in Ireland, linking a masculinist and colonial usage of maps and suggesting that Irish women have been doubly colonized.

Corporeal mapping is the subject of the *Body Map* series, eleven exquisitely detailed ink and watercolor drawings done in 1983 by Prendergast. Maps are talismanic in that they give us our bearings in the physical world, align us with something beyond and greater than ourselves, and at the same time flatter us by giving us a sense of control over the area mapped.

Reading a map requires continuous perceptual adjustment – from imagination to reality, from inner to outer space, from the subjective to the objective. In our pride of accomplishment we lose track of the fact that we are not mastering the physical world but only learning to manipulate another prosthetic device developed by man to allay his fears of the unknown. Prendergast's body maps disturb our belief in correspondences and reveal the very sinister underpinnings of this faith. These are maps of the psychological interconnectedness of the activities of exploration and map-making, the desire to scrutinize, inscribe, and control the female body and the colonial control of other lands through mapping and naming. *Enclosed Worlds in Open Spaces* (1983) is an intricately drawn map of what appears to be a large continental land mass surrounded by a pale blue sea (Figure 5.7). Numerous codes of cartography attest to the veracity of the map: the precision of the drawing, the heavy antique vellum paper, a compass rose indicating the four directions, insignias of sailing ships indicating the separation of the seas from the land mass, and the grids indicating longitudinal and latitudinal lines. These cartographic conventions are all reassuring in their familiar logic and confident scientism, but the land mass that is being mapped is not a continent, but a female torso. This is the body represented as a map, a kind of manifestation of the Nietzschean notion of the body as a surface of social inscriptions. Because Prendergast manages to keep these two registers of meaning operating simultaneously, she is able to reveal the woman's body as a surface of libidinal and erotogenic intensities inscribed and reinscribed by social norms, practices, and values.

The seeming rationalism and objectivity of map-making may be a masquerade, a cover-up that belies an underlying irrationality. The body maps are not as obvious nor as stable as they first appear and they can lead the explorer into dangerous terrain. The torso is traversed from north to south by a minute meandering broken line indicating an overland route from the northernmost volcanic mountain region (breasts), through the valley (chest area), across the desert (stomach and abdomen), through the delta region (pubic area) to the harbor (vulva). The route is dotted with numbers representing station stops. As on a traveler's guide, the caption at the bottom of the map indicates which station stops have stables, which have refreshment rooms, and which have good inns. The torso in the first drawing is life-size and while it is unclear who is traversing this continent, or the purpose of the journey, the travelers must be microscopically tiny, smaller even than Lilliputians in the land of Brobdingnagians. The continent is divided into quadrants, and subsequent maps are enlargements of these four sections. Now the scale is four times as large as life-size, causing the activity depicted on the maps to become correspondingly that much smaller. These maps are subsections of the first map, and they too can be subdivided and enlarged for closer scrutiny on into infinity.

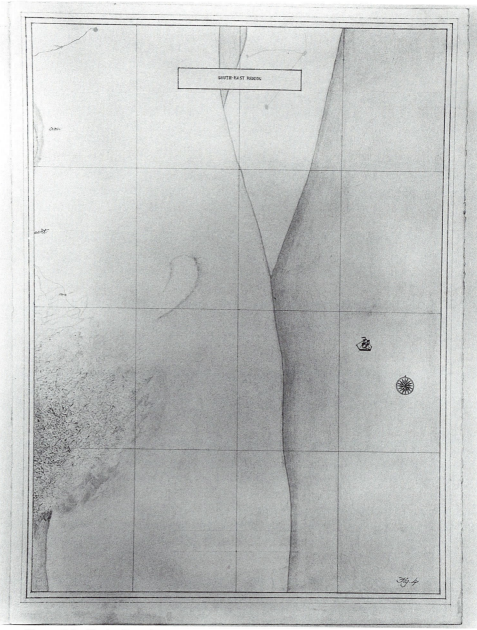

*Figure 5.7* Kathy Prendergast, *Enclosed Worlds in Open Spaces* (watercolor and ink on paper, 76 × 56 cm) 1983 (collection Vincent and Noeleen Ferguson).

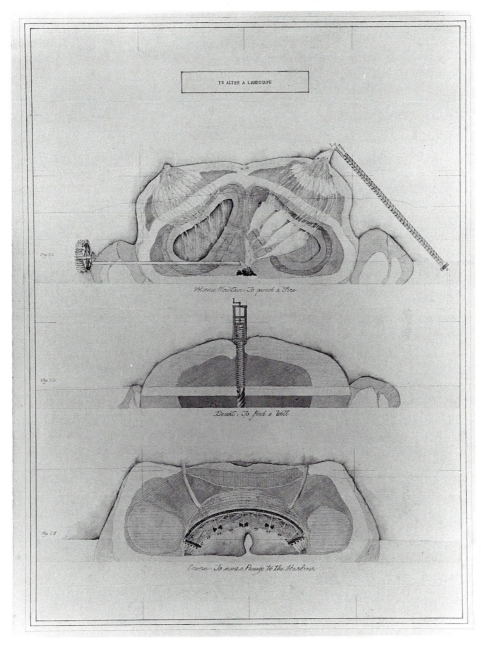

*Figure 5.8* Kathy Prendergast, *To Alter a Landscape* (watercolor and ink on paper, 76 × 56 cm) 1983 (collection Vincent and Noeleen Ferguson).

Ptolemy's and Toscanelli's conceptual organization of the surface of the earth into a rectilinear grid may be reassuring to some, the earth "no longer to be thought of as a heterogeneous assemblage of frightening unknowns," but in Prendergast's works it is the grid formation itself that is frightening. The grid enables, indeed *generates*, this progressive decompartmentalization that results in an expansion of each section of the body. Indeterminacies of scale disturb the order of things. We are accustomed to using the human body as the arbiter of our system of measurement – the hand, the foot, the yard, the furlong, are based on the presumption of man as the measure of all things – but these expanding body parts, on which are detailed ever more minute activities, unsettle our confidence in scale and proportion. The beautifully scripted handwriting and chart markings are very small and faint, forcing the viewer to study the charts intently. When examined through a magnifying glass, the charts reveal yet more detail, suggesting that the exploration could lead to an infinite regression. Meanwhile, at the other end of the scale, the female body grows ever larger, more unfathomable, gargantuan, and grotesque. Like Gulliver, we can imagine falling into the crater of a hair follicle or being drowned by the volcanic emissions of a breast.

As if to alleviate the viewer's/explorer's anxiety about being overwhelmed by the female body, the next series of drawings contains several charts on how to control the landscape and mine its resources (Figure 5.8). While the body in the first series of drawings is seen as a surface to be inscribed, a surface that can be segmented or seen as a part (or parts) of a larger ensemble, in the second series it is the body's latency, depth, and interiority that is explored. The woman's body is understood as a natural resource to be exploited with the aid of science and machinery. The internal workings of the woman's body are to be delved into and understood as a type of machinery with interconnecting organs, flows, and larger ensembles. There are cutaway cross-sectional diagrams of the interior of the female torso that look like stage sets from the movie *The Fantastic Voyage* (1966). Tiny stairs lead down from south of the oasis (below both breasts), through a maze of scaffolding to a cavern (the lung cavity) which in turn is linked to a tunnel (presumably the reproductive system) providing an underground route to the harbor (the vulva). In another, an enormous screw is drilled through the volcanic ducts (the nipples) into the mountain (the breast) to a well below. In one version a windmill is constructed on top of the breast. The function of this construction is described in the dispassionate language of a geological or gynecological report: "Having driven through the water, a well is found. As the desert winds blow, the mill turns, transporting water from the well to the sprinklers which make the land fertile." In another drawing a shaft runs below sea level through the earth (the ribcage) to the fire at the center of the volcanic mountain. The aim here seems to be to bring in

170

water to quench a fire and irrigate the soil. An elaborate system of holding tanks (presumably to contain the steam produced) is connected to pipes running out through the mountain/breast to another, larger shaft leading down below sea level on the opposite side of the continent. These ingeniously designed hybrids of land graphs, civil engineering diagrams, and medical charts seem very familiar; in fact, it is their very familiarity that is frightening, for they invoke the anatomical drawings of female organs that always function, in the name of something – personal hygiene, public health, family planning, medical research, morality, etc. – to control the sexuality of women. Gradually the viewer comes to realize that it is not the female body that is the source of the anxiety – it is the relentlessness of the rational examination itself that is truly terrifying. The pathology thought to inhere in the female body resides instead in the desire to control, the proliferation of methods of exploitation, the obsessional need for more and more detailed information, the constant quest for correspondence to an ideal.

Like Prendergast, **Shirley Irons** invokes the rational discourse of the map, ostensibly to make sense of the world. Her work explores alternative modes of perception: macroscopic/microscopic, interior/exterior. She looks for correspondences between systems of representation, the interworkings of the imagination and the body, naturally occurring formations in organic substances and the landscape. Maps symbolize certainty and a guiding system, but these maps are soon revealed to be perilous guides to an irrational universe. Realizing that all interpretation of observation requires a surrounding confirming theory, Irons invokes Gerald Edelman's model of neuron mapping, a model which suggests that the body itself is engaged in a continuous organic process of mapping. He posits that our brain is composed of maps of nerve bundles, or interconnected series of neuron groups which respond selectively to elemental categories such as movement, touch, sound, and sight. Each sensation produces or alters the maps, strengthening successful perceptions and weakening useless ones, thus building our image of reality. This is a variant of William James's theory that "sensations, once experienced, modify the nervous organisms, so that copies of them arise again in the mind after the original outward stimulus is gone ... [F]antasy, or imagination, are the names given to the faculty of reproducing copies of originals once felt" (1892; 1923 edn: 302). Irons cites these theories in which representation is thought to occur spontaneously, almost like cell division, as a language appropriate for her own working process. Many of her paintings are multiples, usually diptychs or triptychs, of what appear to be different versions of the same scene: a realist painting of a landscape or a seascape, or a suburban scene (Figure 5.9). Often, the focus is on what is usually overlooked or what might be thought of as detritus in the landscape: an ordinary house in a working-class suburb, trucks on the freeway, power lines, an abandoned car by the roadside, the skeletal remains of an old boat half submerged in the sand. The companion paintings in some cases look as if they were derived from slides taken of a detail of the same painting, as if to better illustrate the painterly technique involved or to show what the same visual stimuli would look like if represented microscopically or in the mode of abstract expressionism. The same colors and textures are repeated, but now the view is so myopically focused that external reality seems lost, as in the long digressions in Flaubert's writing when the narrative is suspended and whole pages are given over to the description, say, of the fabric of a dress. This, whether the language is words or paint, is what Kristeva describes as a *desire for language*, a passion for its materiality as opposed to its transparency, "a passion for ventures with meaning and its materials (ranging from colors to sounds ...) in order to carry a theoretical experience to that point where apparent abstraction is revealed as the apex of archaic, oneiric, nocturnal, or corporeal concreteness, to that point where meaning has not yet appeared (the child), no longer is (the insane person), or else functions as a restructuring (writing, art)" (1980: x). In Irons's paintings there is a sense that the process reveals too much, takes us too far beneath the surface, too close to the edge of comprehensibility, too deeply into the pathology of perception, too close to the margins of the mad.

Employing another inadequate descriptive system, Irons writes short stories to accompany some of the paintings:

> That mysterious disease had overtaken Annabel. She looked about her world and saw only strings of inconsequential information, untrustworthy friends, repeated follies, chaos and mud. Desire was the thing that it is. Year after year, sun following cloud, lilies opened and closed and Annabel remained unhappy. The prince, because there is always a prince in fairy tales, came to rescue Annabel. He opened her mind and knit together fibrous chains of lateral geniculate nuclei into a perfect glass sphere. "Here is your new home Annabel." And there in that gift of the imagination Annabel lived happily ever after. Relative to existing theory, the certainty of our sensory experience is only as rich as our interpretations.

Irons's relationship to the mapping structures that form and inform her work is ambiguous. It is as if she agreed to live within a certain perceptual framework but has become forgetful of that constraint and is always pushing through the frontiers of meaning. Though willing to acknowledge that, like the rest of us, she lives in the prisonhouse of language, she treats it as if it were a light sentence, to be served in a diaphanous and expandable terrain.

*Figure 5.9*   Shirley Irons, *Arcadia* (oil, wax, carbon, blood and glue on canvas, 112 × 178 cm) 1992.

*Figure 5.10*   Carrie Mae Weems, "Kids in the Kitchen with Van and Vera,"
from *Family Picture and Stories* (silver print, 36 × 44 cm) 1978–84
(courtesy P.P.O.W Gallery, New York).

**Carrie Mae Weems** is another postcolonial cartographer on a journey of reclamation. She began her journey by going home to visit members of her extended family in Mississippi and Tennessee. As she explains in the text accompanying the first photograph in the series *Family Pictures and Stories* (1978): "I went home this summer. Hadn't seen my folks for awhile, but I'd been thinking about them, felt the need to say something about them, about us, about me and to record something about our family, our history. I was scared. Of what? I don't know, but on my first night back, I was welcomed with so much love from Van and Vera, that I thought to myself, 'Girl, this is your family. Go on and get down.' " Weems uses the format of documentary photography and intimate stories about her own family to portray people who are not likely ever to see themselves represented in a work of art (Figure 5.10). This personal work extends into a meta-narrative on the complexities of race, gender, and class in American life.

In *Ain't Jokin'* (1987–88) Weems tells a series of crude visual and verbal jokes based on racial stereotypes that aren't funny. Photographs of stereo-typical blacks (a man with a watermelon or a woman with a chicken leg) are combined with verbal "jokes" of the following sort: "What are the three

174

**LOOKING INTO THE MIRROR, THE BLACK WOMAN ASKED,
"MIRROR, MIRROR ON THE WALL, WHO'S THE FINEST OF THEM ALL?"
THE MIRROR SAYS, "SNOW WHITE, YOU BLACK BITCH,
AND DON'T YOU FORGET IT!!!"**

*Figure 5.11*  Carrie Mae Weems, *Mirror, Mirror* (silver print, 37 × 37 cm) 1987
(photo: Adam Reich; courtesy P.P.O.W Gallery, New York).

things you can't give a black person? Answer: A black eye, a fat lip and a job." In telling these jokes she is subverting the tendentious joke that depends for its effect upon the differences in the hearers' reactions. "Generally speaking, a tendentious joke calls for three people: in addition to the one who makes the joke, there must be a second who is taken as the object of the hostile or sexual aggressiveness, and a third in whom the joke's aim of producing pleasure is fulfilled" (Freud 1905b: 100). By telling the joke herself, she removes herself from the role of object of the joke and is able to redirect the hostility. Also, in telling the joke herself, she is betraying a class secret: Freud points out that it is only among what he calls the "inferior classes" that the tendentious or smutty joke is told in front of the person (usually a woman) who is the object of the joke. At higher social levels – "civilization and higher education have a large influence in the development of repression" (ibid.: 101) – the joke is told only when the person who is the object of the hostility is not present. Weems tells these jokes to the museum- and gallery-going white middle-class audience – "Only jokes that have a purpose run the risk of meeting with people who do not want to listen to them" (ibid.: 90)." This audience may want to listen to these jokes, but they want to pretend they've never heard them.

Still, telling white trash jokes to a white bourgeois audience is nobody's idea of a good time, as *Mirror, Mirror* (Figure 5.11) makes clear: "Looking into the mirror, the black woman asked, 'Mirror, mirror on the wall, who's the finest of them all?' The mirror says, 'Snow white, you black bitch, and don't you forget it!!!'" Questions asked tend to determine the answers given. The gaze of the Other is not confirming: it does not see you. Looking in the mirror is no way to develop a positive self-image, so Weems went looking elsewhere. She traveled to the same location as Julie Dash did to make her film *Daughters of the Dust* (1991), the islands off the South Carolina–Georgia coast. Here she found in the landscape and household objects evidence of a rich and enduring black community. Its Gullah culture took root on a kind of Ellis Island for African-Americans. Slave ships continued to land on these islands long after the slave trade had been banned; as many West Africans remained where they landed, African culture was maintained. But here one cannot trace one's ancestors through a computer search. Instead, as Weems shows us in *Sea Islands* (1992), some traces of them are more likely to be found reflected in the hubcaps and bicycle wheels hung in trees festooned with Spanish moss. What begins with grim daguerrotype photographs of slaves (originally mug shots taken for slave identification papers, but here rephotographed, enlarged to life-size, mounted in circular frames, and thus given the dignity of portraits) turns into a celebration of an enduring cultural heritage. Weems's own photographs depict mainly environments: neat rooms with simple furniture or storefronts advertising "Awesome hair performance" and "Sweet Potatoe Pies," or simple shacks that have anthropomorized into their inhabitant, like the shack sculptures of Beverly Buchanan. The photographs are combined with red earthenware plates on which the artist has painted texts as poetic as the images, telling a tale of what was lost and what was found as Weems "Went Looking for Africa . . . and found it echoing in the voice of the Geechee's Gullah . . . Went Looking for Africa . . . and found a bowl of butter beans on a grave . . . newspaper walls for the spirits to read . . . rice in the corners a pan of vinegar water up under the bed . . . Went Looking for Africa . . . and found uncombed heads acrylic nails & Afrocentric attitude Africans find laughable."

**Jaune Quick-to-See Smith**, a Flathead Shoshone of Cree ancestry, is also looking at the land for signs of her origin and ancestry, but finds instead a landscape riddled with conflicting land claims. In 1992, in response to that year's celebration of Columbus's "discovery" of America, she painted *Indian Map*, a large-scale map of the United States (Figure 5.12). The painting looks like a combination of Jasper Johns's maps of America and Rauschenberg's compilations of fabrics, advertisements, and newspaper clippings, overlaid with dripped and splashed red and earth-toned paint. The language of American abstract expressionism is only one of the discourses contending for this cultural amalgam. The map is strewn with scraps of paper suggesting that littering the land was a way of laying claim to it. In the collaged newspaper clippings we read reports of land settlements with headlines announcing "It's a steal," or "Best deal of the century." But there are other stories embedded in these paintings that can be unearthed like an archeological dig to reveal the stories of past cultures, suggesting the provisionality of all land claims. Time does not seem to "progress" in this text; rather, history and present-day reality seem to coalesce. In the Atlantic Ocean we find "Columbus Adrift," and the North American continent therefore remains "undiscovered." Beneath some blood-red paint suggestive of a massacre of Indians, Chief Joseph still resides peacefully on the Wallowa prairie. Meanwhile, contemporary accounts of Indian events can be read from bits of the reservation newspaper *Char-Koosta*. The names and stories layered upon the map never take us to the original, indigenous culture; instead of creating a symbol of land ownership, this map is an ongoing perceptual transformation which in turn suggests the provisional nature of cartography.

In *Trade* (*Gifts for Trading Land with White People*) (1992) a silhouette of a canoe is painted over what appears to be a map of Indian country, since one of the newspaper clippings announces "Notes from Indian Country." Again the collaged elements are painted over with dripped red, green, brown, and ochre-colored paint. Out of this textured/textual landscape emerge numerous images of Indians and animals. As the title suggests, the current expedition seems to be about trading back some of the land. The wares strung above the canoe – tomahawks, feathered headdresses, sports pennants, and baseball caps with the insignia of the Washington Redskins, Atlanta Braves, Cleveland Indians, etc. – seem to be the trinkets brought along to trick the white man. It's hard to tell if Smith is a postmodern appropriationalist or if she is just employing the ancient strategies of her tribe, the Montana Flatheads. The creator of this tribe is the trickster coyote whose main trick, she explains, is humor: "Overlying the difficulties we as Indian people face in our daily lives is the key to survival – which is humor, a bittersweet or 'coyote' kind of humor."

*Figure 5.12* Jaune Quick-to-See Smith. *Indian Map* (oil, mixed media, collage on canvas, diptych, 162 × 244 cm) 1992, Collection of Lyn and Jerry Handler (photo: Scott Bowron; courtesy Steinbaum Krauss Gallery, New York).

*Figure 5.13*  Nancy Dwyer, *Big Ego* (polyurethane coated nylon, three parts:
approx. 244 × 142 × 223 cm) 1990 (photo: Ellen Page Wilson).

Words are a plastic material with which one can do all kinds of
things.
   (Freud, *Jokes and Their Relation to the Unconscious* 1905b: 34)

As if taking the plasticity of words literally, **Nancy Dwyer** makes
language laugh by making it concrete, giving words a physical presence
appropriate to their meaning. Words are the subject and substance of her
sculptures and graphic paintings. Rather than mapping words onto a body,
she gives them bodies of their own, which they occupy with a "presence"
appropriate to their power and privilege. In *Big Ego* (1990) the word
EGO is made of huge yellow air-filled balloons that take up all the available space in the room (Figure 5.13). While the words are bigger than the
spectator, their fragility is apparent in that the air-filled words are continually deflating and in need of being pumped up. In a series of paintings

179

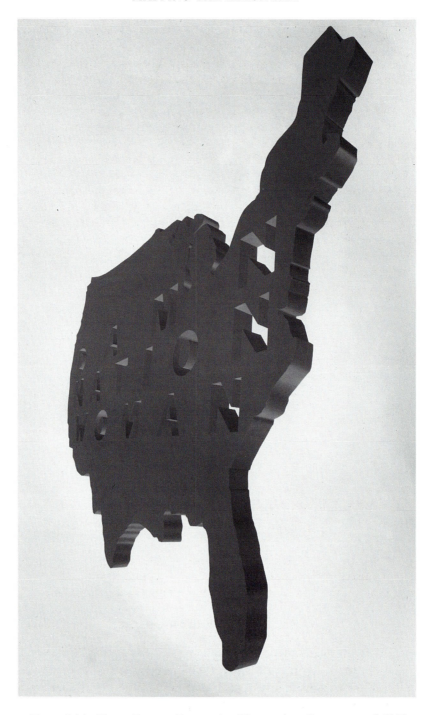

*Figure 5.14*   Nancy Dwyer, *Damnation Woman* (acrylic on canvas) 1990
(courtesy of the artist).

of large maps of the United States, Dwyer explores the effects of language on the land. Viewed from the side, the maps are elongated by perspective and appear to be gigantic three-dimensional objects floating in space, like the *Starship Enterprise*. Words are superimposed or intrude upon the maps, in each case creating a different effect. In one, the words "YOUR NAME HERE" are printed over the map and extend beyond its boundaries. The words echo those found on billboard advertisements, but rather than being a brief intrusion on the landscape, this advertisement with its encircling corporate logo seems to be the ultimate in manifest destiny, completely encircling the continent. In other paintings, other words appear on similar maps, inscribing them differently. The words DAMN NATION WOMAN are printed in red letters one underneath the other (Figure 5.14). They appear to be carved out of the map's three-dimensional structure as if demarcating numerous deep chasms. DAMN NATION WOMAN has cut holes right through the map as if in illustration of Irigaray's argument that woman is the *hole* in men's signifying economy, that all may be endangered by a nothing (1985a: 50).

# 6

# ENCORE

Much as "the woman question" preoccupied social and political theorists of the late nineteenth century when the emancipation of women and the feminine in general was identified as a threat to bourgeois stability, "the question of woman" has become a motif in the discourse of postmodernism. The question has returned like a glitch in the record, causing a "repeat" in the discursive practice. The "repeat" centers around the discussion of hysteria which has returned, not as the subject of a medical discourse, but, appropriately for postmodernism, as a question of representation. Hysteria, an invisible pathology which gained "presence" through the work of Charcot, has now become a simulacrum. Fashion models, dressed in Comme Des Garçons clothing which provides for atrophied appendages, adopt Charcot's *attitudes passionelles*. Anorexia, bulimia, and cosmetic body cutting have lent new meaning to the term "fashion victim." Tina Turner, with disheveled hair and shredded clothing, goes through all the unmotivated gyrations of the *grande attaque hystérique* – posing the question "what's love got to do with it?"

Women who do exist have been disturbing the position of ~~the~~ woman who does not, provoking Lacan to return to the question of woman in his 1972–73 seminar appropriately entitled *Encore*: "There is no woman but excluded by the nature of things which is the nature of words, and it has to be said that there is one thing about which women themselves are complaining at the moment, it's well and truly that, it's just that they do not know what they are saying which is all the difference between them and me" (1972–73: 68). Psychoanalysis may not always be sensitive to Foucault's lesson of the indignity of speaking for others, but the Other has spoken through, has intervened in the theoretical construction psychoanalysis elaborates to contextualize her and has made political claims and demands for social transformation. This chapter is a retelling of the story which intends to foreground what was overlooked – history, the social relations of production and exchange between classes and sexes; that is, the knowledge produced by the hysteric who, as Lacan puts it, "forces the 'signifying matter' to confess" (1975: 38).

The institution of psychoanalysis has always had an uneasy relationship to hysteria in spite of the role hysteria played in the discovery of the unconscious. For Charcot hysteria was too intractable and he sought to bring it into the rule of visibility, into the system of "presence" and representation. For Breuer and Freud it was far too indexical – Breuer's withdrawal from the collaboration with Freud and ultimately from the study of hysteria dates from Anna O.'s hysterical pregnancy . . . with his child! Freud, who navigated the transference more intrepidly, was able to see that hysteria was not a product of femininity. Yet, it is not clear if he was able to see, in spite of Anna O.'s very overt indication (i.e. her pregnancy), that hysteria was the product of patriarchy.

The question of class and patriarchal interests is latent in writings on hysteria. The Salpêtrière Clinic in Paris was an enormous place of confinement for women refused by the general hospitals: "*Dès 1690, trois mille! Trois mille indigentes vagabondes, mendiantes, «femmes caduques», «vieilles femmes filleuses», épileptiques, «femmes en enfance», «innocentes mal taillées et contrefaites», filles incorrigibles, – folles*" (Didi-Huberman 1982: 17). By the 1870s Salpêtrière housed over 4,000 women and approximately one hundred of their children. Institutions such as these, referred to as "lock hospitals" in England, were commonplace by the eighteenth century. Their number points to an important component of the political unconscious as it was developing within patriarchal configurations: the fantasy link between femininity and the pathological. Judith Walkowitz (1980), in her study of the Contagious Diseases Acts of the 1860s, shows how the categorization of femininity as undesirable, insane, diseased, a source of contamination, or just enigmatic served to establish state policy on public hygiene and state control over casual labor – that growing segment of the labor force which was transient, frequently unemployed, and capable at times (such as during the Paris Commune of 1870–71) of formidable collective action. Rather than exploring the idea that poverty and the traffic in women could be reduced by the redistribution of wealth, the state plan for controlling this potentially restive population took the form of controlling reproduction, which in effect meant controlling the sexuality of working-class women and prostitutes. The Contagious Diseases Acts of 1864–68, as they were obliquely entitled, subjected suspected prostitutes and female vagabonds to forcible examination and internment. In 1885 the Criminal Law Amendment Act, which raised the age of consent for girls from thirteen to sixteen, was passed after it had earlier been rejected by parliament. The MPs had rejected it on the grounds that it would curtail their own right of sexual access to young working-class girls, a time-honored prerogative of gentlemen. One member of the House of Lords acknowledged that "very few of their Lordships . . . had not when young men, been guilty of immorality. He hoped they would pause before passing a clause within the range of which their sons might come" (quoted in

Gorham 1978: 366). It was in the context of this legal wrangle for control of the bodies of working-class women that the disease of hysteria was invented.

In his obituary of Charcot written in 1893 Freud expresses his surprise that hysteria was diagnosed in men, particularly in working-class men. Charcot had admitted men to Salpêtrière and "a number of surprising discoveries were made. Hysteria in males, and especially in men of the working class, was found far more often than had been expected; it was convincingly shown that certain conditions which had been put down to alcoholic intoxication or lead-poisoning were of a hysterical nature" (1893: 21). Again in his essay on "The Aetiology of Hysteria" Freud says to the reader: "You will remember, by the way, what a surprisingly large incidence of hysteria was reported by Charcot among working-class *men*" (1896: 210). Though Freud does not refer explicitly to the high unemployment among working-class men at the time, nor to the labor unrest that was making itself felt in Austria and Germany throughout the time he was writing the major body of his work, he does fault Charcot for overestimating heredity as the cause of hysteria while, as he says, "all other noxae of the most various nature and intensity only play the part of incidental causes, of '*agents provocateurs*' " (1896: 184). What is remarkable here in his selection of this particular French term *agents provocateurs*, a term taken from political, not sexual discourse, is the revelation of a momentary rediscovery of another possible "exciting cause." There is no reason why Freud should be exempt from the recurrent turn of mind which takes a narrative, particularly a narrative concerning women and origins, and not only sexualizes it, but in the process depoliticizes it.

Political events take place off stage in Freud's writing, the way they do in a Jane Austen novel. The defeat of the French nation in the Franco-Prussian war and the brutal suppression of the Parisian proletariat during the period of the Paris Commune are mentioned by Freud as events which, according to Freud, Charcot in some measure served to redeem: "People had come to realize that the activities of this man [Charcot] were part of the assets of the nation's '*gloire*', which after the unfortunate war of 1870–1871 was all the more jealously guarded" (1893: 16). It is interesting here that Charcot is called upon to rehabilitate a nationalism which was jeopardized during this period by Aldophe Thiers's action of calling in Bismarck's troops to attack French men and women during the Paris Commune; that is, Charcot is called upon to redeem a time in which class interests had outweighed national interests.

When the *dramatis personae* in Freud's case studies have political careers in their "real" life, this is not mentioned in the case histories. Otto Bauer, the older brother in the Dora case, who as Freud described him "had been the model which her [Dora's] ambitions had striven to follow" (1905: 107), became the leader and chief theoretician of the Austrian

184

Socialist Party between 1918 and 1934. Anna O., the inventor of the "talking cure," was Bertha Pappenheim, a leader of the German Jewish women's movement. In her research into the life of Bertha Pappenheim, Dianne Hunter points out that in the year Freud and Breuer published *Studies on Hysteria*, Pappenheim was appointed director of an orphanage in Isenburg, Germany. This was to be the headquarters for her forty-years' work rescuing and sheltering abandoned and abused women and children who were being sold into prostitution. As Hunter points out, Pappenheim was well known and "had many enemies among orthodox Jewish men who resented her exposure of Jewish complicity in the traffic in women" (1983: 477). It is more than likely that Freud and Pappenheim would have heard of her philanthropic work, yet the fact that Pappenheim devotes her life to opposing the traffic in women does not enter into the discussion of hysteria; it is not seen as part of her "resistance to the Oedipal law which her 'case' inscribes" (Jacobus 1986: 143).

Freud frequently seems to be on the verge of revealing some links between class and hysteria. He names his first case study "Dora" after his maid, the maid who figures in his own dreams. In a number of Freud's case studies the maid or governess is the source of sexual knowledge. Freud points out to Dora her identification first with her own governess and then with the governess Herr K. seduces and dismisses. Freud stresses how deeply impressed Dora was by the fate of the governess, and notes that when Dora decides to end her meetings with him she gives him a fortnight's notice, "just like a governess" (Freud 1905: 107). The ambiguities of that phrase resonate with Freud's own position in this particular cash nexus. At fourteen Dora has the acumen to know that her father is "a man of means," and Freud suspects that behind her use of this phrase its opposite lay concealed, namely, that Dora knows her father was a man without means in a sexual sense – that her father was impotent (ibid.: 47). She suspects him of having entered into a tacit agreement with Herr K. to exchange her for Herr K.'s wife ... perhaps she even suspects him of hiring Freud to persuade her of the wisdom of this arrangement. Her identification with the governess may be the result of her recognition of the obvious similarities in their positions, that she too is part of the "goods" caught up in the traffic in women. As Philip Rieff points out in his introduction to the case study, "Dora did not wish to join hands in this charmless circle – although Freud does, at one point, indicate that she should" (Rieff 1963).[1] Rieff regrets that "Freud bypassed the patient's insight into the rot of her human environment as part of the misleading obvious," when it was, he suggests, "the most important single fact of the matter" (1963: 18). The "misleading obvious" is an apt term for what was not seen in this subtle story. It was not that Freud failed to understand the workings of the transference in time, or that he failed to understand the nature of Dora's attachment to Frau K.; rather, as in the case of Poe's purloined letter, what was not seen was in clear view and needed only an adjustment of the vision – from focusing only on the individual to regarding the individual in her particular position within the economic structure of patriarchy.

The question on which Freud got stuck and to which Lacan returns in *Encore* is the question of woman, or more precisely, "this question of woman *as* representation" (Rose 1978: 12). Freud's work on hysteria began with a rejection of Charcot's reliance on the visual in the diagnostic process – his distrust of symptoms "read off" the body in so unmediated a fashion. Yet Freud was not really successful in his attempt to replace the visual with a verbal mode of knowing, for as Laplanche points out the spectacle is reintroduced in the theory of castration. "It goes without saying, that castration is precisely not a reality, but a thematization of reality. A certain theorization of reality which, for Freud, is so anchored in perception that to deny castration is finally the same thing as denying the perceptual experience itself" (1980: 66). What Gayatri Spivak asks of this "thematization of reality" is why has it been necessary for the figure of woman to be represented constantly in terms of the imagined possibility of the dismemberment of the phallus (1983: 191)? An answer may be provided in an analogy Freud gives in the essay on "Fetishism" (1927a), an analogy that is really a metonymy of the political implications of his thesis. After describing the substitution that is effected to deny the unwelcome perception and to allay the terror the little boy feels when he first discovers that his mother has no penis and hence his own may be in danger, Freud goes on to make an analogy between perceiving a woman's genitals as a revolting sight and an actual political revolt: "In later life a grown man may perhaps experience a similar panic when the cry goes up that Throne and Altar are in danger, and similar illogical consequences will ensue" (1927a: 153). Freud analyzes the function of the sexual substitution, the way the sight of the lack is denied by substituting the fetish, but he does not go on to discuss the "illogical consequences" that follow the perception of a political threat transposed onto the site of a woman's body. A political threat, a threat to property, coming necessarily from those who lack property or other signs of privilege (women, for example) is substituted by the fantasy of an imagined sexual threat. A certain economic "differential" now begins to suggest itself, particularly as the image of woman (or parts of her) has come to be the dominant fetish object of this culture – the image of woman is a cover-up, used to deny women's real political and economic lack. As if able to see the operation more clearly from a distance, Freud refers to a culture that attempts to compensate its women for the loss – "in the Chinese custom of mutilating the female foot and then revering it like a fetish after it has been mutilated. It seems as though the Chinese male wants to thank the woman for having submitted to being castrated" (ibid.: 157). It is within the context of Freud's analogy, extended, with the political and sexual differentials operating together that the history of woman *as* representation needs to be explored.

Charcot had carefully established the representational context in which he wished his own pictures of hysterics in the *Iconographie photographique de la Salpêtrière* to be viewed. In *Les Démoniaques dans l'art* the activity of liberating the mad from the demons which possess them is located in a Christian and high cultural tradition; that is, they are aligned with the standard hegemonic cultural texts. Images of the possessed being exorcized appear in everything from the mosaics of Ravenna, tapestries of Reims, lithographs from Florence, engravings of Brueghel, and reliefs on tombstones, to the grand tableau of Rubens in which Saint Ignatius stands calmly and benevolently with arms outstretched above a crowd of tormented souls writhing below. These form the prefatory chapters to "*Les «Démoniaques Convulsionnaires» D'Aujourd'hui*" and "*La Foi Qui Guérit*," chapters in which the various positions of *la grande attaque hystérique* are illustrated and Charcot's own work is aligned with those early Christian faith-healers. "In the case of hysteria, a doctor is hardly capable of not watching with an artist's eye the overwhelming pain of a body in the throes of the symptoms of hysteria," Georges Didi-Huberman observes in his study of the invention of hysteria. "It is an atrocity, but one is forced to consider hysteria, as it was illustrated at the Salpêtrière, in the last third of the nineteenth century, as a chapter of the history of art" (1982: 10).

Charcot worked under the aegis of Robert Fleury's painting of Pinel delivering the madwomen (Freud mis-perceives them as madmen) of Salpêtrière (Figure 6.1). In his obituary of Charcot, Freud describes the aura this painting added to the very theatrical performance of Charcot's famous *Leçons du mardi*:

> In the hall in which he gave his lectures there hung a picture of the 'citizen' Pinel, having the chains taken off the poor madmen in the Salpêtrière. The Salpêtrière which had witnessed so many horrors during the Revolution, had also been the scene of this most humane of all revolutions. At such lectures Maître Charcot himself made a curious impression. He, who at other times bubbled over with vivacity and cheerfulness, and who always had a joke on his lips, now looked serious and solemn under his little velvet cap; indeed, he even seemed to have grown older. His voice sounded subdued. We could almost understand how ill-disposed strangers could reproach the whole lecture with being theatrical.
>
> (1893: 17)

Fleury's 1878 painting looks more like the genre of pillage, plunder and bondage paintings that were commonplace in the nineteenth century than the documentation of what Freud referred to as a "humane revolution."

*Figure 6.1* Robert Fleury, *Pinel déliverant les folles de la Salpêtrière*, detail, 1878, Bibliothèque Charcot, Salpêtrière.

Although Freud invokes the French Revolution, we are closer in this painting to Delacroix's *Death of Sardanapalus,* with its sensual depiction of bare-breasted women strewn over the ground, than we are to *Liberty Leading the People*. In fact, in spite of the Romantic nature of Fleury's depiction of this scene of liberation, what Freud speaks of is the horror of the French Revolution, not its inspiration.[2] By the time Freud was writing Charcot's obituary, the French Revolution, the 1848 Revolution, and the Paris Commune had been retold in the discourse of patriarchy as a series of anecdotes of proletarian women and common prostitutes displaying monstrous and unknown forms (i.e. their genitals) to a horrified society. Neil Hertz in his essay "Medusa's Head: Male Hysteria under

188

*Figure 6.2    The Fruits of the French Revolution,* English drawing from the period
following the French Revolution.

Political Pressure" provides this passage from Victor Hugo's "Choses vues"
("Things Seen," 1848) as an example of how things were seen. The National
Guard, "more irritated than intimidated," are "resolutely" defending them-
selves against attackers during the June uprising:

> At that moment a woman appeared on the crest of the barricade, a
> young woman, beautiful, dishevelled, terrifying. This woman who was
> a public whore, pulled her dress up to the waist and cried to the guards-
> men, in that dreadful brothel language that one is always obliged to
> translate: "Cowards! Fire if you dare, at the belly of a woman!"
>
> Here things took an awful turn. The National Guard did not
> hesitate. A fusillade toppled the miserable creature. She fell with a
> great cry. There was a horrified silence at the barricade among the
> attackers.
>
> Suddenly a second woman appeared. This one was younger and
> still more beautiful; she was practically a child, barely seventeen.
> What profound misery! She, too, was a public whore. She raised her
> dress, showed her belly, and cried: "Fire you bandits!" They fired.
> She fell, pierced with bullets, on top of the other's body.

That was how this war began.

Nothing is more chilling or more somber. It's a hideous thing, this heroism of abjection.

(365–66)

Narratives such as this were accompanied by cartoons (Figure 6.2) in which the ideals of the French Revolution are represented as pregnant whores, or Democracy is presented as a nude woman sitting with legs spread across a guillotine – an enormous *vagina dentata* (Figure 6.3).

In contrast to Fleury's painting of Pinel freeing the madwomen of Salpêtrière, the painting done by André Brouillet of Charcot delivering his Tuesday lectures with Blanche Wittman as the central exhibit is meant to mark the distance from romance to the realism of the scientific amphitheater (Figure 6.4). As with Eakins's *Gross Clinic* we are shown inside a medical amphitheater, inside the scientific, the objective, the rationally demonstrable. Women in convulsions are not strewn on

*Figure 6.3*  A. Willette, *I am holy Democracy. I await my lovers*, early nineteenth century.

*Figure 6.4*  André Brouillet, *A Clinical Lecture at the Salpêtrière*, 1887:
shows Jean Martin Charcot and Blanche Wittman demonstrating hysteria at
one of the famous Leçons du Mardi. The picture on the wall (top left corner)
is one of Charcot's drawings of an hysteric in convulsion (courtesy of
AP-HP-D.F.C.-Photothèque).

the ground; instead, out of a consideration for decorum, they are depicted
in sketches on the wall. Blanche's dress is around her waist; her off-
the-shoulder undergarments are a faint allusion to that bare-breasted
Amazon of Delacroix's *Liberty*. Whatever threat the revolting women
of Salpêtrière represented either as the insane, as the propertyless, or
as the sexually uncontrollable, by the time we get to Blanche, the
threat is gone. In Brouillet's painting the hysteric is compliant, saved and
aestheticized.

"Somatic compliance" is Freud's term for the process whereby the body
complies with the psychical demands by providing the material for the
inscription of its signs. "Blank" Blanche is totally compliant; she has col-
lapsed, but is effortlessly supported by Charcot, who remains intent on
his lecture, on his inscription. She has joined the ranks of the endlessly
repeated images of helpless ecstatics, prostrate women who are seemingly
unable to stand up straight; that is, Fleury paints her in the pose of any
number of salon models of the time. Bram Dijkstra has devoted a section
of his book *Idols of Perversity* to images of collapsing women or women
with broken backs:

191

The word *opisthotonus*, used in the nineteenth century by pathologists to designate, in the words of the *Oxford English Dictionary*, a "spasm of muscles of the neck, back, and legs, in which the body is bent backward," might indeed serve as a generic designation for the many paintings of women shown in terminal backward spasms of uncontrollable sexual desire which began to litter the walls of the yearly exhibitions in the 1870s and continued to do so well into the twentieth century.

(1986: 101)

The search for the erotic that lay at the heart of what they called the Convulsive Beauty led the Surrealists to celebrate the hysterics of Salpêtrière. "We Surrealists are anxious to celebrate here the quinquagenary of hysteria, the greatest poetic discovery of the end of the nineteenth century," Aragon and Breton write in *La Révolution surréaliste* of 1928. Hysteria, they claim, is the subversion of the "relations which are established between the subject and the moral world." But just in case we think we are close to a consideration of the political potential of hysteria, we are reminded that while the Surrealists may have been at the service of the revolution, the only revolution the hysterics were to be at the service of was the sexual, which by now we know is not one. This is Breton's and Aragon's account of what was revolutionary about the hysterics of Salpêtrière: "Does Freud, who owes so much to Charcot, remember the time – confirmed by the survivors – when the interns at Salpêtrière confused their professional duties and their taste for love, after nightfall, when the patients met them outside or received them in their beds? Afterwards those women patiently recounted, for the good of the medical cause which does not defend itself, their (supposedly pathological) mental attitudes under the influence of passion, which were so precious to them and are still precious to us as humans beings" (1928: 20–22). While Surrealism invested its faith in the revolutionary potential of the repressed (male) desire, the role for women was that of agent or sexually liberal muse, not fellow revolutionary. However, several women artists working within the Surrealist movement attempted a displacement rather than a liberation along the lines of sexual iconography: for example, Meret Oppenheim's famous fur-lined teacup, or her fetishistic shoes in bondage, significantly entitled (if we recall the importance of the maid in Freud's case studies) *Ma Gouvernante, My Nurse, Mein Kindermädchen* (Figure 6.5). In each case the joke, like the fetishized woman, earns its keep by keeping back an awareness of lack.

Hysteria now is no longer considered an adequate clinical diagnosis. It was a source of too much confusion and was eliminated from the *Diagnostic and Statistical Manual of Mental Disorders* (*DSM II*) in 1952. It has also been part of a cover-up; the diagnosis for what was not understood, or

*Figure 6.5* Meret Oppenheim, *Ma Gouvernante, My Nurse, Mein Kindermädchen* (mixed media) 1936 (Moderna Museet, Stockholm).

perhaps for what was understood too well, the *méconnaissance*, it seems, perpetuated not only by the hysterical analysand, but also by the analyst. While doing follow-up research on patients who had gone through the wards of the National Hospital in England during the early 1950s, E.T.O. Slater and E. Glithero discovered that an alarmingly high percentage of the patients diagnosed as hysterics had died. "One does not expect patients suffering from hysteria to die in considerable numbers after a relatively short interval, and you will ask for some further explanation"(Glithero and Slater 1965: 12). One explanation Slater and Glithero give is that the doctor will misinterpret organic ailments as hysterical symptoms if he has an unfavorable reaction to the patient. Certain personality disorders, they suggest, "lead directly to an unfavorable reaction on the part of the clinician. . . . In some sense it is true to say that 'hysteria' is a label assigned to a particular relationship between observer and observed; it appears on the case-sheet most readily if the doctor has found himself at a loss, if the case is obscure and if treatment is unsuccessful." Hysteria's displacement suggests some of the limits and the impossibilities of the institution of psychoanalysis, but it also raises the question asked by Jacqueline Rose: "Whether in fact only an institution that knows the necessity and impossibility of its own limits and, like the subject, can only operate on that edge, might be – instead of the antithesis of all politics – the precondition or site where any politics must take place" (1986: 22).

Psychoanalysis may have failed, as Stephen Heath alleges, to include – in the theoretical construction and concepts it elaborates – history, the social relations of production, classes, sexes (1978: 61), or even to reflect upon its own role in structuring a discursive field where history, like the woman, does not exist, but the hysteric, who after all was the inventor of "the talking cure," repeatedly points to this lack. My point here in retelling this tale of hysteria is not to accuse psychoanalysis of a failure to produce justice, or even an adequate account of how women are fitted into place within patriarchy. What I am making is a variation of the request Walter Benjamin makes at the end of "The Work of Art in the Age of Mechanical Reproduction" when he asked that the aestheticization of politics be answered by a politicization of art. If it is true that hysteria has been presented as a chapter in the history of art, then it may be that art can provide a political reading of hysteria.

## TO PLAY WITH MIMESIS

To play with mimesis is thus, for a woman, to try to recover the place of her exploitation by discourse, without allowing herself simply to be reduced to it. It means to resubmit herself – inasmuch as she is on the side of "perceptible," of "matter" – to "ideas," in particular to ideas about herself, that are elaborated in/by masculine logic, but so as to make "visible," by an effect of playful repetition, what was supposed to remain invisible: the cover-up of a possible operation of the feminine in language. It also means to "unveil" the fact that, if women are such good mimics, it is because they are not simply reabsorbed into this function.

(Irigaray 1985b: 76)

A number of contemporary women artists are exploring the potential and the pitfalls of a cultural politics based upon the possibility of women's strategic mimicry of hysteria as a form of resistance to the demands and requirements of the social and sexual roles assigned to them. They are playing with mimesis in order to destabilize both a theoretical practice and a female body image. In so doing they bring something not subject to the rule of visibility into the system of "presence" and representation. They explore the semantic field generated by Charcot's codification of pathological attitudes in order to focus, not on what is made to appear, but rather on that "delicious game," on the "method that makes anything appear at will."

These artists have returned to this original moment in the theory of the unconscious to reconsider the radical doubt raised by the hysteric, the *failure* of identity. The hysteric, and by extension femininity itself, has been constructed to be watched, but what is revealed by the apparatus of surveillance – amphitheaters, drawings, cameras, mirrors, charts, graphs, maps – is the growing suspicion that all such exploration may be in vain. The subject remains opaque *even* when caught up in intense scrutiny, and all that can be observed is a series of dissimulations. As Elizabeth Grosz argues, the body as well as being the site of the inscription of power and knowledge, is "also a site of resistance, for it exerts a recalcitrance, and always entails the possibility of being self-marked, self-represented in alternative ways" (1990: 64).

> You're born naked, and the rest is drag.
>
> RuPaul

Nietzsche's complaint that woman is always acting, that every woman is an artist, is the underlying premise of **Cindy Sherman**'s work. Sherman is the model for all her images: all her works are self-portraits that ironically reveal the categorical contradiction of the genre. She is Everywoman, and womanliness itself is a masquerade. If this reminds you of Epimenides's paradox of self-reference along the lines of "All women are liars. I am a woman," it shows how far Sherman takes us into the defiles of the signifier. She began in the late 1970s taking black and white photos reminiscent of the *femmes fatales* of *film noir* (Figure 6.6). In these elaborations of images of women caught in the middle of ambiguous narratives, she is a woman demonstrating the representations of woman, and the pose is presented *as* pose. At times she presents herself as genuine, which only means, to borrow a phrase from Stephen Heath, a "certain submissive *in*significance." Mary Ann Doane suggests that the masquerader is in control: "To masquerade is to manufacture a lack in the form of a certain distance between oneself and one's image" (1982: 82). On the other hand, the masquerade may be a form of submission; its reading is always subject to misreading:

> The woman who checks her makeup half a dozen times a day to see if her foundation has caked or her mascara has run, who worries that the wind or rain may spoil her hairdo, who looks frequently to see if her stockings have bagged at the ankle or who, feeling fat, monitors everything she eats, has become, just as surely as the inmate of the Panopticon, a self-policing subject, a self committed to a relentless self-surveillance. This self-surveillance is a form of obedience to patriarchy.
>
> (Bartky 1988: 81)

*Figure 6.6*　Cindy Sherman, *Untitled Film Still #54* (20 × 26 cm) 1980
(courtesy Metro Pictures, New York).

The masquerade of "femininity" may function either as a form of complicity with, or refusal of, patriarchal sexual relations. In a classic Lacanian double-bind, masquerade is the very definition of "femininity" because it is constructed entirely with reference to the male sign. Adopting it as a strategy is a risky gesture. Like the swimmer in Stevie Smith's poem "Not Waving, But Drowning," the masquerader can't be sure they won't think she is just waving, when really she's drowning.

When the mask begins to slip – when the construction of identity shows, as it does in Sherman's later work – the threat behind the mask of womanliness is revealed. Heath argues that hysteria is failed masquerade. Images of Sherman in *Vogue* magazine modeling clothing by the designer Dorothée Bis were part of a proliferation of images of hysterics in high fashion, but Sherman pushes the grotesque too far, turning the fashionable into the pathological, or rather presenting them as part of the same continuum (Figure 6.7). In her latest work the body is replaced either by prosthetic devices or by body fragments which, as Lacan points out in his theory of the imaginary, are the parts we have always mistaken for the whole (Figure 6.8). The body fragments Sherman presents are the bizarre yet familiar fragments that cinema presents us with; the body in

196

*Figure 6.7*    Cindy Sherman, *Untitled #122* (color photograph, 189.2 × 116.2 cm)
1983 (courtesy Metro Pictures, New York).

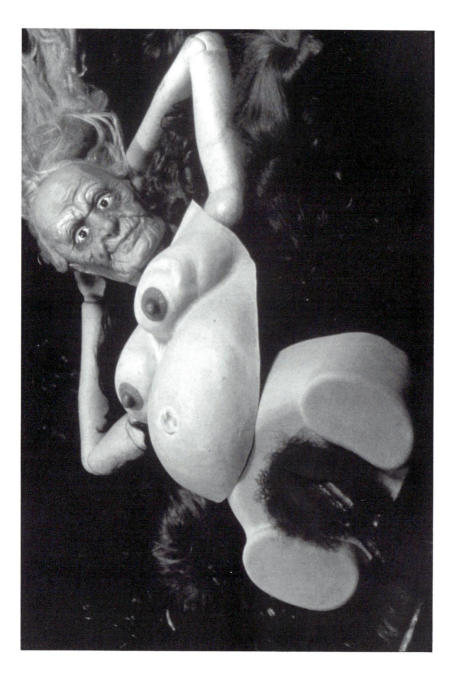

*Figure 6.8*   Cindy Sherman, *Untitled #250* (127 × 177 cm) 1992 (courtesy Metro Pictures, New York).

cinema is either fragmented by the viewing apparatus, or the body itself is chopped up, sawn, rent, or scattered across the visual field. David Lynch's *Blue Velvet* (1986), for example, begins with the discovery of an ear in a vacant lot, and a search is undertaken for the rest of the pieces. Appropriately, it is in a book entitled *Television* that Lacan calls upon us to witness the hysteric:

> Man does not think with his soul, as the Philosopher imagined. He thinks as a consequence of the fact that a structure, that of language – the word implies it – a structure carves up his body, a structure that has nothing to do with anatomy. Witness the hysteric. This shearing happens to the soul through the obsessional symptom: a thought that burdens the soul, that it doesn't know what to do with.
>
> (1973: 10)

Sherman *is* the witness for the hysteric. In her early work language carves up her body the way paper dolls are cut out; she constructed herself through the identities fashioned by the representational modes in which she grew up – Hollywood films and glossy fashion magazines. In the later work this severe repression returns in the somatizing body. At first the split in the subject could be thought of as the split between the subject of the gaze, the socially constructed subject, and the "real" subject it presumably concealed. Hence the fascination with what the "real" Cindy Sherman looks like, but the "real" Cindy Sherman has disappeared into her own appearance. Through her long obsession with identities' undoing she has discovered, not the dispossessed body in the imaginary, but the possessed body of the hysteric: a body that ages, splits, vomits, bleeds, and symptomatizes, a body subject to paralyses and anesthesias. In refusing an identity by proffering multiples, in fragmenting and dispersing the body, in becoming the grotesque, Sherman has adopted the hysteric's gesture of resistance.

**Mary Kelly**'s *Interim* (1983–85) explores representations of aging, specifically the way women entering middle age are represented. Like Meret Oppenheim, Kelly has selected ordinary objects, particularly items of women's clothing, and, following the mechanism of the fetish, has substituted the object for the lack: shoes, the classic fetish object (Figure 6.9); a lacy slip, "underclothing, which are so often chosen as a fetish, crystallize the moment of undressing, the last moment in which the woman could still be regarded as phallic" (Freud 1927a: 155); or the black leather jacket that the narrative tells us is the orthopedic prop worn by the woman attempting to signify "professional artist" (Figure 6.10). The clothes are folded, opened or knotted, and captioned according to Charcot's classifications of the photographs or drawings of women's bodies in the "passionate attitudes" of hysteria in his *Iconographie photographique de la Salpêtrière*: "*Menacé*," "*Appel*," "*Supplication*," "*Erotisme*," "*Extase*." For each attitude there are three positions which are captioned in a

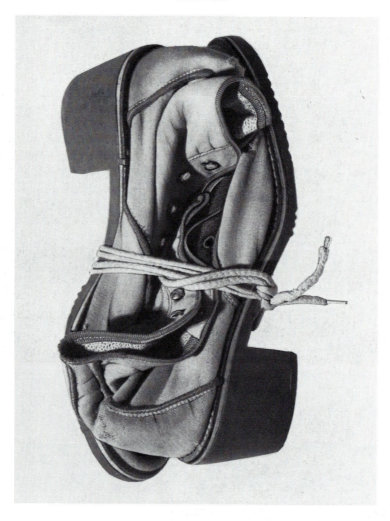

*Figure 6.9* Mary Kelly, *Interim*, "Supplication," 1983–85.

different typeface to suggest the way sexuality is inscribed in a number of discourses, such as fashion and beauty, popular medicine, sexology, or romantic fiction. The images (laminated positives on Perspex) attain a "presence," that is, they cast a shadow on a fleshy pink background suggestive of make-up. They act as a mirror in which the viewer catches her own reflection. This drama reenacts Lacan's mirror stage:

> The mirror stage is a drama whose internal thrust is precipitated from insufficiency to anticipation – and which manufactures for the subject, caught up in the lure of spatial identification, the succession

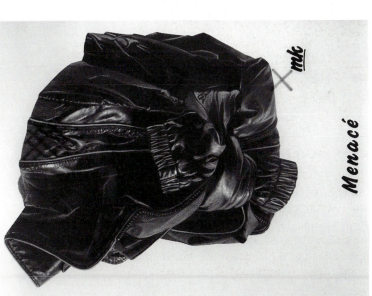

*Figure 6.10* Mary Kelly, *Interim,* "Menacé," 1983–85.

of phantasies that extends from a fragmented body-image to a form of its totality that I shall call orthopaedic – and, lastly, to the assumption of the armour of an alienating identity, which will rank with its rigid structure the subject's entire mental development.

(1949: 4)

In *Interim* Kelly effects a displacement: the identification with the woman observed is transferred to the article of clothing – a metonymy, not a presence. Each image is accompanied by a text, a compilation of conversations with women – women who are *listened to* rather than *looked at* – as in "the talking cure." There are various ways "through" the texts: they can be read as "inner speech," repeated preoccupying phrases, or unconscious thoughts. Some of the phrases have what looks like red lipstick drawn over them – elisions or emphases. The first story is of a fortieth birthday party:

you look great . . . well preserved . . . content . . . how old are you . . . she can't even say it . . . middle age . . . a phobia . . . what to wear . . . get it right . . . the uniform freedom . . . like a man . . . secure . . . surprised to catch a glimpse of myself as others see me.

The second story takes place in a family-planning clinic as a male doctor examines an older woman who fears she may be pregnant:

take off your clothes . . . don't want another child . . . won't listen . . . preoccupied with looking . . . at the facts . . . blind spot . . . being older . . . not wanting . . . to know . . . desires . . . can't wait . . . why is this woman so hysterical . . . ridiculous . . . get dressed.

In the third story an instructor is at a dance with her students at an art college:

want to dance . . . see myself . . . the image grates . . . clothes . . . hair . . . expression . . . arms . . . hips . . . feel silly . . . everyone here so Goddamn young . . . reduced to a voyeur . . . hate them . . . turn them into frogs and vanish.

If the mother who knows sexual pleasure, the subject of Mary Kelly's earlier work *The Post-Partum Document* (1973), is the most severely repressed "feminine" figure in Western culture, then the middle-aged woman runs a close second. If the assumption of an image occasions desire, then middle age marks the loss of that assumed image, of not being the object of man's desire, of being out of sync with how one looks, of alienation from one's image. It is precisely this arbitrary application of significance to image that links *Interim* to the hysterical inscriptions Charcot invented.

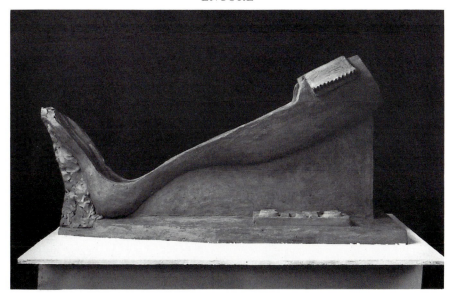

*Figure 6.11*   Jeanne Silverthorne, "Says," from the series *Gossip*
(pigmented plaster, 41x 26 × 57 cm) 1984.

The body is the inscribed surface of events (traced by language and
dissolved by ideas) the locus of a dissociated Self (adopting the illusion of a substantial unity), and volume in perpetual disintegration.

(Foucault 1977: 148)

Language weighs heavily upõn the body in **Jeanne Silverthorne**'s work,
perhaps because she gives it weight, embodies it in sculptural form, or
perhaps because in Silverthorne's work language always represents loss
or damage to the body. The sculptures are extensions of the body, a body
in the process of speaking. The early sculptures, the *Gossip* series (from
1982 to 1984), were modeled on prosthetic devices and linked to small
monosyllabic words: attached to a knee-brace is the word "Too," perhaps
to say "too bad"; a pair of dentures clatter the criticism, "So, So"; a leg
support says "Says" as if implying that it is in on the circuit of who says
what about whom (Figure 6.11). The pairing suggests that language is a
kind of prosthesis enabling the user to extend her influence beyond the
physical limitations of the body, but at the same time there is a sense of
impairment, a recognition of the damage done to the body by language.
Language can be used as a crutch, but a kind of symbiosis sets in: the
body is disfigured by its dependency. In other works, inanimate objects
are anthropomorphized and seem to be on the verge of speech: a hydrocal
faucet issues what looks like a steady stream of water down a drain that
says "Sorry"; a tongue oozing from a hot water bottle gurgles "Please";

*Figure 6.12* Jeanne Silverthorne, *Untitled* (rubber and resin, dimensions variable) 1994.

a mass of budding matter proclaims "UP, UP, UP"; books snore; light bulbs, always the signifier of bright ideas, are given thought bubbles in which they think of themselves as abstractions, pure signifiers; a huge chandelier, a complex ganglion of rubber cords illuminating nothing, becomes a kind of apotheosis of the dysfunctional (Figure 6.12). Conversely, abstractions are given material substance: thoughts, in the form of cartoon bubbles, hang in dense crepuscular rubber masses above doorways while electrical wiring (neural pathways, arteries) link these lofty but weighty thoughts to the ground.

The notion that the body is encoded by language and that this language can be "read off" the body is the underlying assumption of the discovery/invention of DNA. In three DNA models done from 1986 to 1988 Silverthorne attempts to make this biological language model manifest. Masses of interwoven cords cast in hydrocal seem to be surrogates for the human body, embodiments of its encoding. Enmeshed as they are in language, these bodies are inert. Their lack of agency may be what motivated Silverthorne to equip each of the DNA III models with a key of the sort found on wind-up toys. No gender is specified, but DNA I stands erect while DNA II assumes the pose of a *grande horizontale* like one of Ingres's voluptuous odalisques.

Running throughout Silverthorne's sculptural work is a play upon another language, that of art history. Her flaccid rubber versions of commonplace objects are rife with references to Oldenburg; the light bulbs are a direct quotation from Jasper Johns; the clouds are like Bernini's cumulus cushions; while the sexuality implicit in these anthropomorphic inanimate objects speaks to the work of Eva Hesse and Louise Bourgeois. *Correspondences* (1991–), an ongoing series of small sculptures, letters, and photographs, is an attempt to address directly the activity of producing and reproducing a work of art. The small-scale sculptures are themselves modeled upon much smaller fragments of plaster fallen off larger molds, or hardened drippings of excess rubber, or discarded lumps of clay, all from other projects. Always something is left over, something remains in excess of the language intended to encode it. Soon correspondences begin to emerge. Inevitably, once the randomly formed fragments are inserted into an art context (i.e. put on pedestals, exhibited in a gallery), they start to look like other works of art. Many resemble the sculptures of Rodin. Ironically, some even suggest classical statuary.

Exploring expression outside language, what it is like to be speechless matter, was the impetus for a large-scale female fertility figure loosely based on the Venus of Willendorf (Figure 6.13). Skin is the topos of a tale of vulnerability that runs throughout Silverthorne's sculptures. (In 1992 she even made two rubber "portraits" of skin itself: one *Young Collagen* and the other a kind of cautionary tale to sun worshipers, *Sun Damaged Collagen*.) In this sculpture the female body is reduced to its essential components, a fantasy of the mother's body with reproductive organs swollen and dominant. This is woman trapped in biology, encased in grotesque heaps of flesh, with nothing on, nor on her mind. In fact, she has no head at all; it seems to have atrophied like all the rest of her unused appendages. Without arms, legs, or language, she is without agency, but since she is placed on a pedestal (actually a rubber dolly with wheels) she could, if inclined, slip away.

*Figure 6.13*   Jeanne Silverthorne, *Untitled* (hydrocal, rubber, and wheels) 1989.

When a number of Silverthorne sculptures are shown together, the installation looks like a set-up for a series of Rube Goldberg or Fishli-Weiss comic calamities – one accidental occurrence leading inevitably to the next. The only thing required to set it off is for someone or something to slip up. And there on the floor is a black rubber banana peel, something skinned, of course, but also the *deus ex machina* which turns it all into a joke.

Skin, as the key signifier of cultural and racial difference in the stereotype, is the most visible of fetishes, recognized as common knowledge in a range of cultural, political, historical discourses, and plays a public part in the racial drama that is enacted everyday in colonial societies.

(Bhabha 1990: 82)

In the photographs of **Lorna Simpson**, skin is a palimpsest of texts, a social surface of inscription. The skin in Simpson's work is always black, and while the viewer is presented with a synecdoche of body parts, the game is not to construct the whole from the part. Wholeness is never even imagined. The black man or woman is always reduced to what Frantz Fanon calls the epidermal schema. Simpson's work is an ongoing catechism of color. *Twenty Questions* (1986), subtitled "A Sampler," is not an embroidery work for little girls to practice their stitches, but it is about fabrication, the fabrication of black identity. Like most samplers, it is full of adages of the sort children learn by heart. There are four circular photographs of the back of a black woman's head. The question asked of her – "Is she as pretty as a picture?"– is followed by a series of mutually exclusive propositions: "or clear as crystal," "or pure as a lily," "or black as coal," or "sharp as a razor." It is not black identity that Simpson is addressing, but the language games that encode that blackness in negativity. In *Completing the Analogy* (1987) a black woman with her back to the viewer faces a series of riddles, but the answer to every analogy is already there filling in the blank: "hat is to head as darkness is to – skin; scissors are to cloth as razor is to – skin; bow is to arrow as shotgun is to – skin." The analogues are slightly "off," and as the irrationality accumulates, so does a sense of violence.

As Simpson's work has developed, it has become more and more pared down and precise, as if she is writing a fundamental lexicon for the discursive language that writes the black body. *Easy for You to Say* (1989) is a classroom primer teaching children their vowels (Figure 6.14). The letters "A E I O U" are printed on an oval white background. Behind the letters, where we would expect to find a picture of an apple illustrating the letter "A" or an elephant for the letter "E," there is in each case only the head and shoulders of a black woman in a white shift. The letters blot out the face of the woman the way a victim's face is blotted out in televised court trials. In this catechism "A" is for Amnesia, "E" is for Error, "I" is for Indifference, "O" is for Omission, and "U" is for Uncivil. Learning a language is learning to distinguish difference, learning to discriminate. In another guessing game, *Sounds Like* (1988), three identical women, like the three wise monkeys, hear nothing, see nothing, and say nothing; each of the faces is covered from eyebrows to mouth by a tight white bandanna. Embossed on these bandannas are the words "I," "WIT," and "NESS."

In Simpson's work we are shown only a small section of skin, usually the exposed flesh from the neck to the collar of a dress, but this intersection of black skin and white cotton is oddly compelling. "Is not the most erotic portion of the body *where the garment gapes*?" Roland Barthes asked as if providing an explanation for what compels our attention in Simpson's photographs. What is erotic, he suggests, "is the intermittence of skin flashing between two articles of clothing (trousers and sweater), between

*Figure 6.14* Lorna Simpson, *Easy for You to Say* (5 color Polaroids, 10 plastic plaques) 1989.

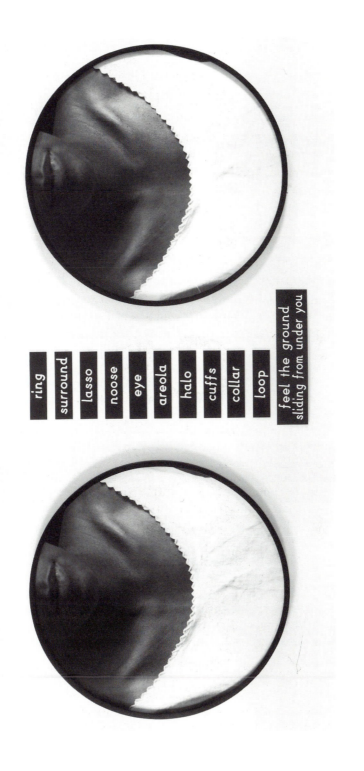

ring
surround
lasso
noose
eye
areola
halo
cuffs
collar
loop
feel the ground
sliding from under you

*Figure 6.15* Lorna Simpson, *Untitled* (2 black-and-white photographs, 91 cm diameter; 11 plastic plaques) 1989.

two edges (the open-necked shirt, the glove and the sleeve); it is this flash which seduces, or rather the staging of an appearance-as-disappearance" (1975: 10). *Untitled* (1989) is the intersection of a white circular neckline with the black skin (Figure 6.15). The edge, the margin, the intersection is all Simpson offers. Placing the body of a black woman on view is in itself a risky gesture, but the eroticism of these images provides a pleasure very different from the voyeuristic pleasure of the striptease which, as Barthes suggests, is like narrative, an "Oedipal pleasure (to denude, to know, to learn the origin and the end)" (ibid.: 10). Simpson is not engaged here in the winnowing out of truths, but in the layering of significance; "ring . . . surround . . . lasso . . . noose . . . eye . . . areola . . . halo . . . cuffs . . . collar . . . loop . . . feel the ground sliding from under you" . . . deep lacerations of language upon the body.

In *Landscape/Body Parts* (1992) Simpson takes us on a black woman's journey through language, through the ideological landscape/landmine of masculinist and colonial discourse (Figure 6.16). The text engraved on the Plexiglas reads like notes logged in a travel journal. The place names prompt a consideration of the connection between landscape, gender, names, and identity ("She passed a sign for a town named Roscoe and remembered that's what he called his dick") as well as the biologism, essentialism, and colonialism inherent in the notion of a feminine or racial closeness to nature ("The guide pointed to a rock formation called 'The Mermaid' and asked did it remind her of a vagina? . . . Seated on a train she realized she had been given a Mississippi Appendectomy."). The woman in the photographs stands headless, wearing red high-heeled shoes on her hands – offering a double fetish. The humor of these images resides just where the body exceeds the demand to conform. The body's resistance to the role assigned lies in this comic compliance.

Throughout Simpson's work we view the same strong woman's body over and over. Her familiar appearance is reassuring, as if we are watching an act of endurance. But what we are really being reassured by is the enormous ability of the body to overreach the framework that attempts to contain it, to exceed the domains of control, to live in excess of language. Simpson is angry, and while the work's overall effect is that of restraint, the anger is there in excess of what could be couched in the worn-out language of aggression, which is too self-defeating, too unproductive of pleasure. Using the skin as parchment Simpson is writing what Barthes would call a "text of bliss: the text that imposes a state of loss, the text that discomforts . . . unsettles the reader's historical, cultural, psychological assumptions, the consistency of his tastes, values, memories, brings to a crisis his relation with language" (Barthes 1975: 14).

> Does not the orgasmic body figure as a body decomposed, dismembered, dissolute, where postures and dynamic axes form and deform

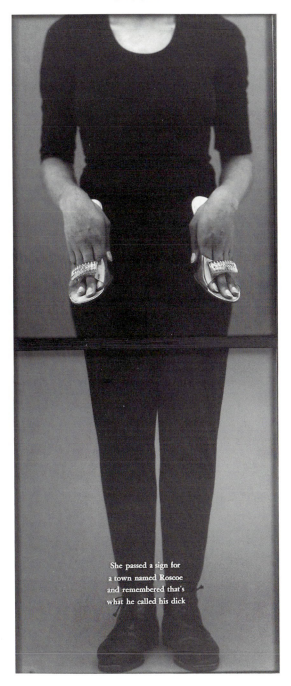

*Figure 6.16* Lorna Simpson, *Landscape/Body Parts III*, triptych
(2 color Polaroids with engraved Plexiglas, 126 × 52 cm) 1992.

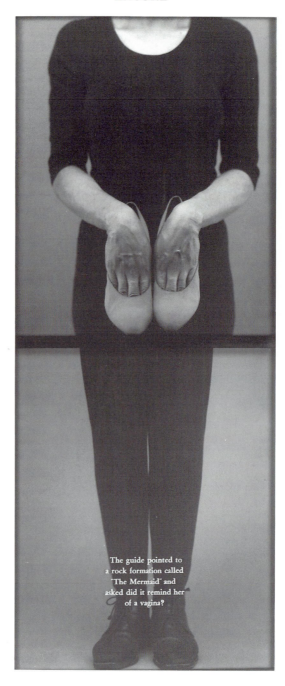

The guide pointed to
a rock formation called
"The Mermaid" and
asked did it remind her
of a vagina?

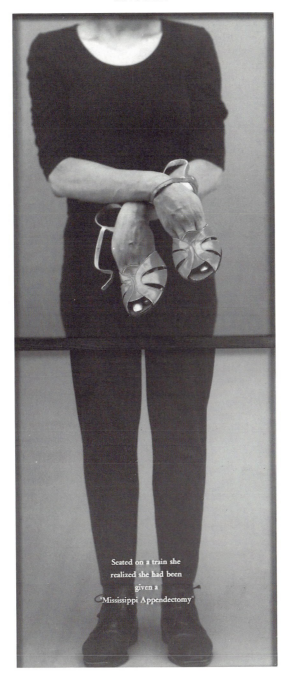

Seated on a train she
realized she had been
given a
"Mississippi Appendectomy"

in the limp indecisiveness of the erotic trouble? Is it not a breaking
down into a mass of exposed organs, secretions, striated muscles,
systems turning into pulp and susceptibility? The orgasmic body is
... the body drifting toward a state on the far side of organization and
sense, a state where action loses its seriousness and becomes play.

(Lingis 1985: 55–56)

Working in the foul rag-and-bone shop of the heart, **Kiki Smith** fashions objects out of the intimate spaces of love and the body: her mother's
feet cast in glass; three generations of death masks taken of her grandmother, father, and sister; a ribcage held together with string as if kept
in the hope of future resurrection; a womb made of bronze; an arm torn
from a shoulder, its skin flayed; a head and hands hung from the ceiling
by straps of burlap; lopped limbs trailing a long train studded with sequin
stars and flowers rising to new life. Lymph glands, minute transmitters of
sensation, are set out on tiny tables; veins and arteries protrude from the
wall and curl upon the floor; jars store bodily fluids; statues of saints,
sinners, and mortals do what mortals do: curl up against the cold, crawl
on all fours, defecate, lactate, ejaculate, urinate (Figure 6.17). Scattered
throughout is a copious collection of gargantuan glass tears – enough,
were they to melt, to wash away the sins of the world.

These are not the kind of bodies and objects we are accustomed to,
not the finished, polished desiring machines produced by modern technology or reproduced on glossy paper or celluloid. They lack the egotism
of the healthy and the beautiful, they lack the imaginary plentitude of the
media image, they lack the patina of self. If they have acquired a polish
it seems to have been the result of age and wear. The breasts and belly
of Mary Magdalene are smooth as if from human touch: not the quick
grope invited by Duchamp's "Please Touch," but the fervent rubbing
of the ancient faithful. These bodies, bones, and broken bits are the
devotional icons of a more credulous era; an old, authentic hunger has
curled around them and clings.

The body, in Smith's work, is always in process, just emerging from, or
on the verge of slipping back into, inchoate matter. Her sculptures are
not made in the classical image of the finished, completed man. "What
about the parts that dangle loose trail behind," she writes in her notebook as if to remind herself of what might slip away: "your hair holds on
you, the shit and the pee and the chafed skin the milk and the cum the
placenta, you can feel your hair in the second person not feeling it in the
first. Tender threads. Haunting ways to remain staining." Her bodies shed
skin or grow excessive hair, fluids ooze from various orifices, vertebrae
protrude outside the flesh, the spine grows vines from which flowers bloom,
arms and legs devolve into branches, or if they break off, she saves the
fragments, but doesn't try to restore wholeness. "That's the cost," she says

214

of a sculpture with a broken hand, leaving it to its accidental fate – there is always a price to be paid for being in this world; why deny it?

A prohibition has long been in place on this form of fetishism. "Object lust" may be accepted, encouraged even, as a necessary vice to fuel consumer society, but Smith isn't making objects for a consumer age, or reflecting upon consumer images. She worries that she may be condemned like the ancient icon makers for making graven images, or burned at the theoretical stake of essentialism. The danger in making figurative work inheres in the body itself. Smith wants to represent the female body, but to represent it in a way that will bring it out of the ghetto and make it neutral, make it universal, make the female body able to stand for "Man." While the feminist prohibition on all representations of the female body has been lifted during the last decade, all artists who enter this field are acutely aware that they are entering a quagmire. Unlike Antony Gormley or Jeff Koons, Smith feels she cannot use her own body because she cannot command her body's readings the way they can. The female body keeps reverting to the particularity of its material being. Its reading is so rigidly encoded that it is extremely difficult to get any other reading than narcissism if the body happens to match the current bodily ideal; or if the body varies from the ideal in any way, then the work must address this variation. Smith thinks her own body is too fat, and therefore sculptures cast from her own body will end up being about weight. (Lorraine O'Grady made a similar observation when she gave up using her own body in her performance because, as she said, now the performance would have to be about aging.) But "the universal" image has much more leeway if the figure is male – Jeff Koons's narcissism along with his paunch seems to have fallen well within the norm.

Female narcissism, Smith observes, thinking of Hannah Wilke, "always has to be paid for." Her statue of Mary Magdalene recalls Donatello's wooden *Penitent Magdalene*, hair covering her body, that source of so much temptation. In Smith's version she is large-boned; the hair seems to have grown as a protection against the elements. She drags a broken chain from one leg, like a dancing bear escaped from the circus, but she is dancing-mad, caught between animal and human heat. When she was making this sculpture Smith had in mind French folk tales of Mary Magdalene's life after the death of Christ. It is one of many cautionary tales every culture tells to repress the sexuality of young girls: "Mary Magdalene lives in the wilderness for seven years to atone for her sins. One day while drinking from a pool she sees her image reflected back to her and is condemned again for her narcissism. Her tears create the seven rivers of Provence."

The cost of inhabiting the female body is something Smith is constantly calculating. While she undertakes a reclamation of women's bodies in very material terms, working in fabric, wax, clay, paper, glass, bronze, iron,

*Figure 6.17* Kiki Smith, *Tale* (wax, pigment, and papier mâché, 160 × 23 × 23 cm) 1992 (courtesy PaceWildenstein).

burlap, beads, etc., she searches for exceptions to our biological determinism in mythopoeic accounts of women. Lilith, for example, that first
female failure or first feminist depending upon who tells the tale – Adam's
first wife who refused to lie under him – clings like a gigantic fly upon
the wall, warily keeping her distance from the fate she has escaped. Her
wraith-like, papier-mâché body seems weathered beyond what paper could
endure, her blue glass eyes peer down upon the female figures below as
if in horror at what her sex has endured. She too is mad. The statue of
the Virgin Mary is given a viscous, sinuous character. The glutinous, ropy
exposed muscles and veins of this wax figure testify to the Virgin's carnality
– this is flesh to make the spirit visible. Smith has a penchant for stories
from the Old Testament, stories of women who led robust, sinful lives,
rather than the more pious circumscribed lives of women in the New.
Lot's wife, looking back and lusting for the fleshpots and then turning
into a pillar of salt, is a character who engages her imagination. Smith
herself is an eclectic pagan. She wants stories writ on a grand scale, images
big enough to fit the female form. The photograph she took of herself is
gargantuan. It is a 360-degree photograph of her own head taken with a
periphery camera in the British Museum. It looks less like a contemporary
photograph than a seventeenth-century anamorphosis with optical alternatives and hidden meanings; her face melts into the blue of the lake, her
eyes become islands, her hair spreads red and black out into the night
sky. Is there a motive for this metaphor, or is this just an image of a
woman slipping free of the A B C of being?

## THE WOMAN WHO "DOES NOT CEDE HER DESIRE"

In the end, the woman pushed to hysteria is the woman who disturbs
and is nothing but disturbance.

(Cixous 1990: 352)

No closure to this project is possible. Since I began writing this book there
has erupted a riot of women artists exploring the potential of laughter,
hysteria, the grotesque and the carnivalesque. The work being produced
is in excess of any one writer's ability to provide supportive commentary.
Excess, positive exaggeration, hyperbolization, transgression is what most
of the work is about, particularly the grotesque's ability to transgress even
its own body.

Some, like **Nancy Davidson**, explore the comic excess at the intersection
of exaggeration and eroticism. Like a clown at the carnival, Davidson
presents the audience with balloons, gargantuan weather balloons over six
feet in diameter. The balloons take over the space, threatening to engulf
the viewer. Each balloon is dressed in a tutu with fetishistic straps that
bifurcate it into the two halves of a grotesquely fat derrière floating, lighter

than air, up to the ceiling (Figure 6.18). **Marie Baronnet** also "moons" the spectator; sticking her upturned naked body rear-first into the lens of the camera, she turns her ostensibly normal body into something uncanny like antic parsnips photographed by Edward Weston (Figure 6.19). **Catherine Opie** photographs herself and other lesbians, gays, transvestites, and trans-sexuals who, through the use of hormones, tattoos, body piercing, and cross-

*Figure 6.18*  Nancy Davidson, *Overly Natural* (fabric, latex, wire, dimensions variable) 1993.

dressing, are transforming their bodies into whatever gender they want. The French performance artist **Orlan** undergoes repeated operations for plastic surgery in order to make her facial features resemble famous paintings, such as the *Mona Lisa*. **Jenny Saville** paints full-bodied femininity: enormous trunks of women, viewed from the thighs upward, tower above the viewer (Figure 6.20). These are women who have given themselves over to excess, and excess in woman is always viewed as a threat. The grotesque "body swallows the world and is itself swallowed by the world." On the other hand, in **Maureen O'Connor**'s *Thinner than You* the body has disappeared entirely; we are left with only a disembodied diaphanous dress on a hanger. Hardly conceivable, the lady has vanished. These women may strike the viewer as freakish oddities, but ultimately they may only be extreme versions of the way every woman responds to the obstacles and repressions imposed upon her. These are women who, as Slavoj Žižek

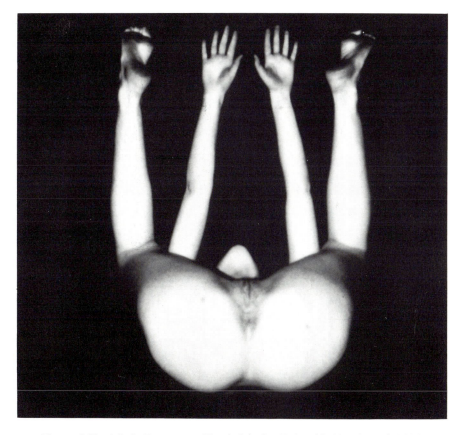

*Figure 6.19*   Marie Baronnet, *Untitled* (color Polaroid, 20 × 21 cm) 1994.

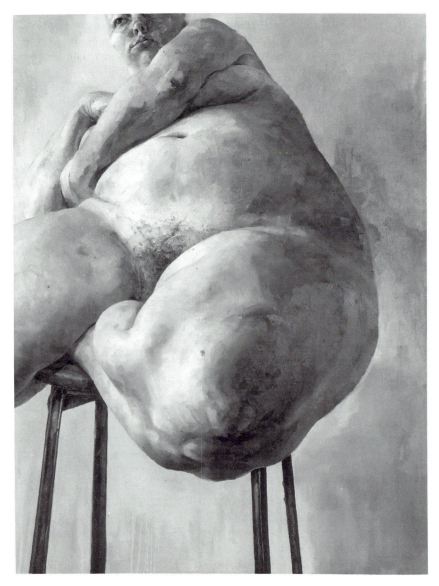

*Figure 6.20*  Jenny Saville, *Prop* (oil on canvas, 213.5 × 183 cm) 1993
(courtesy Saatchi Collection, London).

would put it, have assumed their own fate. They have the courage to be exactly who they want to be, or with blunt unsparing realism, show exactly who they are. **Nancy Fried** sculpts larger than life-size terra cotta torsos of her own body after it had undergone a radical mastectomy. The torsos are all headless, one cradles a mask of mourning in its arms like an infant, in another the masks are hoisted on the hips like baggage a traveller is determined to carry. In *The Picture of Health? 1982 Onwards* **Jo Spence** embarked on a photographic documentation of her fight with breast cancer, or perhaps it would be more accurate to say her confrontation with the medical orthodoxy and its system of representing her and her disease. These works are triumphant, not because the women win the battle; for the most part they don't. They are triumphant in their challenge to society's obsession with masking loss, in their willingness to look steadily at the "disappearance that everybody denies" (Žižek 1991: 79).

> Men say that there are two unrepresentable things: death and the feminine sex. That's because they need femininity to be associated with death; it's the jitters that give them a hard-on!
>
> (Cixous 1975: 255)

The assumption of hysteria as a way to slip out of the consigned position in the spectacle may be the most ontologically destabilizing gesture available to women, but it is not without risk, for in this strategy of "assuming her own fate," Žižek points out the woman "*assumes* her nonexistence," her invisibility, even her death. I wish to use his analysis of the *femme fatale*'s strategy in relation to the symbolic order to draw my own writing on hysteria to conclusion. The *femme fatale*, the ambiguous woman capable of many disguises, is the character in *film noir* who most embodies deception and deceitfulness, "a woman whose promise of surplus enjoyment conceals mortal danger . . . . What is the precise dimension of this danger? Our answer is that, contrary to appearance, the *femme fatale* embodies a radical *ethical* attitude, that of 'not ceding one's desire,' of persisting in it to the very end when its true nature as the death drive is revealed" (Žižek 1991: 63).

The artist who perhaps best exemplifies the destiny of the *femme fatale* and whose work elucidates what is meant by the "ethical attitude" of the woman who "does not cede her desire" is **Hannah Wilke**. Her early performances were condemned for their exhibitionism and narcissistic indulgence. This was a woman who could endlessly manipulate herself, who displayed a liberated sensuality, who maintained a primary narcissism. Her power was seen as a threat, a threat she played upon in all of her works. Wilke exemplified perfectly the Lacanian proposition that "the Woman does not exist," that she is nothing but "the symptom of man." However, as Peggy Phelan has argued, "performance is the art form which most fully understands the generative possibilities of disappearance" (1993:

27). In so far as Wilke would enter the frame of a particular fantasy she embodied pathological enjoyment, but she would always "traverse" the fantasy. In response to the audience's demand to "take it off" – she was the girl who went too far.

In *Hannah Wilke: Super-T-Art* she photographed herself in a progression of twenty poses through which she transforms herself from the image of a martyred saint, hands held outward as if to reveal stigmata, to the burlesque dancer doing a seductive striptease, and finally to the image of Christ at the crucifixion, the drapery she had been using as a prop throughout now wrapped as a simple loincloth. The same facial expressions are interpreted differently as she runs the gamut from saint to sinner and back again. In the introspective persona of the saint the downcast eyes are read as contemplation, but in the frame in which she fondles her nipple the same expression is read as masturbatory self-indulgence. As the striptease continues she becomes the uncontrollable hysteric, her arms flail purposelessly around her body and gradually assume their horizontal posture in the crucifixion. She becomes the martyred Christ, not just because there can be no female Passion that is not punished, but because there is no pose for female Passion. Women cannot "play with themselves"; women's sexual pleasure cannot be visualized as anything other than the hysteric – as reason's excess, absence, and abjection. This is underscored by the fact that the sexualized image of the female is ultimately consigned to the conventions of masculine visual pleasure or martyrdom. Inevitably, female pleasure is exchanged for amazing male Grace. By crucifying herself, Wilke makes it clear that this innocuous masquerade has taken a toll and martyred her to the visual expectations of the audience. There is a price to be paid for this spectacular rise.

All of Wilke's work insists that gender and sexuality are indeterminate processes of signification which are inscribed on the surface of the body. In a 1977 video performance entitled *Intercourse with . . .* her naked torso is inscribed with other people's names. In *S.O.S. – Starification Object Series* it is scarred with wads of chewing gum shaped in the form of female genitalia. The "plastic" nature of the vulvae shows how attempts to render woman's sexuality visible ultimately consign it to the artificial while at the same time suggesting that which we can objectify (either aesthetically or medically) as woman's sexual anatomy is purely a construct. Each frame figures her in some stereotypically feminine pose: a cowgirl, a vamp, a movie star, an Islamic woman wearing a headdress and veil. In this image, Wilke exposes the irony of another culture's cover-up which, while seeming to hide and repress female sexuality, has succeeded in creating it in very predetermined and disciplined ways. Even the deification of the movie "stars" asserts that an intelligible system of signification of sexuality is achieved only through performative violence. Female sexuality is made visible only through starification/scarification; ultimately it leads to her call for help, "S.O.S."

Life, Walter Benjamin observes, acquires definable meaning only at and through death. Wilke's final exhibition, *INTRA-VENUS*, was a dramatic instance of the power of the last act to radically rewrite the meaning of an entire life's *opus*. Yet when her earlier work is looked at through the retrospective lens of the last exhibition, it seems to be part of a continuum that leads with all the economy and precision of a Greek play to this particular climax. Shown posthumously, *INTRA-VENUS* documents, in thirteen larger-than-life photographs, set out like the stations of the cross, her confrontation with her own death from lymphatic cancer. In her signature style of humorous self-assured exhibitionist, she plays her last role – that of the grotesque dying crone. Bald, naked, bloated, scarred by chemotherapy and bone marrow treatments, hooked to IV tubes, Wilke assumes the whole array of stereotypical poses she has always assumed: rigging herself up in the same calendar girl contortions she assumed in her 1975 *Invasion Performance*, or the martyred beatitude of the Virgin Mary with downcast eyes and bent head shrouded in a blue shawl. Sometimes she simply sits there staring vacuously into some middle distance, her body traversed by medical apparatus; or, balancing a bouquet of plastic flowers on her head, she clowns like Carmen Miranda (Figure 6.21). Wilke's last work is the clearest example we are likely to get of what Freud calls the "triumph of narcissism" which occurs as a result of "the grandeur" of humor. "Humour has something liberating about it; but it also has something of grandeur and elevation. . . . The grandeur in it clearly lies in *the triumph of narcissism,* the victorious assertion of the ego's invulnerability. The ego refuses to be distressed by the provocations of reality, to let itself be compelled to suffer. It insists that it cannot be affected by the traumas of the external world; it shows, in fact, that such traumas are no more than the occasions for it to gain pleasure" (1927a: 162).

Along with the return to the question of woman in *Encore*, there is another feature in Lacan's seminar that, as Žižek notes, must appear "somewhat strange from the point of view of the 'standard' Lacanian theory. That is to say, the entire effort of the 'standard' Lacanian theory of the signifier is to make us see the pure contingency on which the process of symbolization depends, i.e., to 'denaturalize' the effect of meaning by demonstrating how it results from a series of contingent encounters, how it is always 'overdetermined.' In *Encore*, however, Lacan surprisingly *rehabilitates the notion of the sign*, of the sign conceived precisely in its opposition to the signifier, i.e., as preserving the continuity with the real" (1991: 39). It is important to remember that this surprising theoretical shift occurs in the seminar in which Lacan returns to the question of woman. According to Žižek's reading of Lacan, what is so threatening about the *femme fatale* is not the boundless enjoyment that overwhelms

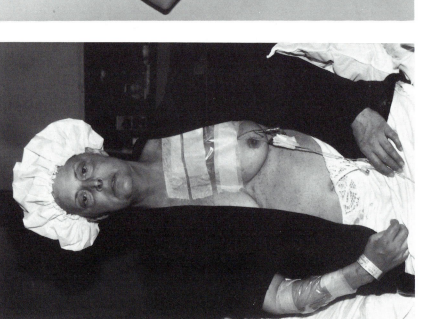

*Figure 6.21* Hannah Wilke, *June 15, 1992/ January 30, 1992: #1 from INTRA-VENUS* 2 panels; chromagenic supergloss prints, 182 × 244 cm) 1992–93 (photo: Dennis Cowley; courtesy Ronald Feldman Fine Arts Inc., New York).

the man, nor that she is so immersed in deception, but the threat that she will go too far, let the masks all fall off, reveal "the real." The moment of the hysterical breakdown designates the moment at which she assumes an ethical status, accepting without reserve the imminence of her own death. In assuming her nonexistence, she constitutes herself as "subject." "In other words, what is really menacing about the *femme fatale* is not that she is fatal for men but that she presents a case of a 'pure,' nonpathological subject fully assuming her own fate" (ibid.: 66). When the whole ontological consistency of Woman as "the symptom of man" is dissolved, man is left to confront the void of his own nonexistence. Such a confrontation, Cixous suggests, is enough to set half the world laughing: "You only have to look at the Medusa straight on to see her. And she is not deadly. She's beautiful and she's laughing" (1975: 255).

At the beginning of this century Virginia Woolf explained women's absence from history and from cultural production in terms of the metaphor of the mirror: "Women have served all these centuries as looking-glasses possessing the magic and delicious power of reflecting the figure of man at twice its natural size." It was an important role, she argues; it enabled men to go out on the stage of history and do what needed to be done. We have begun to look for ourselves in this mirror but have found little in the way of real resemblance, only readymade reflections. Still, the process of looking for ourselves has revealed something of the workings of this apparatus. We fashion and refashion ourselves through these necessary and repeated encounters with the mirror, an apparatus that can provide only fragmentary misrecognitions that are nevertheless constitutive. In an interesting linguistic coincidence Lacan would appreciate, *mir* in Russian means "world."[3] The question that feminists on both sides of the *mir* are now considering is what the *mir* would look like if we were to take "that magic and delicious power" women have perfected through centuries of service to man and turn it to reflect the figure of woman at, say, just its natural size.

# NOTES

## INTRODUCTION

1 Danto asks this question, but he does not fall into the question's trap. Danto's essay surveys the work women artists have done over the past three decades, making it clear that women did not simply enter the mainstream, they redefined it.

## 1 THE REVOLUTIONARY POWER OF WOMEN'S LAUGHTER

1 Ironically, modern technology supports Freud's speculations about Leonardo's identification with his mother – X-rays of the Mona Lisa have revealed another portrait underneath, one that is thought to be Leonardo's self-portrait. Most appropriately, this discovery was featured on an episode of the American television series *Unsolved Mysteries*.

2 See also Sarah Kofman, "Narcissistic Woman," in *The Enigma of Woman: Woman in Freud's Writings* (1985).

3 For an assessment of how successful Bakhtin was in his attempts to exonerate Rabelais from the charge of antifeminism, see Wayne C. Booth, "Freedom of Interpretation: Bakhtin and the Challenge of Feminist Criticism" (1986).

4 Bakhtin's theory of the collective social body has been read by some Russian readers as a prescription for socialist collectivity. The non-individualized body is discussed again in Chapter 3 of this book with reference to the formation of the collective identity of the Soviet citizen under Stalinism.

5 Craig Owens in "The Discourse of Others: Feminism and Postmodernism" (1983) and Alice Jardine in *Gynesis* (1985) explore the modernism vs. postmodernism debate in terms of sexual difference. They argue that the feminist critique of patriarchy has fueled the postmodernist critique of representation, resulting in the loss of credibility in what Lyotard calls the *grands récits* of modernity – the master narratives of Western culture which, as Owens points out, are always narratives of mastery.

6 I owe this reference to Baudrillard to Tania Modleski's essay "Femininity as Mas(s)querade: A Feminist Approach to Mass Culture" (1986). Although Modleski acknowledges that Baudrillard does not denigrate either the masses or femininity and goes on to extend the "contemporary psychoanalytic definitions of woman to a political analysis of the masses"(1986: 49), she is dubious about the "possibilities of a revolution based on the mute tactics of the eternal 'feminine'"(ibid.: 51).

7 "Among country people or in inns of the humbler sort it will be noticed that it is not until the entrance of the barmaid or the innkeeper's wife that smuttiness starts up. Only at higher social levels is the opposite found, and the presence of a woman brings smut to an end" (Freud 1905b: 99).

## 2 ART HISTORY AND ITS (DIS)CONTENT

1 "Woman as Sign" is the title of a 1978 essay by Elizabeth Cowie reprinted in Adams and Cowie (1990: 253–273).
2 For more on this subject, see Emily Apter, "Female Trouble in the Colonial Harem" (1992), and Marilynn Lincoln Board, "Constructing Myths and Ideologies in Matisse's Odalisques" (1989).
3 See Sarah Wilson's *Matisse* (1992) for a detailed account of French acquisition policies during this period.
4 Currently, *The Origin of the World* is on display in Paris at the Musée d'Orsay.
5 As I was writing this chapter, National Public Radio reported the problems that natural history museums were having in dealing with the obvious and embarrassing gender and cultural biases of their exhibits. One director explained that there simply wasn't enough money to "correct" all the mistakes in displays such as elaborate dioramas. Instead, he has invented what he calls the "dilemma label" for those that are incorrect or misleading. For example, a diorama showing a lioness at home with her cub while the male lion is off hunting a zebra would be given a "dilemma label" explaining that it was the female lion that did the hunting. The male, he said, "was usually more of a couch potato."
6 I am indebted in this discussion to Lennard Davis's unpublished essay "'No Fable in Their Case': New World Explorers and the Problem of Narration"(1992). I am also grateful to Lennard for bringing to my attention the photograph from the *New York Times*.

## 3 REFLECTIONS OF RESISTANCE: WOMEN ARTISTS ON THE OTHER SIDE OF THE *MIR*

1 While Irina Sandomirskaya points out in her essay "Around Б: Power and the Magic of Writing" (1992) that the legislative reforms that took place during the Soviet period, according women equal access with men to education and professional training, equal opportunities in employment, remuneration, social and political activity, etc., were more often proclaimed than enacted, the very fact of having this equity written into law marks an advance on the majority of industrialized countries even now. *Canadian Woman Studies* (Winter 1989) provides a detailed comparison between the conditions of Canadian and Soviet women.
2 See Yelena Khanga, "No Matryoshkas Need Apply" (1991: 19); and Margot Hornblower, "Skin Trade," *Time* 141 (21 June 1993) 44–51. One of the rapidly growing jobs for women in Russia is prostitution. Hornblower quotes one man's explanation for the increase in customers: "Married men do not want to practice what they see in porno movies with their wives," he explains. "But they can with Natashas."
3 The Decembrists attempted to liberalize Russia's political, economic, and social systems by staging an abortive coup in December 1825.

## 6 ENCORE

1 For further discussion of Freud's politics see Rieff (1954, 1956).
2 Freud sees Pinel's act as a means of expiation for the French Revolution, just as he sees Charcot's work as a means of reclaiming French glory lost in the 1870–71 war.
3 In a further coincidence, *mir* also means "peace." *Miru mir* is "peace to the world."

# BIBLIOGRAPHY

Alchuk, Anna (1991) "The Silent Sex," in *A Chicken is No Bird*, Amsterdam: Picaron Editions.

Alloula, Malek (1986) *The Colonial Harem*, Minneapolis: University of Minnesota Press.

Apter, Emily (1992) "Female Trouble in the Colonial Harem," *Differences: A Journal of Feminist Cultural Studies* 4, 1 (Spring): 205–224.

Aragon, Louis and Breton, André (1928) "Le cinquantenaire de l'hystérie," *La Révolution surréaliste* no. 11: 20–22.

Atkinson, Alexander Dallin and Lapidus, Gail Warshosky (eds) (1977) *Women in Russia*, Stanford: Stanford University Press.

Attie, David (1977) *Russian Self-Portraits*, New York: Harper and Row.

Bakhtin, Mikhail (1968) *Rabelais and His World*, trans. Helen Iswolsky, Cambridge, Mass.: MIT Press.

Barr, Alfred H. (1966) *Matisse: His Art and His Public*, New York: Arno Press.

Barthes, Roland (1964) *Critical Essays*, trans. Richard Howard (1972), Evanston, Ill.: Northwestern University Press.

—— (1974) *S/Z*, trans. Richard Miller, New York: Hill and Wang.

—— (1975) *The Pleasure of the Text*, trans. Richard Miller, New York: Hill and Wang.

—— (1981) *Camera Lucida*, trans. Richard Howard, New York: Hill and Wang.

Bartky, Sandra Lee (1988) "Foucault, Femininity and the Modernization of Patriarchal Power," in Irene Diamond and Lee Quinby (eds) *Feminism and Foucault: Reflections on Resistance*, Boston: Northeastern University Press.

Baudrillard, Jean (1983) *In the Shadow of the Silent Majorities, or the End of the Social, and Other Essays*, trans. Paul Foss, Paul Patton and John Johnston, New York: Semiotext(e) Foreign Agents Series.

Baudry, Jean-Louis (1986) "The Apparatus: Metapsychological Approaches to the Impression of Realism in the Cinema," in Philip Rosen (ed.) *Narrative, Apparatus, Ideology: A Film Theory Reader*, New York: Columbia University Press.

Bendavid-Val, Leah (1991) *Changing Reality: Recent Soviet Photography*, Washington, DC: Starwood Publishing in association with the Corcoran Gallery of Art.

Benjamin, Walter (1968) "The Work of Art in the Age of Mechanical Reproduction," in Hannah Arendt (ed.) *Illuminations*, New York: Harcourt, Brace and World.

—— (1969) "The Storyteller: Reflections on the Work of Nikolai Leskov," in Hannah Arendt (ed.) *Illuminations*, trans. Harry Zohn, New York: Schocken Books.

—— (1978) "The Author as Producer," in Peter Demetz (ed.) *Reflections: Essays, Aphorisms, Autobiographical Writings*, New York: Schocken Books.

Bhabha, Homi K. (1990) "The Other Question: Difference, Discrimination and the Discourse of Colonialism," in Russell Ferguson *et al.* (eds) *Out There: Marginalization and Contemporary Cultures*, Cambridge, Mass.: MIT Press.

Bird, Jon (1987) "Rites of Passage," in *Nancy Spero*, London: ICA/Fruitmarket Gallery/Orchard Gallery/Foyle Arts Project.

Board, Marilynn Lincoln (1989) "Constructing Myths and Ideologies in Matisse's Odalisques," *Genders* no. 5 (Summer): 22–49.

Booth, Wayne C. (1986) "Freedom of Interpretation: Bakhtin and the Challenge of Feminist Criticism," in Gary Saul Morson (ed.) *Bakhtin: Essays and Dialogues on His Work*, Chicago: University of Chicago Press.

Bowers, Susan R.(1993) "The Witch's Garden: The Feminist Grotesque," in Roland Dotterer and Susan R. Bowers (eds) *Sexuality, The Female Gaze, and the Arts: Women, the Arts and Society*, Cranbury, NJ: Susquehanna University Press.

Bryson, Norman (1983) *Vision and Painting: The Logic of the Gaze*, New Haven: Yale University Press.

Cameron, Dan (1987) "Post-Feminism," *Flash Art* no. 132 (February/March): 80–83.

Cixous, Hélène (1975) "The Laugh of the Medusa," in Elaine Marks and Isabelle de Courtivron (eds) (1981) *New French Feminisms: An Anthology*, New York: Schocken Books.

—— (1990) "Castration or Decapitation?" in Russell Ferguson *et al.* (eds) *Out There: Marginalization and Contemporary Cultures*, Cambridge, Mass.: MIT Press.

Clark, Timothy J. (1980) "Preliminaries to a Possible Treatment of 'Olympia' in 1865," *Screen* 21,1 (Spring): 18–41.

Connor, Steven (1989) *Postmodernist Culture: An Introduction to Theories of the Contemporary*, Oxford: Blackwell.

Cowie, Elizabeth (1978) "Woman as Sign," in Parveen Adams and Elizabeth Cowie (eds) (1990) *The Woman in Question M/F*, Cambridge, Mass.: MIT Press.

Danto, Arthur (1989) "Women Artists, 1970–85," *The Nation*, 25 December, 794–798.

Davis, Lennard (1992) "'No Fable in Their Case': New World Explorers and the Problem of Narration," unpublished essay.

Deitcher, David (1991) "Barbara Kruger: Resisting Arrest," *Artforum* 29, 6 (February): 84–91.

de Mazia, Violette (1986) *The Lure and Trap of Color Slides in Art Education: The Time-Released Venom of Their Make-Believe*, Merion, Penn.: Barnes Foundation.

Derrida, Jacques (1979) *Spurs: Nietzsche's Styles*, trans. Barbara Harlow, Chicago: University of Chicago Press.

Didi-Huberman, Georges (1982) *Invention de l'hystérie*, Paris: Editions Macula.

Dijkstra, Bram (1986) *Idols of Perversity: Fantasies of Feminine Evil in Fin-de-Siècle Culture*, New York: Oxford University Press.

Doane, Mary Ann (1982) "Film and Masquerade: Theorizing the Female Spectator," Screen 23, 3/4 (September/October): 74–87.

Eagleton, Terry (1976) *Marxism and Literary Criticism*, London: Methuen.

—— (1981) *Walter Benjamin or Towards a Revolutionary Criticism*, London: Verso.

—— (1983) *Literary Theory: An Introduction*, Minneapolis: University of Minnesota Press.

Edgerton, Samuel (1974) "Florentine Interest in Ptolemaic Geography as Background for Renaissance Painting, Architecture and the Discovery of America," *Journal of the Society of Architectural Historians* no. 33: 275–292.

—— (1980) "The Renaissance Artist as Quantifier," in Margaret A. Hagen (ed.) *The Perception of Pictures, Alberti's Window: The Projective Model of Pictorial Information,* New York: Academic Press.

Engel, Barbara Alpern (1987) *Mothers and Daughters: Women of the Intelligentsia in Nineteenth Century Russia,* Cambridge: Cambridge University Press.

Ferguson, Bruce (1986) "Wordsmith: An Interview with Jenny Holzer," *Art in America* no. 74: 108–115.

Flam, Jack D. (ed.) (1973) *Matisse on Art,* London: Phaidon Press.

—— (1986) *Matisse: The Man and His Art 1869–1918,* Ithaca, NY: Cornell University Press.

Flaubert, Gustave (1856) *Madame Bovary,* trans. Merloyd Lawrence (1969), Boston: Houghton Mifflin.

Foucault, Michel (1977) "Nietzsche, Genealogy, History," in Donald Bouchard (ed.) *Language, Counter-Memory, Practice: Selected Essays and Interviews,* Ithaca, NY: Cornell University Press.

—— (1978) *The History of Sexuality,* vol. 1, trans. Robert Hurley, New York: Pantheon.

—— (1984) "What is an Author?" in Paul Rabinow (ed.) *The Foucault Reader,* New York: Pantheon.

Freud, Sigmund (1893) "Charcot," in *The Standard Edition of the Complete Psychological Works of Sigmund Freud* vol. 3, trans. J. Strachey (1957), London: Hogarth Press.

—— (1895) "Studies on Hysteria," in *Standard Edition* vol. 2.

—— (1896) "The Aetiology of Hysteria," in *Standard Edition* vol. 3.

—— (1900) "Infantile Material as a Source of Dreams," in *Standard Edition* vol. 4.

—— (1905a) "Fragment of an Analysis of a Case of Hysteria," in *Standard Edition* vol. 7.

—— (1905b) "Jokes and Their Relation to the Unconscious," in *Standard Edition* vol. 8.

—— (1910) "Leonardo da Vinci and a Memory of His Childhood," in *Standard Edition* vol. 11.

—— (1914) "On Narcissism," in *Standard Edition* vol. 14.

—— (1927a) "Fetishism," in *Standard Edition* vol. 21.

—— (1927b) "Humour," in *Standard Edition* vol. 21.

—— (1930) "Civilization and Its Discontents," in *Standard Edition* vol. 21.

—— (1931) "Female Sexuality," in *Standard Edition* vol. 21.

—— (1932) "Femininity," in *New Introductory Lectures* vol. 22 of *Standard Edition.*

Gardner, Helen Louise (1980) *Art through the Ages,* 7th edn, New York: Harcourt Brace Jovanovich.

Glithero, E. and Slater, E.T.O. (1965) "A Follow-Up of Patients Diagnosed as Suffering from 'Hysteria'," *Journal of Psychosomatic Research* no. 9: 12.

Gokhale, Shanta (1981) *The New Generation 1960–1980,* ed. Uma da Cunda, New Delhi: Directorate of Film Festivals.

Goncharova, Natalya (1913) "Preface to Catalogue of One-Man Exhibition, 1913," in John Bowlt (ed.) (1976) *Russian Art of the Avant Garde, Theory and Criticism: 1902–1935,* New York: Viking.

Gorham, Deborah (1978) "The 'Maiden Tribute of Modern Babylon' Reexamined: Child Prostitution and the Idea of Childhood in Late-Victorian England," *Victorian Studies* no. 21: 353–379.

Gray, Francine Duplessix (1990) *Soviet Women: Walking the Tightrope,* New York: Doubleday.

Grimes, Nancy (1989) "Barbara Kruger," *ARTnews* 88, 4 (April): 200.

Grosz, Elizabeth (1990) "Inscriptions and Body-maps: Representations and the Corporeal," in Terry Threadgold and Anne Cranny-Francis (eds) *Feminine/ Masculine and Representation*, Sydney: Allen and Unwin.

—— (1994) *Volatile Bodies: Toward a Corporeal Feminism*, Bloomington: Indiana University Press.

Hadjinicolaou, Nicos (1973) *Art History and Class Struggle*, trans. L. Asmal (1978), London, Pluto Press.

Handy, Ellen (1991) "Barbara Kruger," *Arts Magazine* 65, 8 (April): 79.

Haraway, Donna J. (1991) *Simians, Cyborgs, and Women: The Reinvention of Nature*, New York: Routledge.

H.D. (1974) *Tribute to Freud, Writing on the Wall*, Boston: Godine.

Heath, Stephen (1974) "Lessons from Brecht," *Screen* 15, 2: 103–128.

—— (1978) "Difference," *Screen* 19, 3: 51–112.

Hilton, Alison (1980) "'Bases of the New Creation'; Women Artists and Constructivism," *Arts Magazine* 56, 2 (October): 142–145.

Hobhouse, Janet (1987) "What Did These Sensuous Images Really Mean to Matisse?" *Connoisseur* 217, 1 (January): 61–67.

Hugo, Victor (1848) "Choses vues," in *Oeuvres complètes* vol. 32, Paris: Imprimerie nationale, 1955. Quoted in Neil Hertz (1983) "Medusa's Head: Male Hysteria under Political Pressure," *Representations* no. 4 (Fall): 27–57.

Hunter, Dianne (1983) "Hysteria, Psychoanalysis and Feminism: The Case of Anna O.," *Feminist Studies* 9, 3: 464–488.

Huyssen, Andreas (1986) "Mass Culture as Woman: Modernism's Other," in *After the Great Divide: Modernism, Mass Culture, Postmodernism*, Bloomington: Indiana University Press.

Irigaray, Luce (1985a) *Speculum of the Other Woman*, trans. Gillian C. Gill, Ithaca, NY: Cornell University Press.

—— (1985b) *This Sex Which is Not One*, trans. Catherine Porter, Ithaca, NY: Cornell University Press.

Jacobus, Mary (1986) *Reading Woman: Essays in Feminist Criticism*, New York: Columbia University Press.

James, William (1892) *Psychology, Briefer Course*, reprint (1923), New York: Henry Holt.

Jameson, Fredric (1972) *The Prison House of Language: A Critical Account of Structuralism and Russian Formalism*, Princeton, NJ: Princeton University Press.

Janus (ed.) (1980) *Man Ray: The Photographic Image*, trans. Murtha Baca, London: Gordon Fraser Gallery.

Jardine, Alice (1985) *Gynesis: Configurations of Woman and Modernity*, Ithaca, NY: Cornell University Press.

Joyce, James (1922) *Ulysses*, reprint (1946), New York: Modern Library.

Kermode, Frank (1967) *The Sense of an Ending; Studies in the Theory of Fiction*, New York: Oxford University Press.

Khanga, Yelena (1991) "No Matryoshkas Need Apply," *New York Times*, 25 November, Op-Ed section.

Kofman, Sarah (1985) *The Enigma of Woman: Woman in Freud's Writings*, trans. Catherine Porter, Ithaca, NY: Cornell University Press.

Kozloff, Max (1991) "The Discreet Voyeur," *Art in America* 79, 7 (July): 100–107.

Kramer, Hilton (1981) in *New York Times Magazine*, Section 6, 11 October.

Krauss, Rosalind (1993) "Cindy Sherman's Gravity: A Critical Fable," *Artforum* 32, 1 (September): 163–165, 206.

Kristeva, Julia (1977) *About Chinese Women*, trans. Anita Barrows, London: Urizen Books.

—— (1980) *Desire in Language: A Semiotic Approach to Literature and Art*, trans.

Alice Jardine, Thomas Gora and Leon S. Roudiez, New York: Columbia University Press.

—— (1986) "Stabat Mater," trans. Arthur Goldhammer, in Susan Rubin Suleiman (ed.) *The Female Body in Western Culture*, Cambridge, Mass.: Harvard University Press.

Kruger, Barbara (1983) *Remote Control: Power, Cultures and the World of Appearances*, Cambridge, Mass: MIT Press.

Kuspit, Donald (1987) "Barbara Kruger," *Artscribe International* no. 65 (September/October): 75–77.

Lacan, Jacques (1949) "The Mirror Stage as Formative of the Function of the I as Revealed in Psychoanalytic Experience," in *Ecrits: A Selection*, trans. Alan Sheridan (1977), New York: Norton.

—— (1964) "Anamorphosis," [*Le séminare XI: Les quatres concepts fondamentaux de la psychanalyse*, Paris: Seuil, 1973] in *The Four Fundamental Concepts of Psychoanalysis*, trans. Alan Sheridan (1977), New York: Norton.

—— (1972–73) "A Love Letter," "God and the Jouissance of the Woman," and "Seminar XX: Encore," trans. Jacqueline Rose, in Juliet Mitchell and Jacqueline Rose (eds) (1982) *Feminine Sexuality: Jacques Lacan and the école freudienne*, New York: Norton.

—— (1973) *Télévision* [Paris: Seuil, 1974] trans. Denis Hollier, Rosalind Krauss, and Annette Michelson as 'Television', *October* no. 40 (Spring 1987): 7–50.

—— (1975) "Conference, Yale University 1975," *Scilicet* no. 6/7.

—— (1977) *The Four Fundamental Concepts of Psychoanalysis*, trans. Alan Sheridan, New York: Norton.

Laplanche, Jean (1980) *Problématiques II/Castration-Symbolisations*, vol. 2 of *Problématiques*, Paris: Presses universitaires de France.

Lee, Rosa (1987) "Resisting Amnesia: Feminism, Painting and Postmodernism," *Feminist Review* no. 26 (July): 5–27.

Le Guin, Ursula (1989) *Dancing at the Edge of the World: Thoughts on Words, Women, Places*, New York: Grove.

Lingis, Alphonso (1985) *Libido: The French Existential Theories*, Bloomington: Indiana University Press.

Lippard, Lucy (1990) *Mixed Blessings: New Art in a Multicultural America*, New York: Pantheon.

Livshits, Benedikt (1933) *Polutoraglazy strelets*, Moscow and Leningrad.

Lydon, Mary (1988) "Foucault and Feminism: A Romance of Many Dimensions," in Irene Diamond and Lee Quinby (eds) *Feminism and Foucault: Reflections on Resistance*, Boston: Northeastern University Press.

MacCabe, Colin (ed.) (1986) *High Theory, Low Culture: Analysing Popular Television and Film*, Manchester: University of Manchester Press.

Matisse, Henri (1972) *Ecrits*, Paris: Herman.

Michgelsen, Pauline (1991) "Belles des artes," in *A Chicken Is No Bird*, Amsterdam: Picaron Editions.

Mitchell, Juliet and Rose, Jacqueline (eds) (1982) *Feminine Sexuality: Jacques Lacan and the école freudienne*, New York: Norton.

Modleski, Tania (1986) "Femininity as Mas(s)querade: A Feminist Approach to Mass Culture," in Colin MacCabe (ed.) *High Culture, Low Culture: Analysing Popular Television and Film*: Manchester: University of Manchester Press.

Montrelay, Michèle (1990) "Inquiry into Femininity," in Parveen Adams and Elizabeth Cowie (eds) *The Woman in Question: M/F*, Cambridge, Mass.: MIT Press.

Nairne, Sandy (1987) *State of the Art: Ideas and Images of the 1980s*, London: Chatto and Windus.

Nochlin, Linda (1988) "Courbet's Real Allegory: Rereading *The Painter's Studio*," in Sarah Faunce and Linda Nochlin, *Courbet Reconsidered*, Brooklyn: Brooklyn Museum.

O'Grady, Lorraine (1992) "Olympia's Maid: Reclaiming Black Female Subjectivity," *Afterimage* 20, 1 (Summer): 14–19.

Owens, Craig (1983) "The Discourse of Others: Feminism and Postmodernism," in Hal Foster (ed.) *The Anti-Aesthetic: Essays on Postmodern Culture*, Port Townsend, Wash.: Bay Press.

—— (1984) "The Medusa Effect or, The Specular Ruse," *Art in America* 72, 1 (January): 97–105.

Parker, Rozsika and Pollock, Griselda (1981) *Old Mistresses: Women, Art and Ideology*, London: Routledge and Kegan Paul.

Phelan, Peggy (1993) *Unmarked: The Politics of Performance*, London and New York: Routledge.

Pollock, Griselda (1982) "Vision Voice and Power: Feminist Art History and Marxism," *Block* no. 6: 2–21.

—— (1988) *Vision and Difference: Femininity, Feminism and the Histories of Art*, New York: Routledge.

Rich, Adrienne (1976) *Of Woman Born: Motherhood as Experience and Institution*, New York: Norton.

Rieff, Philip (1954) "Psychology and Politics: The Freudian Connection," *World Politics* no. 7: 293–305.

—— (1956) "The Origins of Freud's Political Philosophy," *Journal of the History of Ideas* 17: 235–249.

—— (1963) "Introduction," in Sigmund Freud *Dora: An Analysis of a Case of Hysteria*, New York: Collier.

Rose, Jacqueline (1978) "Dora – Fragment of an Analysis," *m/f* no. 2: 5–21.

—— (1983) 'Feminity and its Discontents,' *Feminist Review* 14: 5–21.

—— (1986) *Sexuality in the Field of Vision*, London: Verso.

Russo, Mary (1986) "Female Grotesques: Carnival and Theory," in Teresa de Lauretis (ed.) *Feminist Studies/Critical Studies*, vol. 8 of Kathleen Woodward (ed.) *Theories of Contemporary Culture*, Bloomington: Indiana University Press.

Ryklin, Mikhail K. (1993) "Bodies of Terror: Theses toward a Logic of Violence," *New Literary History* no. 24: 57–58.

Safouan, Mustapha (1980) "In Praise of Hysteria," in Stuart Schneiderman (ed. and trans.) *Returning to Freud: Clinical Psychoanalysis in the School of Lacan*, New Haven: Yale University Press.

Sandomirskaya, Irina (1992) "Around *Б*: Power and the Magic of Writing," *Heresies* no. 26: 44–60.

Smith, Jaune Quick-to-See (1993) "Parameters," catalogue essay Northampton, Mass.: Smith College of Art.

Sobko, N.P. (1886) "Russkoe iskusstvo v 1886," fond 708, ed krh 62, Leningrad: Public Library, Manuscript Division.

Sontag, Susan (1973) *On Photography*, reprint (1990), New York: Doubleday.

Spero, Nancy (1985) "Defying the Death Machine: An Interview with Nancy Spero by Nicole Jolicoeur and Nell Tenhaaf," *Parachute* no. 39 (June/July/August): 50–55.

Spivak, Gayatri Chakravorty (1983) "Displacement and the Discourse of Woman," in Mark Krupnick (ed.) *Displacement: Derrida and After*, vol. 5 of Kathleen Woodward (ed.) *Theories of Contemporary Culture*, Bloomington: Indiana University Press.

Squiers, Carol (1987) "Diversionary (Syn)Tactics,"*ARTnews* 86, 2 (February): 76–85.

Stallybrass, Peter and White, Allon (1986) *The Politics and Poetics of Transgression*, Ithaca, NY: Cornell University. Press.

Stein, Gertrude (1935) "Portraits and Repetition," in *Lectures in America*, New York: Random House.

Tallman, Susan (1989) "Counting Pretty Ponies: Barbara Kruger and Stephen King Make Book," *Arts Magazine*, 63, 7 (March): 19- 20.

Tickner, Lisa (1987a) "Images of Women and *la peinture féminine*," in *Nancy Spero*, London: ICA/Fruitmarket Gallery/Orchard Gallery/Foyle Arts Project: 5–19.

—— (1987b) *The Spectacle of Women: Imagery of the Suffrage Campaign 1907–1914*, London: Chatto and Windus.

Todorov, Tzvetan (1984) *The Conquest of America: The Question of the Other*, trans. Richard Howard, New York: Harper and Row.

Tolstaya, Tatyana (1991) "An Interview with Tatyana Tolstaya," *Border/Lines* no. 20/21 (Winter): 20–21.

Turner, Victor (1977) "Frame, Flow and Reflection: Ritual and Drama as Public Liminality," in Michel Benamou and Charles Caramello (eds) *Performance in Postmodern Culture*, vol. 1 of Kathleen Woodward (ed.) *Theories of Contemporary Culture*, Madison: Coda Press.

Vachtova, Ludmilla (1979) "The Russian Woman and Her Avant-Garde," in *Women Artists of the Russian Avant-Garde, 1910–1930*, Cologne: Galerie Gmurzynska.

Vogel, Lise (1974) "Fine Arts and Feminism: The Awakening Consciousness," *Feminist Studies* 2,1: 3–37.

Walkowitz, Judith (1980) *Prostitution and Victorian Society – Woman, Class and the State*, Cambridge: Cambridge University Press.

Williams, Linda (1989) *Hard Core: Power, Pleasure and the "Frenzy of the Visible"*, Berkeley: University of California Press.

Williams, Raymond (1977) *Marxism and Literature*, Oxford: Oxford University Press.

Williams, William Carlos (1954) "A1 Pound Stein," in *Selected Essays of William Carlos Williams*, New York: New Directions.

Wilson, Sarah (1992) *Matisse*, New York: Rizzoli.

Wood, Paul (1992) "The Politics of the Avant-Garde," in *The Great Utopia: The Russian and Soviet Avant-Garde, 1915–1932*, New York: Guggenheim Museum.

Woolf, Virginia (1929) *A Room of One's Own*, Harmondsworth, Middlesex: Penguin Books, 1963.

Žižek, Slavoj (1991) *Looking Awry: An Introduction to Jacques Lacan through Popular Culture*, Cambridge Mass.: MIT Press.

# INDEX

Page numbers in *italic* refer to pages with illustrations.